Just The facts101

Textbook Key Facts

Australia Intelligence, Security Activities & Operations Handbook

by Cram101

Texbook NOT Included

Table of Contents

Just The Facts101

Exam Prep for

Australia Intelligence, Security Activities & Operations Handbook

Just The Facts101 Exam Prep

eAIN 444346

Foundations of Business

A business, also known as an enterprise, agency or a firm, is an entity involved in the provision of goods and/or services to consumers. Businesses are prevalent in capitalist economies, where most of them are privately owned and provide goods and services to customers in exchange for other goods, services, or money.

:: Rhetoric ::

_________ is the pattern of narrative development that aims to make vivid a place, object, character, or group. _________ is one of four rhetorical modes , along with exposition, argumentation, and narration. In practice it would be difficult to write literature that drew on just one of the four basic modes.

Exam Probability: **Medium**

1. *Answer choices:*

(see index for correct answer)

- a. Polysyndeton
- b. Rhetorical criticism
- c. Description
- d. Zeugma

Guidance: level 1

:: Commerce ::

_________ relates to "the exchange of goods and services, especially on a large scale". It includes legal, economic, political, social, cultural and technological systems that operate in a country or in international trade.

Exam Probability: **High**

2. *Answer choices:*

(see index for correct answer)

- a. Organ trade
- b. Real prices and ideal prices
- c. V-commerce
- d. Commerce

Guidance: level 1

:: Management occupations ::

_________ is the process of designing, launching and running a new business, which is often initially a small business. The people who create these businesses are called entrepreneurs.

Exam Probability: **High**

3. *Answer choices:*

(see index for correct answer)

- a. Chief sustainability officer
- b. entrepreneurial
- c. Chief diversity officer
- d. General counsel

Guidance: level 1

:: Income ::

__________ is a ratio between the net profit and cost of investment resulting from an investment of some resources. A high ROI means the investment`s gains favorably to its cost. As a performance measure, ROI is used to evaluate the efficiency of an investment or to compare the efficiencies of several different investments. In purely economic terms, it is one way of relating profits to capital invested. __________ is a performance measure used by businesses to identify the efficiency of an investment or number of different investments.

Exam Probability: **High**

4. *Answer choices:*

(see index for correct answer)

- a. Return on investment
- b. Gratuity
- c. Aggregate expenditure
- d. Independent income

Guidance: level 1

:: Debt ::

__________ is the trust which allows one party to provide money or resources to another party wherein the second party does not reimburse the first party immediately , but promises either to repay or return those resources at a later date. In other words, __________ is a method of making reciprocity formal, legally enforceable, and extensible to a large group of unrelated people.

Exam Probability: **High**

5. *Answer choices:*

(see index for correct answer)

- a. Internal debt
- b. External debt
- c. Credit
- d. Student debt

Guidance: level 1

:: Human resource management ::

_________ is the corporate management term for the act of reorganizing the legal, ownership, operational, or other structures of a company for the purpose of making it more profitable, or better organized for its present needs. Other reasons for _________ include a change of ownership or ownership structure, demerger, or a response to a crisis or major change in the business such as bankruptcy, repositioning, or buyout. _________ may also be described as corporate _________ , debt _________ and financial _________ .

Exam Probability: **Medium**

6. *Answer choices:*
(see index for correct answer)

- a. Simultaneous recruiting of new graduates
- b. Restructuring
- c. Mentorship
- d. Job sharing

Guidance: level 1

:: Management ::

The term _________ refers to measures designed to increase the degree of autonomy and self-determination in people and in communities in order to enable them to represent their interests in a responsible and self-determined way, acting on their own authority. It is the process of becoming stronger and more confident, especially in controlling one`s life and claiming one`s rights. _________ as action refers both to the process of self- _________ and to professional support of people, which enables them to overcome their sense of powerlessness and lack of influence, and to recognize and use their resources. To do work with power.

Exam Probability: **Low**

7. *Answer choices:*
(see index for correct answer)

- a. Certified Energy Manager
- b. Risk management
- c. Goal
- d. Complementary assets

Guidance: level 1

:: Business ::

A _________ is a mathematical object used to count, measure, and label. The original examples are the natural _________ s 1, 2, 3, 4, and so forth. A written symbol like "5" that represents a _________ is called a numeral. A numeral system is an organized way to write and manipulate this type of symbol, for example the Hindu–Arabic numeral system allows combinations of numerical digits like "5" and "0" to represent larger _________ s like 50. A numeral in linguistics can refer to a symbol like 5, the words or phrase that names a _________ , like "five hundred", or other words that mean a specific _________ , like "dozen". In addition to their use in counting and measuring, numerals are often used for labels , for ordering , and for codes . In common usage, _________ may refer to a symbol, a word or phrase, or the mathematical object.

Exam Probability: **Medium**

8. *Answer choices:*

(see index for correct answer)

- a. Number
- b. Professional services
- c. Business as usual
- d. Operating subsidiary

Guidance: level 1

:: Management ::

A _________ is a formal written document containing business goals, the methods on how these goals can be attained, and the time frame within which these goals need to be achieved. It also describes the nature of the business, background information on the organization, the organization`s financial projections, and the strategies it intends to implement to achieve the stated targets. In its entirety, this document serves as a road map that provides direction to the business.

Exam Probability: **Low**

9. *Answer choices:*

(see index for correct answer)

- a. Industrial democracy
- b. Business plan

- c. Stewardship theory
- d. Swarm Development Group

Guidance: level 1

:: Business ::

The seller, or the provider of the goods or services, completes a sale in response to an acquisition, appropriation, requisition or a direct interaction with the buyer at the point of sale. There is a passing of title of the item, and the settlement of a price, in which agreement is reached on a price for which transfer of ownership of the item will occur. The seller, not the purchaser typically executes the sale and it may be completed prior to the obligation of payment. In the case of indirect interaction, a person who sells goods or service on behalf of the owner is known as a salesman or saleswoman or salesperson, but this often refers to someone _________ goods in a store/shop, in which case other terms are also common, including salesclerk, shop assistant, and retail clerk.

Exam Probability: **Medium**

10. *Answer choices:*

(see index for correct answer)

- a. Selling
- b. Business partnering
- c. Ametek
- d. Hellenic Australian Business Council

Guidance: level 1

:: ::

_________ is the collection of techniques, skills, methods, and processes used in the production of goods or services or in the accomplishment of objectives, such as scientific investigation. _________ can be the knowledge of techniques, processes, and the like, or it can be embedded in machines to allow for operation without detailed knowledge of their workings. Systems applying _________ by taking an input, changing it according to the system`s use, and then producing an outcome are referred to as _________ systems or technological systems.

Exam Probability: **High**

11. *Answer choices:*

(see index for correct answer)

- a. Sarbanes-Oxley act of 2002
- b. process perspective
- c. Technology
- d. cultural

Guidance: level 1

:: Product management ::

A _________ , trade mark, or trade-mark is a recognizable sign, design, or expression which identifies products or services of a particular source from those of others, although _________ s used to identify services are usually called service marks. The _________ owner can be an individual, business organization, or any legal entity. A _________ may be located on a package, a label, a voucher, or on the product itself. For the sake of corporate identity, _________ s are often displayed on company buildings. It is legally recognized as a type of intellectual property.

Exam Probability: **Low**

12. *Answer choices:*

(see index for correct answer)

- a. Product manager
- b. Trademark
- c. Crossing the Chasm
- d. Trademark look

Guidance: level 1

:: International trade ::

An _________ is a good brought into a jurisdiction, especially across a national border, from an external source. The party bringing in the good is called an _________ er. An _________ in the receiving country is an export from the sending country. _________ ation and exportation are the defining financial transactions of international trade.

Exam Probability: **Low**

13. *Answer choices:*

(see index for correct answer)

- a. Rybczynski theorem
- b. Import
- c. Concertina model
- d. Trade preference

Guidance: level 1

:: Stock market ::

_________ is freedom from, or resilience against, potential harm caused by others. Beneficiaries of _________ may be of persons and social groups, objects and institutions, ecosystems or any other entity or phenomenon vulnerable to unwanted change by its environment.

Exam Probability: **Low**

14. *Answer choices:*

(see index for correct answer)

- a. Security
- b. Beneficial ownership
- c. Small-order execution system
- d. The Congressional Effect

Guidance: level 1

:: Payments ::

A _________ is the trade of value from one party to another for goods, or services, or to fulfill a legal obligation.

Exam Probability: **Low**

15. *Answer choices:*

(see index for correct answer)

- a. Direct Payments
- b. Deficiency payments
- c. VersaPay
- d. Payment

Guidance: level 1

:: ::

An _________ is a contingent motivator. Traditional _________ s are extrinsic motivators which reward actions to yield a desired outcome. The effectiveness of traditional _________ s has changed as the needs of Western society have evolved. While the traditional _________ model is effective when there is a defined procedure and goal for a task, Western society started to require a higher volume of critical thinkers, so the traditional model became less effective. Institutions are now following a trend in implementing strategies that rely on intrinsic motivations rather than the extrinsic motivations that the traditional _________ s foster.

Exam Probability: **Medium**

16. *Answer choices:*

(see index for correct answer)

- a. hierarchical
- b. co-culture
- c. Character
- d. Incentive

Guidance: level 1

:: Meetings ::

An _________ is a group of people who participate in a show or encounter a work of art, literature , theatre, music , video games , or academics in any medium. _________ members participate in different ways in different kinds of art; some events invite overt _________ participation and others allowing only modest clapping and criticism and reception.

Exam Probability: **Low**

17. *Answer choices:*

(see index for correct answer)

- a. Middle East Electricity
- b. Ex officio member
- c. Audience
- d. Function hall

Guidance: level 1

:: Accounting terminology ::

__________ is a legally enforceable claim for payment held by a business for goods supplied and/or services rendered that customers/clients have ordered but not paid for. These are generally in the form of invoices raised by a business and delivered to the customer for payment within an agreed time frame. __________ is shown in a balance sheet as an asset. It is one of a series of accounting transactions dealing with the billing of a customer for goods and services that the customer has ordered. These may be distinguished from notes receivable, which are debts created through formal legal instruments called promissory notes.

Exam Probability: **Medium**

18. *Answer choices:*

(see index for correct answer)

- a. Accounts receivable
- b. Record to report
- c. managerial accounting
- d. Fund accounting

Guidance: level 1

:: ::

__________ is the administration of an organization, whether it is a business, a not-for-profit organization, or government body. __________ includes the activities of setting the strategy of an organization and coordinating the efforts of its employees to accomplish its objectives through the application of available resources, such as financial, natural, technological, and human resources. The term " __________ " may also refer to those people who manage an organization.

Exam Probability: **Low**

19. *Answer choices:*

(see index for correct answer)

- a. functional perspective
- b. open system
- c. similarity-attraction theory
- d. empathy

Guidance: level 1

:: ::

__________ is the production of products for use or sale using labour and machines, tools, chemical and biological processing, or formulation. The term may refer to a range of human activity, from handicraft to high tech, but is most commonly applied to industrial design, in which raw materials are transformed into finished goods on a large scale. Such finished goods may be sold to other manufacturers for the production of other, more complex products, such as aircraft, household appliances, furniture, sports equipment or automobiles, or sold to wholesalers, who in turn sell them to retailers, who then sell them to end users and consumers.

Exam Probability: **Low**

20. *Answer choices:*

(see index for correct answer)

- a. Manufacturing
- b. similarity-attraction theory
- c. open system
- d. functional perspective

Guidance: level 1

:: ::

__________ is a means of protection from financial loss. It is a form of risk management, primarily used to hedge against the risk of a contingent or uncertain loss

Exam Probability: **Low**

21. *Answer choices:*

(see index for correct answer)

- a. interpersonal communication
- b. Insurance
- c. deep-level diversity
- d. empathy

Guidance: level 1

:: Association of Southeast Asian Nations ::

The Association of Southeast Asian Nations is a regional intergovernmental organization comprising ten countries in Southeast Asia, which promotes intergovernmental cooperation and facilitates economic, political, security, military, educational, and sociocultural integration among its members and other countries in Asia. It also regularly engages other countries in the Asia-Pacific region and beyond. A major partner of Shanghai Cooperation Organisation, _________ maintains a global network of alliances and dialogue partners and is considered by many as a global powerhouse, the central union for cooperation in Asia-Pacific, and a prominent and influential organization. It is involved in numerous international affairs, and hosts diplomatic missions throughout the world.

Exam Probability: **Medium**

22. *Answer choices:*
(see index for correct answer)

- a. Association of Southeast Asian Nations
- b. Accession of East Timor to the Association of Southeast Asian Nations
- c. ASEAN
- d. The ASEAN Way

Guidance: level 1

:: Non-profit technology ::

Instituto del Tercer Mundo is a Non-Governmental Organization that performs information, communication and education activities. _________ , which was established in 1989, shares the same secretariat and coordinating personnel as Social Watch and is based in Montevideo, Uruguay.

Exam Probability: **High**

23. *Answer choices:*
(see index for correct answer)

- a. Entertainment Consumers Association
- b. League for Programming Freedom
- c. Community technology center
- d. Charon

Guidance: level 1

:: Currency ::

A _________ , in the most specific sense is money in any form when in use or circulation as a medium of exchange, especially circulating banknotes and coins. A more general definition is that a _________ is a system of money in common use, especially for people in a nation. Under this definition, US dollars , pounds sterling , Australian dollars , European euros , Russian rubles and Indian Rupees are examples of currencies. These various currencies are recognized as stores of value and are traded between nations in foreign exchange markets, which determine the relative values of the different currencies. Currencies in this sense are defined by governments, and each type has limited boundaries of acceptance.

Exam Probability: **High**

24. *Answer choices:*

(see index for correct answer)

- a. Unidad de Fomento
- b. Nomisma
- c. Currency
- d. Reserve currency

Guidance: level 1

:: Investment ::

In finance, the benefit from an _________ is called a return. The return may consist of a gain realised from the sale of property or an _________ , unrealised capital appreciation , or _________ income such as dividends, interest, rental income etc., or a combination of capital gain and income. The return may also include currency gains or losses due to changes in foreign currency exchange rates.

Exam Probability: **Medium**

25. *Answer choices:*

(see index for correct answer)

- a. Internal rate of return
- b. VISTA
- c. Advisors Sentiment
- d. Lawcard

Guidance: level 1

:: Project management ::

__________ is the right to exercise power, which can be formalized by a state and exercised by way of judges, appointed executives of government, or the ecclesiastical or priestly appointed representatives of a God or other deities.

Exam Probability: **High**

26. *Answer choices:*

(see index for correct answer)

- a. Risk management plan
- b. Authority
- c. Akihabara syndrome
- d. Student syndrome

Guidance: level 1

:: Generally Accepted Accounting Principles ::

In accounting, __________ is the income that a business have from its normal business activities, usually from the sale of goods and services to customers. __________ is also referred to as sales or turnover.Some companies receive __________ from interest, royalties, or other fees. __________ may refer to business income in general, or it may refer to the amount, in a monetary unit, earned during a period of time, as in "Last year, Company X had __________ of $42 million". Profits or net income generally imply total __________ minus total expenses in a given period. In accounting, in the balance statement it is a subsection of the Equity section and __________ increases equity, it is often referred to as the "top line" due to its position on the income statement at the very top. This is to be contrasted with the "bottom line" which denotes net income .

Exam Probability: **Medium**

27. *Answer choices:*

(see index for correct answer)

- a. Shares outstanding
- b. Net realizable value

- c. Indian Accounting Standards
- d. Access to finance

Guidance: level 1

:: Fraud ::

In law, _________ is intentional deception to secure unfair or unlawful gain, or to deprive a victim of a legal right. _________ can violate civil law , a criminal law , or it may cause no loss of money, property or legal right but still be an element of another civil or criminal wrong. The purpose of _________ may be monetary gain or other benefits, for example by obtaining a passport, travel document, or driver`s license, or mortgage _________ , where the perpetrator may attempt to qualify for a mortgage by way of false statements.

Exam Probability: **Medium**

28. *Answer choices:*

(see index for correct answer)

- a. Accreditation mill
- b. Hitler Diaries
- c. Insurance fraud
- d. Identity theft

Guidance: level 1

:: Business law ::

A _________ is a group of people who jointly supervise the activities of an organization, which can be either a for-profit business, nonprofit organization, or a government agency. Such a board`s powers, duties, and responsibilities are determined by government regulations and the organization`s own constitution and bylaws. These authorities may specify the number of members of the board, how they are to be chosen, and how often they are to meet.

Exam Probability: **Medium**

29. *Answer choices:*

(see index for correct answer)

- a. Registered agent

- b. Board of directors
- c. Certificate of incorporation
- d. Lessor

Guidance: level 1

:: Insolvency ::

_________ is a legal process through which people or other entities who cannot repay debts to creditors may seek relief from some or all of their debts. In most jurisdictions, _________ is imposed by a court order, often initiated by the debtor.

Exam Probability: **High**

30. *Answer choices:*
(see index for correct answer)

- a. Insolvency law of Russia
- b. George Samuel Ford
- c. Bankruptcy
- d. United Kingdom insolvency law

Guidance: level 1

:: Television commercials ::

_________ is a phenomenon whereby something new and somehow valuable is formed. The created item may be intangible or a physical object .

Exam Probability: **Low**

31. *Answer choices:*
(see index for correct answer)

- a. Slim Jeans
- b. Life
- c. Creativity
- d. Pretty

Guidance: level 1

:: Generally Accepted Accounting Principles ::

Expenditure is an outflow of money to another person or group to pay for an item or service, or for a category of costs. For a tenant, rent is an _________ . For students or parents, tuition is an _________ . Buying food, clothing, furniture or an automobile is often referred to as an _________ . An _________ is a cost that is "paid" or "remitted", usually in exchange for something of value. Something that seems to cost a great deal is "expensive". Something that seems to cost little is "inexpensive". " _________ s of the table" are _________ s of dining, refreshments, a feast, etc.

Exam Probability: **Low**

32. *Answer choices:*

(see index for correct answer)

- a. Statement of recommended practice
- b. Expense
- c. Standard Business Reporting
- d. Chinese accounting standards

Guidance: level 1

:: ::

In regulatory jurisdictions that provide for it , _________ is a group of laws and organizations designed to ensure the rights of consumers as well as fair trade, competition and accurate information in the marketplace. The laws are designed to prevent the businesses that engage in fraud or specified unfair practices from gaining an advantage over competitors. They may also provides additional protection for those most vulnerable in society. _________ laws are a form of government regulation that aim to protect the rights of consumers. For example, a government may require businesses to disclose detailed information about products—particularly in areas where safety or public health is an issue, such as food.

Exam Probability: **Medium**

33. *Answer choices:*

(see index for correct answer)

- a. Consumer Protection
- b. Sarbanes-Oxley act of 2002
- c. empathy
- d. functional perspective

Guidance: level 1

:: Interest rates ::

An _________ is the amount of interest due per period, as a proportion of the amount lent, deposited or borrowed . The total interest on an amount lent or borrowed depends on the principal sum, the _________ , the compounding frequency, and the length of time over which it is lent, deposited or borrowed.

Exam Probability: **Medium**

34. *Answer choices:*

(see index for correct answer)

- a. Rate
- b. Reference rate
- c. Interest rate
- d. LIBO rate

Guidance: level 1

:: Business law ::

_________ is where a person`s financial liability is limited to a fixed sum, most commonly the value of a person`s investment in a company or partnership. If a company with _________ is sued, then the claimants are suing the company, not its owners or investors. A shareholder in a limited company is not personally liable for any of the debts of the company, other than for the amount already invested in the company and for any unpaid amount on the shares in the company, if any. The same is true for the members of a _________ partnership and the limited partners in a limited partnership. By contrast, sole proprietors and partners in general partnerships are each liable for all the debts of the business .

Exam Probability: **Medium**

35. *Answer choices:*

(see index for correct answer)

- a. Equity of redemption
- b. Limited liability
- c. Consignment agreement
- d. Starting a Business Index

Guidance: level 1

:: Marketing analytics ::

__________ is a long-term, forward-looking approach to planning with the fundamental goal of achieving a sustainable competitive advantage. Strategic planning involves an analysis of the company`s strategic initial situation prior to the formulation, evaluation and selection of market-oriented competitive position that contributes to the company`s goals and marketing objectives.

Exam Probability: **Medium**

36. *Answer choices:*

(see index for correct answer)

- a. Mission-driven marketing
- b. Return on marketing investment
- c. Marketing strategy
- d. Gross rating point

Guidance: level 1

:: Energy and fuel journals ::

In physics, energy is the quantitative property that must be transferred to an object in order to perform work on, or to heat, the object. Energy is a conserved quantity; the law of conservation of energy states that energy can be converted in form, but not created or destroyed. The SI unit of energy is the joule, which is the energy transferred to an object by the work of moving it a distance of 1 metre against a force of 1 newton.

Exam Probability: **High**

37. *Answer choices:*

(see index for correct answer)

- a. Flow, Turbulence and Combustion
- b. Renewable and Sustainable Energy Reviews
- c. Advanced Energy Materials
- d. Energies

Guidance: level 1

:: Identity management ::

__________ is the ability of an individual or group to seclude themselves, or information about themselves, and thereby express themselves selectively. The boundaries and content of what is considered private differ among cultures and individuals, but share common themes. When something is private to a person, it usually means that something is inherently special or sensitive to them. The domain of __________ partially overlaps with security , which can include the concepts of appropriate use, as well as protection of information. __________ may also take the form of bodily integrity.

Exam Probability: **Medium**

38. *Answer choices:*

(see index for correct answer)

- a. Identity verification service
- b. DigiD
- c. Mobile signature
- d. Privacy

Guidance: level 1

:: Financial accounting ::

__________ is a financial metric which represents operating liquidity available to a business, organisation or other entity, including governmental entities. Along with fixed assets such as plant and equipment, __________ is considered a part of operating capital. Gross __________ is equal to current assets. __________ is calculated as current assets minus current liabilities. If current assets are less than current liabilities, an entity has a __________ deficiency, also called a __________ deficit.

Exam Probability: **High**

39. *Answer choices:*

(see index for correct answer)

- a. Accounting identity
- b. Equity method
- c. Commuted cash value
- d. Working capital

Guidance: level 1

:: Alchemical processes ::

In chemistry, a _________ is a special type of homogeneous mixture composed of two or more substances. In such a mixture, a solute is a substance dissolved in another substance, known as a solvent. The mixing process of a _________ happens at a scale where the effects of chemical polarity are involved, resulting in interactions that are specific to solvation. The _________ assumes the phase of the solvent when the solvent is the larger fraction of the mixture, as is commonly the case. The concentration of a solute in a _________ is the mass of that solute expressed as a percentage of the mass of the whole _________. The term aqueous _________ is when one of the solvents is water.

Exam Probability: **Medium**

40. *Answer choices:*

(see index for correct answer)

- a. Digestion
- b. Putrefying bacteria
- c. Solution
- d. Ceration

Guidance: level 1

:: Mathematical finance ::

In economics and finance, _________ , also known as present discounted value, is the value of an expected income stream determined as of the date of valuation. The _________ is always less than or equal to the future value because money has interest-earning potential, a characteristic referred to as the time value of money, except during times of negative interest rates, when the _________ will be more than the future value. Time value can be described with the simplified phrase, "A dollar today is worth more than a dollar tomorrow". Here, `worth more` means that its value is greater. A dollar today is worth more than a dollar tomorrow because the dollar can be invested and earn a day`s worth of interest, making the total accumulate to a value more than a dollar by tomorrow. Interest can be compared to rent. Just as rent is paid to a landlord by a tenant without the ownership of the asset being transferred, interest is paid to a lender by a borrower who gains access to the money for a time before paying it back. By letting the borrower have access to the money, the lender has sacrificed the exchange value of this money, and is compensated for it in the form of interest. The initial amount of the borrowed funds is less than the total amount of money paid to the lender.

Exam Probability: **Low**

41. *Answer choices:*
(see index for correct answer)

- a. Forward measure
- b. Implied volatility
- c. Black model
- d. Fugit

Guidance: level 1

:: Human resource management ::

_________ are the people who make up the workforce of an organization, business sector, or economy. "Human capital" is sometimes used synonymously with " _________ ", although human capital typically refers to a narrower effect . Likewise, other terms sometimes used include manpower, talent, labor, personnel, or simply people.

Exam Probability: **Medium**

42. *Answer choices:*
(see index for correct answer)

- a. Human resources
- b. Disciplinary probation
- c. Contextual performance
- d. Succession planning

Guidance: level 1

:: Free trade agreements ::

A _________ is a wide-ranging taxes, tariff and trade treaty that often includes investment guarantees. It exists when two or more countries agree on terms that helps them trade with each other. The most common _________ s are of the preferential and free trade types are concluded in order to reduce tariffs, quotas and other trade restrictions on items traded between the signatories.

Exam Probability: **Low**

43. *Answer choices:*

(see index for correct answer)

- a. Trans-Pacific Partnership
- b. Ouchy Convention
- c. New West Partnership
- d. Trade, Development and Cooperation Agreement

Guidance: level 1

:: Regression analysis ::

A _________ often refers to a set of documented requirements to be satisfied by a material, design, product, or service. A _________ is often a type of technical standard.

Exam Probability: **Low**

44. *Answer choices:*

(see index for correct answer)

- a. Truncated regression model
- b. Non-linear least squares
- c. Smoothing spline
- d. Specification

Guidance: level 1

:: Security compliance ::

A _________ is a communicated intent to inflict harm or loss on another person. A _________ is considered an act of coercion. _________ s are widely observed in animal behavior, particularly in a ritualized form, chiefly in order to avoid the unnecessary physical violence that can lead to physical damage or the death of both conflicting parties.

Exam Probability: **Medium**

45. *Answer choices:*

(see index for correct answer)

- a. Threat
- b. Month of bugs
- c. Vulnerability management
- d. Security Content Automation Protocol

Guidance: level 1

:: Occupations ::

An _________ is a person who has a position of authority in a hierarchical organization. The term derives from the late Latin from officiarius, meaning "official".

Exam Probability: **Medium**

46. *Answer choices:*

(see index for correct answer)

- a. Middleware analyst
- b. Clockmaker
- c. Shoeshiner
- d. Officer

Guidance: level 1

:: Evaluation ::

_________ is the practice of being honest and showing a consistent and uncompromising adherence to strong moral and ethical principles and values.In ethics, _________ is regarded as the honesty and truthfulness or accuracy of one`s actions. _________ can stand in opposition to hypocrisy, in that judging with the standards of _________ involves regarding internal consistency as a virtue, and suggests that parties holding within themselves apparently conflicting values should account for the discrepancy or alter their beliefs. The word _________ evolved from the Latin adjective integer, meaning whole or complete. In this context, _________ is the inner sense of "wholeness" deriving from qualities such as honesty and consistency of character. As such, one may judge that others "have _________ " to the extent that they act according to the values, beliefs and principles they claim to hold.

Exam Probability: **High**

47. *Answer choices:*

(see index for correct answer)

- a. Summative assessment
- b. Encomium
- c. Cryptographic Module Testing Laboratory
- d. Review

Guidance: level 1

:: Project management ::

Contemporary business and science treat as a _________ any undertaking, carried out individually or collaboratively and possibly involving research or design, that is carefully planned to achieve a particular aim.

Exam Probability: **High**

48. *Answer choices:*

(see index for correct answer)

- a. Critical path drag
- b. Project
- c. The Goal
- d. Concurrent engineering

Guidance: level 1

:: Derivatives (finance) ::

_________ is any bodily activity that enhances or maintains physical fitness and overall health and wellness. It is performed for various reasons, to aid growth and improve strength, preventing aging, developing muscles and the cardiovascular system, honing athletic skills, weight loss or maintenance, improving health and also for enjoyment. Many individuals choose to _________ outdoors where they can congregate in groups, socialize, and enhance well-being.

Exam Probability: **Medium**

49. *Answer choices:*

(see index for correct answer)

- a. Net volatility
- b. Financial future
- c. Exercise
- d. Triple witching hour

Guidance: level 1

:: ::

A _________ is any person who contracts to acquire an asset in return for some form of consideration.

Exam Probability: **High**

50. *Answer choices:*

(see index for correct answer)

- a. Buyer
- b. process perspective
- c. hierarchical
- d. Character

Guidance: level 1

:: Management ::

_________ is the practice of initiating, planning, executing, controlling, and closing the work of a team to achieve specific goals and meet specific success criteria at the specified time.

Exam Probability: **Low**

51. *Answer choices:*

(see index for correct answer)

- a. Tacit knowledge
- b. Porter five forces analysis
- c. Project management
- d. Visual learning

Guidance: level 1

:: Stock market ::

The _________ of a corporation is all of the shares into which ownership of the corporation is divided. In American English, the shares are commonly known as " _________ s". A single share of the _________ represents fractional ownership of the corporation in proportion to the total number of shares. This typically entitles the _________ holder to that fraction of the company's earnings, proceeds from liquidation of assets , or voting power, often dividing these up in proportion to the amount of money each _________ holder has invested. Not all _________ is necessarily equal, as certain classes of _________ may be issued for example without voting rights, with enhanced voting rights, or with a certain priority to receive profits or liquidation proceeds before or after other classes of shareholders.

Exam Probability: **Medium**

52. *Answer choices:*

(see index for correct answer)

- a. Mosaic theory
- b. High-frequency trading
- c. Stock Catalyst
- d. Stock

Guidance: level 1

:: Business terms ::

A __________ is a short statement of why an organization exists, what its overall goal is, identifying the goal of its operations: what kind of product or service it provides, its primary customers or market, and its geographical region of operation. It may include a short statement of such fundamental matters as the organization`s values or philosophies, a business`s main competitive advantages, or a desired future state—the "vision".

Exam Probability: **Medium**

53. *Answer choices:*

(see index for correct answer)

- a. churn rate
- b. operating cost
- c. back office
- d. granular

Guidance: level 1

:: Management ::

In business, a __________ is the attribute that allows an organization to outperform its competitors. A __________ may include access to natural resources, such as high-grade ores or a low-cost power source, highly skilled labor, geographic location, high entry barriers, and access to new technology.

Exam Probability: **Low**

54. *Answer choices:*

(see index for correct answer)

- a. Technology scouting
- b. Competitive advantage
- c. Energy monitoring and targeting
- d. Middle management

Guidance: level 1

:: Summary statistics ::

_________ is the number of occurrences of a repeating event per unit of time. It is also referred to as temporal _________ , which emphasizes the contrast to spatial _________ and angular _________ . The period is the duration of time of one cycle in a repeating event, so the period is the reciprocal of the _________ . For example: if a newborn baby's heart beats at a _________ of 120 times a minute, its period—the time interval between beats—is half a second . _________ is an important parameter used in science and engineering to specify the rate of oscillatory and vibratory phenomena, such as mechanical vibrations, audio signals , radio waves, and light.

Exam Probability: **Low**

55. *Answer choices:*
(see index for correct answer)

- a. Robin Hood index
- b. Frequency
- c. Quartile
- d. Multiple of the median

Guidance: level 1

:: Strategic alliances ::

A _________ is an agreement between two or more parties to pursue a set of agreed upon objectives needed while remaining independent organizations. A _________ will usually fall short of a legal partnership entity, agency, or corporate affiliate relationship. Typically, two companies form a _________ when each possesses one or more business assets or have expertise that will help the other by enhancing their businesses. _________ s can develop in outsourcing relationships where the parties desire to achieve long-term win-win benefits and innovation based on mutually desired outcomes.

Exam Probability: **Medium**

56. *Answer choices:*
(see index for correct answer)

- a. Strategic alliance
- b. Defensive termination
- c. International joint venture
- d. Cross-licensing

Guidance: level 1

:: Shareholders ::

A __________ is a payment made by a corporation to its shareholders, usually as a distribution of profits. When a corporation earns a profit or surplus, the corporation is able to re-invest the profit in the business and pay a proportion of the profit as a __________ to shareholders. Distribution to shareholders may be in cash or, if the corporation has a __________ reinvestment plan, the amount can be paid by the issue of further shares or share repurchase. When __________ s are paid, shareholders typically must pay income taxes, and the corporation does not receive a corporate income tax deduction for the __________ payments.

Exam Probability: **High**

57. *Answer choices:*

(see index for correct answer)

- a. Institutional Shareholder Services
- b. Shareholder Executive
- c. Activist shareholder
- d. Shareholder oppression

Guidance: level 1

:: Loans ::

In finance, a __________ is the lending of money by one or more individuals, organizations, or other entities to other individuals, organizations etc. The recipient incurs a debt, and is usually liable to pay interest on that debt until it is repaid, and also to repay the principal amount borrowed.

Exam Probability: **High**

58. *Answer choices:*

(see index for correct answer)

- a. Marketing assistance loans
- b. Beverly Loan Company
- c. Loan
- d. Second lien

Guidance: level 1

:: ::

__________ is an abstract concept of management of complex systems according to a set of rules and trends. In systems theory, these types of rules exist in various fields of biology and society, but the term has slightly different meanings according to context. For example.

Exam Probability: **High**

59. *Answer choices:*

(see index for correct answer)

- a. hierarchical perspective
- b. Sarbanes-Oxley act of 2002
- c. surface-level diversity
- d. levels of analysis

Guidance: level 1

Management

Management is the administration of an organization, whether it is a business, a not-for-profit organization, or government body. Management includes the activities of setting the strategy of an organization and coordinating the efforts of its employees (or of volunteers) to accomplish its objectives through the application of available resources, such as financial, natural, technological, and human resources.

:: ::

_________ is a kind of action that occur as two or more objects have an effect upon one another. The idea of a two-way effect is essential in the concept of _________ , as opposed to a one-way causal effect. A closely related term is interconnectivity, which deals with the _________ s of _________ s within systems: combinations of many simple _________ s can lead to surprising emergent phenomena. _________ has different tailored meanings in various sciences. Changes can also involve _________ .

Exam Probability: **Low**

1. *Answer choices:*

(see index for correct answer)

- a. Interaction
- b. Sarbanes-Oxley act of 2002
- c. co-culture
- d. functional perspective

Guidance: level 1

:: Management ::

The term _________ refers to measures designed to increase the degree of autonomy and self-determination in people and in communities in order to enable them to represent their interests in a responsible and self-determined way, acting on their own authority. It is the process of becoming stronger and more confident, especially in controlling one`s life and claiming one`s rights. _________ as action refers both to the process of self- _________ and to professional support of people, which enables them to overcome their sense of powerlessness and lack of influence, and to recognize and use their resources. To do work with power.

Exam Probability: **High**

2. *Answer choices:*

(see index for correct answer)

- a. Mission critical
- b. Empowerment
- c. Design management
- d. Knowledge ecosystem

Guidance: level 1

:: International trade ::

_________ involves the transfer of goods or services from one person or entity to another, often in exchange for money. A system or network that allows _________ is called a market.

Exam Probability: **Low**

3. *Answer choices:*

(see index for correct answer)

- a. Outward Processing Arrangement
- b. Single-window system
- c. Indian Ocean trade
- d. Trade

Guidance: level 1

:: Export and import control ::

" _________ " means the Government Service which is responsible for the administration of _________ law and the collection of duties and taxes and which also has the responsibility for the application of other laws and regulations relating to the importation, exportation, movement or storage of goods.

Exam Probability: **Low**

4. *Answer choices:*

(see index for correct answer)

- a. Canadian Export and Import Controls Bureau
- b. CoCom
- c. International Traffic in Arms Regulations
- d. Wassenaar Arrangement

Guidance: level 1

:: Business models ::

A _________ , _________ company or daughter company is a company that is owned or controlled by another company, which is called the parent company, parent, or holding company. The _________ can be a company, corporation, or limited liability company. In some cases it is a government or state-owned enterprise. In some cases, particularly in the music and book publishing industries, subsidiaries are referred to as imprints.

Exam Probability: **Low**

5. *Answer choices:*

(see index for correct answer)

- a. Collective business system
- b. Subsidiary
- c. Meta learning
- d. Subscription business model

Guidance: level 1

:: ::

In production, research, retail, and accounting, a _________ is the value of money that has been used up to produce something or deliver a service, and hence is not available for use anymore. In business, the _________ may be one of acquisition, in which case the amount of money expended to acquire it is counted as _________ . In this case, money is the input that is gone in order to acquire the thing. This acquisition _________ may be the sum of the _________ of production as incurred by the original producer, and further _________ s of transaction as incurred by the acquirer over and above the price paid to the producer. Usually, the price also includes a mark-up for profit over the _________ of production.

Exam Probability: **Low**

6. *Answer choices:*

(see index for correct answer)

- a. process perspective
- b. surface-level diversity
- c. information systems assessment
- d. similarity-attraction theory

Guidance: level 1

:: Statistical terminology ::

_________ is the magnitude or dimensions of a thing. _________ can be measured as length, width, height, diameter, perimeter, area, volume, or mass.

Exam Probability: **High**

7. *Answer choices:*

(see index for correct answer)

- a. Epps effect
- b. Size
- c. Data generating process
- d. Cause of death

Guidance: level 1

:: Management accounting ::

In economics, _________ s, indirect costs or overheads are business expenses that are not dependent on the level of goods or services produced by the business. They tend to be time-related, such as interest or rents being paid per month, and are often referred to as overhead costs. This is in contrast to variable costs, which are volume-related and unknown at the beginning of the accounting year. For a simple example, such as a bakery, the monthly rent for the baking facilities, and the monthly payments for the security system and basic phone line are _________ s, as they do not change according to how much bread the bakery produces and sells. On the other hand, the wage costs of the bakery are variable, as the bakery will have to hire more workers if the production of bread increases. Economists reckon _________ as a entry barrier for new entrepreneurs.

Exam Probability: **High**

8. *Answer choices:*

(see index for correct answer)

- a. Variable cost
- b. Managerial risk accounting
- c. Fixed cost
- d. Chartered Cost Accountant

Guidance: level 1

:: Monopoly (economics) ::

_________ is a category of property that includes intangible creations of the human intellect. _________ encompasses two types of rights: industrial property rights and copyright. It was not until the 19th century that the term " _________ " began to be used, and not until the late 20th century that it became commonplace in the majority of the world.

Exam Probability: **High**

9. *Answer choices:*

(see index for correct answer)

- a. Barriers to exit
- b. Patent portfolio
- c. Ramsey problem
- d. Intellectual property

Guidance: level 1

:: Business law ::

A _________ is an arrangement where parties, known as partners, agree to cooperate to advance their mutual interests. The partners in a _________ may be individuals, businesses, interest-based organizations, schools, governments or combinations. Organizations may partner to increase the likelihood of each achieving their mission and to amplify their reach. A _________ may result in issuing and holding equity or may be only governed by a contract.

Exam Probability: **Low**

10. *Answer choices:*

(see index for correct answer)

- a. Power harassment
- b. Limited partnership
- c. Business.gov
- d. Partnership

Guidance: level 1

:: Production economics ::

_________ is the joint use of a resource or space. It is also the process of dividing and distributing. In its narrow sense, it refers to joint or alternating use of inherently finite goods, such as a common pasture or a shared residence. Still more loosely, " _________ " can actually mean giving something as an outright gift: for example, to "share" one`s food really means to give some of it as a gift. _________ is a basic component of human interaction, and is responsible for strengthening social ties and ensuring a person's well-being.

Exam Probability: **Medium**

11. *Answer choices:*

(see index for correct answer)

- a. Hicks-neutral technical change
- b. Marginal rate of technical substitution
- c. Producer's risk
- d. Isocost

Guidance: level 1

:: Business terms ::

A __________ is a short statement of why an organization exists, what its overall goal is, identifying the goal of its operations: what kind of product or service it provides, its primary customers or market, and its geographical region of operation. It may include a short statement of such fundamental matters as the organization`s values or philosophies, a business`s main competitive advantages, or a desired future state—the "vision".

Exam Probability: **Low**

12. *Answer choices:*

(see index for correct answer)

- a. noncommercial
- b. back office
- c. Personal selling
- d. organic growth

Guidance: level 1

:: Project management ::

A __________ is a team whose members usually belong to different groups, functions and are assigned to activities for the same project. A team can be divided into sub-teams according to need. Usually __________ s are only used for a defined period of time. They are disbanded after the project is deemed complete. Due to the nature of the specific formation and disbandment, __________ s are usually in organizations.

Exam Probability: **Medium**

13. *Answer choices:*

(see index for correct answer)

- a. LibrePlan
- b. Multidisciplinary approach
- c. Technology roadmap
- d. Organizational project management

Guidance: level 1

:: Belief ::

__________ is the study of general and fundamental questions about existence, knowledge, values, reason, mind, and language. Such questions are often posed as problems to be studied or resolved. The term was probably coined by Pythagoras . Philosophical methods include questioning, critical discussion, rational argument, and systematic presentation. Classic philosophical questions include: Is it possible to know anything and to prove it What is most real Philosophers also pose more practical and concrete questions such as: Is there a best way to live Is it better to be just or unjust Do humans have free will

Exam Probability: **Medium**

14. *Answer choices:*
(see index for correct answer)

- a. Urdoxa
- b. Epistemic closure
- c. Wish fulfillment
- d. Philosophy

Guidance: level 1

:: Poker strategy ::

__________ is any measure taken to guard a thing against damage caused by outside forces. __________ can be provided to physical objects, including organisms, to systems, and to intangible things like civil and political rights. Although the mechanisms for providing __________ vary widely, the basic meaning of the term remains the same. This is illustrated by an explanation found in a manual on electrical wiring.

Exam Probability: **High**

15. *Answer choices:*
(see index for correct answer)

- a. Steal
- b. Slow play
- c. Protection
- d. Position

Guidance: level 1

:: Social networks ::

_________ broadly refers to those factors of effectively functioning social groups that include such things as interpersonal relationships, a shared sense of identity, a shared understanding, shared norms, shared values, trust, cooperation, and reciprocity. However, the many views of this complex subject make a single definition difficult.

Exam Probability: **Low**

16. *Answer choices:*

(see index for correct answer)

- a. International Network for Social Network Analysis
- b. Friend of a friend
- c. Online learning community
- d. Social capital

Guidance: level 1

:: ::

_________ , known in Europe as research and technological development , refers to innovative activities undertaken by corporations or governments in developing new services or products, or improving existing services or products. _________ constitutes the first stage of development of a potential new service or the production process.

Exam Probability: **Medium**

17. *Answer choices:*

(see index for correct answer)

- a. interpersonal communication
- b. Character
- c. Research and development
- d. corporate values

Guidance: level 1

:: ::

In communications and information processing, _________ is a system of rules to convert information—such as a letter, word, sound, image, or gesture—into another form or representation, sometimes shortened or secret, for communication through a communication channel or storage in a storage medium. An early example is the invention of language, which enabled a person, through speech, to communicate what they saw, heard, felt, or thought to others. But speech limits the range of communication to the distance a voice can carry, and limits the audience to those present when the speech is uttered. The invention of writing, which converted spoken language into visual symbols, extended the range of communication across space and time.

Exam Probability: **High**

18. *Answer choices:*
(see index for correct answer)

- a. Code
- b. corporate values
- c. empathy
- d. cultural

Guidance: level 1

:: Financial risk ::

_________ is a type of risk faced by investors, corporations, and governments that political decisions, events, or conditions will significantly affect the profitability of a business actor or the expected value of a given economic action. _________ can be understood and managed with reasoned foresight and investment.

Exam Probability: **Low**

19. *Answer choices:*
(see index for correct answer)

- a. Reputational risk
- b. Age at risk
- c. Over-the-counter
- d. Political risk

Guidance: level 1

:: Organizational theory ::

A _________ is an organizational theory that claims that there is no best way to organize a corporation, to lead a company, or to make decisions. Instead, the optimal course of action is contingent upon the internal and external situation. A contingent leader effectively applies their own style of leadership to the right situation.

Exam Probability: **Medium**

20. *Answer choices:*

(see index for correct answer)

- a. Battlefield promotion
- b. Seagull manager
- c. Requisite organization
- d. Contingency theory

Guidance: level 1

:: Leadership ::

_________ /Management is a part of a style of leadership that focuses on supervision, organization, and performance; it is an integral part of the Full Range Leadership Model. _________ is a style of leadership in which leaders promote compliance by followers through both rewards and punishments. Through a rewards and punishments system, transactional leaders are able to keep followers motivated for the short-term. Unlike transformational leaders, those using the transactional approach are not looking to change the future, they look to keep things the same. Leaders using _________ as a model pay attention to followers` work in order to find faults and deviations.

Exam Probability: **Medium**

21. *Answer choices:*

(see index for correct answer)

- a. Servant leadership
- b. Sex differences in leadership
- c. Maintenance actions
- d. Transactional leadership

Guidance: level 1

:: Lean manufacturing ::

_________ is the Sino-Japanese word for "improvement". In business, _________ refers to activities that continuously improve all functions and involve all employees from the CEO to the assembly line workers. It also applies to processes, such as purchasing and logistics, that cross organizational boundaries into the supply chain. It has been applied in healthcare, psychotherapy, life-coaching, government, and banking.

Exam Probability: **Medium**

22. *Answer choices:*
(see index for correct answer)

- a. Lean laboratory
- b. No value added
- c. Kaizen
- d. Lean enterprise

Guidance: level 1

:: Production economics ::

_________ is the creation of a whole that is greater than the simple sum of its parts. The term _________ comes from the Attic Greek word sea synergia from synergos, , meaning "working together".

Exam Probability: **Low**

23. *Answer choices:*
(see index for correct answer)

- a. Post-Fordism
- b. Partial productivity
- c. Marginal cost of capital schedule
- d. Marginal product

Guidance: level 1

:: ::

_________ is the amount of time someone works beyond normal working hours. The term is also used for the pay received for this time. Normal hours may be determined in several ways.

Exam Probability: **Low**

24. *Answer choices:*
(see index for correct answer)

- a. Character
- b. Overtime
- c. process perspective
- d. hierarchical perspective

Guidance: level 1

:: Systems theory ::

A _________ is a set of policies, processes and procedures used by an organization to ensure that it can fulfill the tasks required to achieve its objectives. These objectives cover many aspects of the organization's operations . For instance, an environmental _________ enables organizations to improve their environmental performance and an occupational health and safety _________ enables an organization to control its occupational health and safety risks, etc.

Exam Probability: **Low**

25. *Answer choices:*
(see index for correct answer)

- a. Management system
- b. subsystem
- c. process system
- d. Viable System Model

Guidance: level 1

:: Outsourcing ::

_________ is the relocation of a business process from one country to another—typically an operational process, such as manufacturing, or supporting processes, such as accounting. Typically this refers to a company business, although state governments may also employ _________ . More recently, technical and administrative services have been offshored.

Exam Probability: **Medium**

26. *Answer choices:*

(see index for correct answer)

- a. Offshoring
- b. Divestiture
- c. Strategic sourcing
- d. Chris Ducker

Guidance: level 1

:: Information technology management ::

__________ is a collective term for all approaches to prepare , support and help individuals, teams, and organizations in making organizational change. The most common change drivers include: technological evolution, process reviews, crisis, and consumer habit changes; pressure from new business entrants, acquisitions, mergers, and organizational restructuring. It includes methods that redirect or redefine the use of resources, business process, budget allocations, or other modes of operation that significantly change a company or organization. Organizational __________ considers the full organization and what needs to change, while __________ may be used solely to refer to how people and teams are affected by such organizational transition. It deals with many different disciplines, from behavioral and social sciences to information technology and business solutions.

Exam Probability: **Medium**

27. *Answer choices:*

(see index for correct answer)

- a. Change management
- b. Iteraplan
- c. Enterprise information management
- d. Business transaction performance

Guidance: level 1

:: ::

_________ is the process of two or more people or organizations working together to complete a task or achieve a goal. _________ is similar to cooperation. Most _________ requires leadership, although the form of leadership can be social within a decentralized and egalitarian group. Teams that work collaboratively often access greater resources, recognition and rewards when facing competition for finite resources.

Exam Probability: **High**

28. *Answer choices:*

(see index for correct answer)

- a. Collaboration
- b. personal values
- c. Sarbanes-Oxley act of 2002
- d. interpersonal communication

Guidance: level 1

:: Cash flow ::

_________ s are narrowly interconnected with the concepts of value, interest rate and liquidity.A _________ that shall happen on a future day tN can be transformed into a _________ of the same value in t0.

Exam Probability: **Medium**

29. *Answer choices:*

(see index for correct answer)

- a. Valuation using discounted cash flows
- b. Propequity
- c. Cash flow
- d. Cash carrier

Guidance: level 1

:: ::

__________ , in its broadest context, includes both the attainment of that which is just and the philosophical discussion of that which is just. The concept of __________ is based on numerous fields, and many differing viewpoints and perspectives including the concepts of moral correctness based on ethics, rationality, law, religion, equity and fairness. Often, the general discussion of __________ is divided into the realm of social __________ as found in philosophy, theology and religion, and, procedural __________ as found in the study and application of the law.

Exam Probability: **High**

30. *Answer choices:*

(see index for correct answer)

- a. cultural
- b. interpersonal communication
- c. Justice
- d. information systems assessment

Guidance: level 1

:: Management ::

A __________ is someone who engages in facilitation—any activity that makes a social process easy or easier. A __________ often helps a group of people to understand their common objectives and assists them to plan how to achieve these objectives; in doing so, the __________ remains "neutral", meaning he/she does not take a particular position in the discussion. Some __________ tools will try to assist the group in achieving a consensus on any disagreements that preexist or emerge in the meeting so that it has a strong basis for future action.

Exam Probability: **Medium**

31. *Answer choices:*

(see index for correct answer)

- a. Facilitator
- b. Corticon
- c. Event management
- d. Target culture

Guidance: level 1

:: ::

Business is the activity of making one`s living or making money by producing or buying and selling products . Simply put, it is "any activity or enterprise entered into for profit. It does not mean it is a company, a corporation, partnership, or have any such formal organization, but it can range from a street peddler to General Motors."

Exam Probability: **Medium**

32. *Answer choices:*
(see index for correct answer)

- a. cultural
- b. Firm
- c. co-culture
- d. empathy

Guidance: level 1

:: ::

__________ or haggling is a type of negotiation in which the buyer and seller of a good or service debate the price and exact nature of a transaction. If the __________ produces agreement on terms, the transaction takes place. __________ is an alternative pricing strategy to fixed prices. Optimally, if it costs the retailer nothing to engage and allow __________ , s/he can divine the buyer`s willingness to spend. It allows for capturing more consumer surplus as it allows price discrimination, a process whereby a seller can charge a higher price to one buyer who is more eager . Haggling has largely disappeared in parts of the world where the cost to haggle exceeds the gain to retailers for most common retail items. However, for expensive goods sold to uninformed buyers such as automobiles, __________ can remain commonplace.

Exam Probability: **Medium**

33. *Answer choices:*
(see index for correct answer)

- a. hierarchical perspective
- b. interpersonal communication
- c. Bargaining
- d. surface-level diversity

Guidance: level 1

:: ::

A _________ is the ability to carry out a task with determined results often within a given amount of time, energy, or both. _________ s can often be divided into domain-general and domain-specific _________ s. For example, in the domain of work, some general _________ s would include time management, teamwork and leadership, self-motivation and others, whereas domain-specific _________ s would be used only for a certain job. _________ usually requires certain environmental stimuli and situations to assess the level of _________ being shown and used.

Exam Probability: **High**

34. *Answer choices:*

(see index for correct answer)

- a. Character
- b. open system
- c. interpersonal communication
- d. Sarbanes-Oxley act of 2002

Guidance: level 1

:: Behavior modification ::

In psychotherapy and mental health, _________ has a positive sense of empowering individuals, or a negative sense of encouraging dysfunctional behavior.

Exam Probability: **Low**

35. *Answer choices:*

(see index for correct answer)

- a. Enabling
- b. behavioural change

Guidance: level 1

:: Scientific method ::

In the social sciences and life sciences, a _________ is a research method involving an up-close, in-depth, and detailed examination of a subject of study , as well as its related contextual conditions.

Exam Probability: **Low**

36. *Answer choices:*

(see index for correct answer)

- a. pilot project
- b. explanatory research
- c. Preference test
- d. Case study

Guidance: level 1

:: Project management ::

Some scenarios associate "this kind of planning" with learning "life skills". _________ s are necessary, or at least useful, in situations where individuals need to know what time they must be at a specific location to receive a specific service, and where people need to accomplish a set of goals within a set time period.

Exam Probability: **Medium**

37. *Answer choices:*

(see index for correct answer)

- a. Project cycle management
- b. Gantt chart
- c. Project network
- d. DICE framework

Guidance: level 1

:: ::

_________ or standardisation is the process of implementing and developing technical standards based on the consensus of different parties that include firms, users, interest groups, standards organizations and governments. _________ can help maximize compatibility, interoperability, safety, repeatability, or quality. It can also facilitate commoditization of formerly custom processes. In social sciences, including economics, the idea of _________ is close to the solution for a coordination problem, a situation in which all parties can realize mutual gains, but only by making mutually consistent decisions. This view includes the case of "spontaneous _________ processes", to produce de facto standards.

Exam Probability: **High**

38. *Answer choices:*
(see index for correct answer)

- a. process perspective
- b. information systems assessment
- c. Standardization
- d. empathy

Guidance: level 1

:: Marketing ::

_________ is based on a marketing concept which can be adopted by an organization as a strategy for business expansion. Where implemented, a franchisor licenses its know-how, procedures, intellectual property, use of its business model, brand, and rights to sell its branded products and services to a franchisee. In return the franchisee pays certain fees and agrees to comply with certain obligations, typically set out in a Franchise Agreement.

Exam Probability: **Low**

39. *Answer choices:*
(see index for correct answer)

- a. Klondike Big Inch Land Promotion
- b. Content Curation Marketing
- c. Emailing
- d. Franchising

Guidance: level 1

:: Leadership ::

__________ is a theory of leadership where a leader works with teams to identify needed change, creating a vision to guide the change through inspiration, and executing the change in tandem with committed members of a group; it is an integral part of the Full Range Leadership Model. __________ serves to enhance the motivation, morale, and job performance of followers through a variety of mechanisms; these include connecting the follower`s sense of identity and self to a project and to the collective identity of the organization; being a role model for followers in order to inspire them and to raise their interest in the project; challenging followers to take greater ownership for their work, and understanding the strengths and weaknesses of followers, allowing the leader to align followers with tasks that enhance their performance.

Exam Probability: **Low**

40. *Answer choices:*

(see index for correct answer)

- a. Ethical leadership
- b. Maintenance actions
- c. Servant leadership
- d. Three levels of leadership model

Guidance: level 1

:: Human resource management ::

__________ is a core function of human resource management and it is related to the specification of contents, methods and relationship of jobs in order to satisfy technological and organizational requirements as well as the social and personal requirements of the job holder or the employee. Its principles are geared towards how the nature of a person`s job affects their attitudes and behavior at work, particularly relating to characteristics such as skill variety and autonomy. The aim of a __________ is to improve job satisfaction, to improve through-put, to improve quality and to reduce employee problems .

Exam Probability: **Medium**

41. *Answer choices:*

.ect answer)

- a. Human resource accounting
- b. Illness rate
- c. Adecco Group North America
- d. Job design

Guidance: level 1

:: Monopoly (economics) ::

A _________ is a form of intellectual property that gives its owner the legal right to exclude others from making, using, selling, and importing an invention for a limited period of years, in exchange for publishing an enabling public disclosure of the invention. In most countries _________ rights fall under civil law and the _________ holder needs to sue someone infringing the _________ in order to enforce his or her rights. In some industries _________ s are an essential form of competitive advantage; in others they are irrelevant.

Exam Probability: **Medium**

42. *Answer choices:*
(see index for correct answer)

- a. Tesco Town
- b. Intellectual property
- c. Patent
- d. Herfindahl index

Guidance: level 1

:: ::

A _________ is a professional who provides expert advice in a particular area such as security , management, education, accountancy, law, human resources, marketing , finance, engineering, science or any of many other specialized fields.

Exam Probability: **High**

43. *Answer choices:*
(see index for correct answer)

- a. empathy

- b. personal values
- c. hierarchical perspective
- d. Consultant

Guidance: level 1

:: ::

_________ is the administration of an organization, whether it is a business, a not-for-profit organization, or government body. _________ includes the activities of setting the strategy of an organization and coordinating the efforts of its employees to accomplish its objectives through the application of available resources, such as financial, natural, technological, and human resources. The term " _________ " may also refer to those people who manage an organization.

Exam Probability: **Medium**

44. *Answer choices:*

(see index for correct answer)

- a. Management
- b. empathy
- c. information systems assessment
- d. Character

Guidance: level 1

:: ::

The _________ is a political and economic union of 28 member states that are located primarily in Europe. It has an area of 4,475,757 km2 and an estimated population of about 513 million. The EU has developed an internal single market through a standardised system of laws that apply in all member states in those matters, and only those matters, where members have agreed to act as one. EU policies aim to ensure the free movement of people, goods, services and capital within the internal market, enact legislation in justice and home affairs and maintain common policies on trade, agriculture, fisheries and regional development. For travel within the Schengen Area, passport controls have been abolished. A monetary union was established in 1999 and came into full force in 2002 and is composed of 19 EU member states which use the euro currency.

Exam Probability: **Low**

45. *Answer choices:*

(see index for correct answer)

- a. personal values
- b. imperative
- c. Sarbanes-Oxley act of 2002
- d. corporate values

Guidance: level 1

:: Management occupations ::

_________ ship is the process of designing, launching and running a new business, which is often initially a small business. The people who create these businesses are called _________ s.

Exam Probability: **Low**

46. *Answer choices:*

(see index for correct answer)

- a. Geospatial information officer
- b. Entrepreneurship
- c. Adjutant general
- d. Entrepreneur

Guidance: level 1

:: Project management ::

A _________ is a professional in the field of project management. _________ s have the responsibility of the planning, procurement and execution of a project, in any undertaking that has a defined scope, defined start and a defined finish; regardless of industry. _________ s are first point of contact for any issues or discrepancies arising from within the heads of various departments in an organization before the problem escalates to higher authorities. Project management is the responsibility of a _________ . This individual seldom participates directly in the activities that produce the end result, but rather strives to maintain the progress, mutual interaction and tasks of various parties in such a way that reduces the risk of overall failure, maximizes benefits, and minimizes costs.

Exam Probability: **High**

47. *Answer choices:*

(see index for correct answer)

- a. Constructability
- b. Precedence diagram method
- c. The Chicken and the Pig
- d. Project manager

Guidance: level 1

:: Game theory ::

To _________ is to make a deal between different parties where each party gives up part of their demand. In arguments, _________ is a concept of finding agreement through communication, through a mutual acceptance of terms—often involving variations from an original goal or desires.

Exam Probability: **Medium**

48. *Answer choices:*

(see index for correct answer)

- a. Bandwidth-sharing game
- b. Compromise
- c. Lewis signaling game
- d. Michael Taylor

Guidance: level 1

:: Evaluation ::

_________ is the practice of being honest and showing a consistent and uncompromising adherence to strong moral and ethical principles and values.In ethics, _________ is regarded as the honesty and truthfulness or accuracy of one`s actions. _________ can stand in opposition to hypocrisy, in that judging with the standards of _________ involves regarding internal consistency as a virtue, and suggests that parties holding within themselves apparently conflicting values should account for the discrepancy or alter their beliefs. The word _________ evolved from the Latin adjective integer, meaning whole or complete. In this context, _________ is the inner sense of "wholeness" deriving from qualities such as honesty and consistency of character. As such, one may judge that others "have _________ " to the extent that they act according to the values, beliefs and principles they claim to hold.

Exam Probability: **Medium**

49. *Answer choices:*

(see index for correct answer)

- a. Server Efficiency Rating Tool
- b. XTS-400
- c. Integrity
- d. Goddard College

Guidance: level 1

:: Office administration ::

An _________ is generally a room or other area where an organization`s employees perform administrative work in order to support and realize objects and goals of the organization. The word " _________ " may also denote a position within an organization with specific duties attached to it ; the latter is in fact an earlier usage, _________ as place originally referring to the location of one`s duty. When used as an adjective, the term " _________ " may refer to business-related tasks. In law, a company or organization has _________ s in any place where it has an official presence, even if that presence consists of a storage silo rather than an establishment with desk-and-chair. An _________ is also an architectural and design phenomenon: ranging from a small _________ such as a bench in the corner of a small business of extremely small size , through entire floors of buildings, up to and including massive buildings dedicated entirely to one company. In modern terms an _________ is usually the location where white-collar workers carry out their functions. As per James Stephenson, " _________ is that part of business enterprise which is devoted to the direction and co-ordination of its various activities."

Exam Probability: **Medium**

50. *Answer choices:*

(see index for correct answer)

- a. Inter departmental communication
- b. Office administration
- c. Fish! Philosophy
- d. Activity management

Guidance: level 1

:: Credit cards ::

The _________ Company, also known as Amex, is an American multinational financial services corporation headquartered in Three World Financial Center in New York City. The company was founded in 1850 and is one of the 30 components of the Dow Jones Industrial Average. The company is best known for its charge card, credit card, and traveler`s cheque businesses.

Exam Probability: **Medium**

51. *Answer choices:*

(see index for correct answer)

- a. American Express
- b. Visa Black Card
- c. InteliSpend Prepaid Solutions
- d. Gravity Payments

Guidance: level 1

:: Internet privacy ::

An _________ is a private network accessible only to an organization`s staff. Often, a wide range of information and services are available on an organization`s internal _________ that are unavailable to the public, unlike the Internet. A company-wide _________ can constitute an important focal point of internal communication and collaboration, and provide a single starting point to access internal and external resources. In its simplest form, an _________ is established with the technologies for local area networks and wide area networks . Many modern _________ s have search engines, user profiles, blogs, mobile apps with notifications, and events planning within their infrastructure.

Exam Probability: **High**

52. *Answer choices:*

(see index for correct answer)

- a. Anonymous web browsing
- b. Digitalcourage
- c. Web bug
- d. Anonymity application

Guidance: level 1

:: Organizational behavior ::

_________ is the term now used more commonly in business management, particularly human resource management. _________ refers to the number of subordinates a supervisor has.

Exam Probability: **Low**

53. *Answer choices:*

(see index for correct answer)

- a. Span of control

- b. Ownership
- c. Nut Island effect
- d. Managerial grid model

Guidance: level 1

:: Leadership ::

__________ Theory, or the __________ Model, is a model created by Paul Hersey and Ken Blanchard, developed while working on Management of Organizational Behavior. The theory was first introduced in 1969 as "life cycle theory of leadership". During the mid-1970s, life cycle theory of leadership was renamed " __________ Theory."

Exam Probability: **Medium**

54. *Answer choices:*

(see index for correct answer)

- a. Transactional leadership
- b. servant leader
- c. Situational leadership
- d. The Intangibles of Leadership

Guidance: level 1

:: ::

__________ is the reason for people`s actions, willingness and goals. __________ is derived from the word motive in the English language which is defined as a need that requires satisfaction. These needs could also be wants or desires that are acquired through influence of culture, society, lifestyle, etc. or generally innate. __________ is one`s direction to behaviour, or what causes a person to want to repeat a behaviour, a set of force that acts behind the motives. An individual`s __________ may be inspired by others or events or it may come from within the individual . __________ has been considered as one of the most important reasons that inspires a person to move forward in life. __________ results from the interaction of both conscious and unconscious factors. Mastering __________ to allow sustained and deliberate practice is central to high levels of achievement e.g. in the worlds of elite sport, medicine or music.

Exam Probability: **High**

55. *Answer choices:*
(see index for correct answer)

- a. co-culture
- b. hierarchical perspective
- c. Motivation
- d. information systems assessment

Guidance: level 1

:: Management ::

The _________ is a strategy performance management tool – a semi-standard structured report, that can be used by managers to keep track of the execution of activities by the staff within their control and to monitor the consequences arising from these actions.

Exam Probability: **Medium**

56. *Answer choices:*
(see index for correct answer)

- a. Balanced scorecard
- b. Virtual customer environment
- c. Certified Energy Manager
- d. Competitive heterogeneity

Guidance: level 1

:: ::

According to Torrington, a _________ is usually developed by conducting a job analysis, which includes examining the tasks and sequences of tasks necessary to perform the job. The analysis considers the areas of knowledge and skills needed for the job. A job usually includes several roles. According to Hall, the _________ might be broadened to form a person specification or may be known as "terms of reference". The person/job specification can be presented as a stand-alone document, but in practice it is usually included within the _________ . A _________ is often used by employers in the recruitment process.

Exam Probability: **High**

57. *Answer choices:*
(see index for correct answer)

- a. Job description
- b. process perspective
- c. information systems assessment
- d. corporate values

Guidance: level 1

:: Business ethics ::

__________ is a type of harassment technique that relates to a sexual nature and the unwelcome or inappropriate promise of rewards in exchange for sexual favors. __________ includes a range of actions from mild transgressions to sexual abuse or assault. Harassment can occur in many different social settings such as the workplace, the home, school, churches, etc. Harassers or victims may be of any gender.

Exam Probability: **High**

58. *Answer choices:*
(see index for correct answer)

- a. United Nations Global Compact
- b. Marketing ethics
- c. Sexual harassment
- d. Voluntary compliance

Guidance: level 1

:: Supply chain management terms ::

In business and finance, __________ is a system of organizations, people, activities, information, and resources involved inmoving a product or service from supplier to customer. __________ activities involve the transformation of natural resources, raw materials, and components into a finished product that is delivered to the end customer. In sophisticated __________ systems, used products may re-enter the __________ at any point where residual value is recyclable. __________ s link value chains.

Exam Probability: **High**

59. *Answer choices:*

(see index for correct answer)

- a. Final assembly schedule
- b. Supply-chain management
- c. Stockout
- d. Work in process

Guidance: level 1

Business law

Corporate law (also known as business law) is the body of law governing the rights, relations, and conduct of persons, companies, organizations and businesses. It refers to the legal practice relating to, or the theory of corporations. Corporate law often describes the law relating to matters which derive directly from the life-cycle of a corporation. It thus encompasses the formation, funding, governance, and death of a corporation.

:: Real property law ::

_________ is the judicial process whereby a will is "proved" in a court of law and accepted as a valid public document that is the true last testament of the deceased, or whereby the estate is settled according to the laws of intestacy in the state of residence [or real property] of the deceased at time of death in the absence of a legal will.

Exam Probability: **Medium**

1. *Answer choices:*
(see index for correct answer)

- a. Edwards v. Habib
- b. Probate
- c. Orphan bridge
- d. Atrisco Land Grant

Guidance: level 1

:: ::

_________ is the study and management of exchange relationships. _________ is the business process of creating relationships with and satisfying customers. With its focus on the customer, _________ is one of the premier components of business management.

Exam Probability: **High**

2. *Answer choices:*

(see index for correct answer)

- a. Marketing
- b. process perspective
- c. similarity-attraction theory
- d. information systems assessment

Guidance: level 1

:: ::

_________ Motor Company is an American multinational automaker that has its main headquarter in Dearborn, Michigan, a suburb of Detroit. It was founded by Henry _________ and incorporated on June 16, 1903. The company sells automobiles and commercial vehicles under the _________ brand and most luxury cars under the Lincoln brand. _________ also owns Brazilian SUV manufacturer Troller, an 8% stake in Aston Martin of the United Kingdom and a 32% stake in Jiangling Motors. It also has joint-ventures in China , Taiwan , Thailand , Turkey , and Russia . The company is listed on the New York Stock Exchange and is controlled by the _________ family; they have minority ownership but the majority of the voting power.

Exam Probability: **High**

3. *Answer choices:*

(see index for correct answer)

- a. Ford
- b. interpersonal communication
- c. empathy
- d. co-culture

Guidance: level 1

:: ::

The _________ to the United States Constitution prevents the government from making laws which respect an establishment of religion, prohibit the free exercise of religion, or abridge the freedom of speech, the freedom of the press, the right to peaceably assemble, or the right to petition the government for redress of grievances. It was adopted on December 15, 1791, as one of the ten amendments that constitute the Bill of Rights.

Exam Probability: **High**

4. *Answer choices:*

(see index for correct answer)

- a. interpersonal communication
- b. Sarbanes-Oxley act of 2002
- c. First Amendment
- d. hierarchical perspective

Guidance: level 1

:: Decision theory ::

Within economics the concept of _________ is used to model worth or value, but its usage has evolved significantly over time. The term was introduced initially as a measure of pleasure or satisfaction within the theory of utilitarianism by moral philosophers such as Jeremy Bentham and John Stuart Mill. But the term has been adapted and reapplied within neoclassical economics, which dominates modern economic theory, as a _________ function that represents a consumer`s preference ordering over a choice set. As such, it is devoid of its original interpretation as a measurement of the pleasure or satisfaction obtained by the consumer from that choice.

Exam Probability: **Low**

5. *Answer choices:*

(see index for correct answer)

- a. Choquet integral
- b. Utility
- c. Value of information
- d. Social and Decision Sciences

Guidance: level 1

:: ::

In legal terminology, a _________ is any formal legal document that sets out the facts and legal reasons that the filing party or parties believes are sufficient to support a claim against the party or parties against whom the claim is brought that entitles the plaintiff to a remedy . For example, the Federal Rules of Civil Procedure that govern civil litigation in United States courts provide that a civil action is commenced with the filing or service of a pleading called a _________ . Civil court rules in states that have incorporated the Federal Rules of Civil Procedure use the same term for the same pleading.

Exam Probability: **Low**

6. *Answer choices:*

(see index for correct answer)

- a. cultural
- b. levels of analysis
- c. Complaint
- d. imperative

Guidance: level 1

:: Business law ::

A _________ , also known as the sole trader, individual entrepreneurship or proprietorship, is a type of enterprise that is owned and run by one person and in which there is no legal distinction between the owner and the business entity. A sole trader does not necessarily work `alone`—it is possible for the sole trader to employ other people.

Exam Probability: **Low**

7. *Answer choices:*

(see index for correct answer)

- a. Commercial law
- b. Apparent authority
- c. Negative option billing
- d. Process agent

Guidance: level 1

:: Contract law ::

A _________ cannot be enforced by law. _________ s are different from voidable contracts, which are contracts that may be nullified. However, when a contract is being written and signed, there is no automatic mechanism available in every situation that can be utilized to detect the validity or enforceability of that contract. Practically, a contract can be declared to be void by a court of law. So the main question is that under what conditions can a contract be deemed as void

Exam Probability: **Medium**

8. *Answer choices:*
(see index for correct answer)

- a. Void contract
- b. Shrink wrap contract
- c. Garnishment
- d. Collateral warranty

Guidance: level 1

:: ::

A federation is a political entity characterized by a union of partially self-governing provinces, states, or other regions under a central _________ . In a federation, the self-governing status of the component states, as well as the division of power between them and the central government, is typically constitutionally entrenched and may not be altered by a unilateral decision of either party, the states or the federal political body. Alternatively, federation is a form of government in which sovereign power is formally divided between a central authority and a number of constituent regions so that each region retains some degree of control over its internal affairs. It is often argued that federal states where the central government has the constitutional authority to suspend a constituent state`s government by invoking gross mismanagement or civil unrest, or to adopt national legislation that overrides or infringe on the constituent states` powers by invoking the central government`s constitutional authority to ensure "peace and good government" or to implement obligations contracted under an international treaty, are not truly federal states.

Exam Probability: **Medium**

9. *Answer choices:*

(see index for correct answer)

- a. similarity-attraction theory
- b. interpersonal communication
- c. empathy
- d. Sarbanes-Oxley act of 2002

Guidance: level 1

:: Legal doctrines and principles ::

The _________ rule is a rule in the Anglo-American common law that governs what kinds of evidence parties to a contract dispute can introduce when trying to determine the specific terms of a contract. The rule also prevents parties who have reduced their agreement to a final written document from later introducing other evidence, such as the content of oral discussions from earlier in the negotiation process, as evidence of a different intent as to the terms of the contract. The rule provides that "extrinsic evidence is inadmissible to vary a written contract". The term "parol" derives from the Anglo-Norman French parol or parole, meaning "word of mouth" or "verbal", and in medieval times referred to oral pleadings in a court case.

Exam Probability: **High**

10. *Answer choices:*

(see index for correct answer)

- a. Attractive nuisance doctrine
- b. Parol evidence
- c. unconscionable contract
- d. Contributory negligence

Guidance: level 1

:: ::

_________ is a legal term which, in its broadest sense, is a synonym for anyone in a position of trust and so can refer to any person who holds property, authority, or a position of trust or responsibility for the benefit of another. A _________ can also refer to a person who is allowed to do certain tasks but not able to gain income. Although in the strictest sense of the term a _________ is the holder of property on behalf of a beneficiary, the more expansive sense encompasses persons who serve, for example, on the board of _________ s of an institution that operates for a charity, for the benefit of the general public, or a person in the local government.

Exam Probability: **High**

11. *Answer choices:*

(see index for correct answer)

- a. levels of analysis
- b. hierarchical perspective
- c. cultural
- d. Trustee

Guidance: level 1

:: ::

The _________ is the highest court within the hierarchy of courts in many legal jurisdictions. Other descriptions for such courts include court of last resort, apex court, and high court of appeal. Broadly speaking, the decisions of a _________ are not subject to further review by any other court. _________ s typically function primarily as appellate courts, hearing appeals from decisions of lower trial courts, or from intermediate-level appellate courts.

Exam Probability: **High**

12. *Answer choices:*

(see index for correct answer)

- a. hierarchical perspective
- b. information systems assessment
- c. levels of analysis
- d. Supreme Court

Guidance: level 1

:: ::

In law, an _________ is the process in which cases are reviewed, where parties request a formal change to an official decision. _________ s function both as a process for error correction as well as a process of clarifying and interpreting law. Although appellate courts have existed for thousands of years, common law countries did not incorporate an affirmative right to _________ into their jurisprudence until the 19th century.

Exam Probability: **Medium**

13. *Answer choices:*

(see index for correct answer)

- a. functional perspective
- b. Appeal
- c. empathy
- d. hierarchical

Guidance: level 1

:: ::

_________ is a judicial device in common law legal systems whereby a court may prevent, or "estop" a person from making assertions or from going back on his or her word; the person being sanctioned is "estopped". _________ may prevent someone from bringing a particular claim. Legal doctrines of _________ are based in both common law and equity.

Exam Probability: **High**

14. *Answer choices:*

(see index for correct answer)

- a. hierarchical
- b. personal values
- c. Sarbanes-Oxley act of 2002
- d. Estoppel

Guidance: level 1

:: Insurance law ::

__________ exists when an insured person derives a financial or other kind of benefit from the continuous existence, without repairment or damage, of the insured object . A person has an __________ in something when loss of or damage to that thing would cause the person to suffer a financial or other kind of loss.Normally, __________ is established by ownership, possession, or direct relationship. For example, people have __________ s in their own homes and vehicles, but not in their neighbors` homes and vehicles, and almost certainly not those of strangers.

Exam Probability: **Low**

15. *Answer choices:*

(see index for correct answer)

- a. Commissioner v. First Security Bank of Utah, N.A.
- b. Marine Insurance Act 1906
- c. Insurable interest
- d. QC clause

Guidance: level 1

:: Corporate finance ::

__________ is a contract law concept about the purchase of the release from a debt obligation. It is one of the methods by which parties to a contract may terminate their agreement. The release is completed by the transfer of valuable consideration that must not be the actual performance of the obligation itself. The accord is the agreement to discharge the obligation and the satisfaction is the legal "consideration" which binds the parties to the agreement. A valid accord does not discharge the prior contract; instead it suspends the right to enforce it in accordance with the terms of the accord contract, in which satisfaction, or performance of the contract will discharge both contracts . If the creditor breaches the accord, then the debtor will be able to bring up the existence of the accord in order to enjoin any action against him.

Exam Probability: **Medium**

16. *Answer choices:*

(see index for correct answer)

- a. Accord and satisfaction
- b. Capital structure
- c. Market timing hypothesis

- d. Managerial finance

Guidance: level 1

:: Industrial agreements ::

__________ is a process of negotiation between employers and a group of employees aimed at agreements to regulate working salaries, working conditions, benefits, and other aspects of workers` compensation and rights for workers. The interests of the employees are commonly presented by representatives of a trade union to which the employees belong. The collective agreements reached by these negotiations usually set out wage scales, working hours, training, health and safety, overtime, grievance mechanisms, and rights to participate in workplace or company affairs.

Exam Probability: **High**

17. *Answer choices:*

(see index for correct answer)

- a. Collective bargaining
- b. Compulsory arbitration
- c. Enterprise bargaining agreement
- d. Federal Labor Relations Act

Guidance: level 1

:: ::

__________ is that part of a civil law legal system which is part of the jus commune that involves relationships between individuals, such as the law of contracts or torts , and the law of obligations . It is to be distinguished from public law, which deals with relationships between both natural and artificial persons and the state, including regulatory statutes, penal law and other law that affects the public order. In general terms, __________ involves interactions between private citizens, whereas public law involves interrelations between the state and the general population.

Exam Probability: **High**

18. *Answer choices:*

(see index for correct answer)

- a. imperative
- b. interpersonal communication
- c. Sarbanes-Oxley act of 2002
- d. Private law

Guidance: level 1

:: Real estate ::

_________ , real estate, realty, or immovable property In English common law refers to landed properties belonging to some person. It include all structures, crops, buildings, machinery, wells, dams, ponds, mines, canals, and roads, among other things. The term is historic, arising from the now-discontinued form of action, which distinguish between _________ disputes and personal property disputes. Personal property was, and continues to refer to all properties that are not real properties.

Exam Probability: **Low**

19. *Answer choices:*
(see index for correct answer)

- a. FIABCI
- b. Re-trade
- c. County surveyor
- d. Boutique brokerage

Guidance: level 1

:: ::

An _________ , commonly called an appeals court, court of appeals , appeal court , court of second instance or second instance court, is any court of law that is empowered to hear an appeal of a trial court or other lower tribunal. In most jurisdictions, the court system is divided into at least three levels: the trial court, which initially hears cases and reviews evidence and testimony to determine the facts of the case; at least one intermediate _________ ; and a supreme court which primarily reviews the decisions of the intermediate courts. A jurisdiction's supreme court is that jurisdiction's highest _________ . _________ s nationwide can operate under varying rules.

Exam Probability: **Low**

20. *Answer choices:*

(see index for correct answer)

- a. Sarbanes-Oxley act of 2002
- b. Appellate Court
- c. surface-level diversity
- d. hierarchical

Guidance: level 1

:: American legal terms ::

The phrase "by _________ " is a legal term that indicates that a right or liability has been created for a party, irrespective of the intent of that party, because it is dictated by existing legal principles. For example, if a person dies without a will, his or her heirs are determined by _________ . Similarly, if a person marries or has a child after his or her will has been executed, the law writes this pretermitted spouse or pretermitted heir into the will if no provision for this situation was specifically included. Adverse possession, in which title to land passes because non-owners have occupied it for a certain period of time, is another important right that vests by _________ .

Exam Probability: **High**

21. *Answer choices:*

(see index for correct answer)

- a. Operation of law
- b. Chilling effect

Guidance: level 1

:: Business ::

An _________ is a key document used by limited liability companies to outline the business` financial and functional decisions including rules, regulations and provisions. The purpose of the document is to govern the internal operations of the business in a way that suits the specific needs of the business owners. Once the document is signed by the members of the limited liability company, it acts as an official contract binding them to its terms. _________ is mandatory as per laws only in 5 states - California, Delaware, Maine, Missouri, and New York LLCs operating without an _________ are governed by the state`s default rules contained in the relevant statute and developed through state court decisions. An _________ is similar in function to corporate by-laws, or analogous to a partnership agreement in multi-member LLCs. In single-member LLCs, an _________ is a declaration of the structure that the member has chosen for the company and sometimes used to prove in court that the LLC structure is separate from that of the individual owner and thus necessary so that the owner has documentation to prove that he or she is indeed separate from the entity itself.

Exam Probability: **Medium**

22. *Answer choices:*

(see index for correct answer)

- a. Business analysis
- b. Post-transaction marketing
- c. Countertrade
- d. Business as usual

Guidance: level 1

:: Business law ::

A _________ is a contractual arrangement calling for the lessee to pay the lessor for use of an asset. Property, buildings and vehicles are common assets that are _________d. Industrial or business equipment is also _________d.

Exam Probability: **High**

23. *Answer choices:*

(see index for correct answer)

- a. Operating lease
- b. Lease
- c. Independent contractor

- d. Free agent

Guidance: level 1

:: Contract law ::

__________ is the act of recall or annulment. It is the cancelling of an act, the recalling of a grant or privilege, or the making void of some deed previously existing.

Exam Probability: **Low**

24. *Answer choices:*
(see index for correct answer)

- a. Morals clause
- b. Revocation
- c. End-user license agreement
- d. Verbal contract

Guidance: level 1

:: Fraud ::

__________ is the deliberate use of someone else`s identity, usually as a method to gain a financial advantage or obtain credit and other benefits in the other person`s name, and perhaps to the other person`s disadvantage or loss. The person whose identity has been assumed may suffer adverse consequences, especially if they are held responsible for the perpetrator`s actions. __________ occurs when someone uses another`s personally identifying information, like their name, identifying number, or credit card number, without their permission, to commit fraud or other crimes. The term __________ was coined in 1964. Since that time, the definition of __________ has been statutorily prescribed throughout both the U.K. and the United States as the theft of personally identifying information, generally including a person's name, date of birth, social security number, driver's license number, bank account or credit card numbers, PIN numbers, electronic signatures, fingerprints, passwords, or any other information that can be used to access a person's financial resources.

Exam Probability: **Low**

25. *Answer choices:*
(see index for correct answer)

- a. Wangiri
- b. Identity theft
- c. Regummed stamp
- d. Age fabrication

Guidance: level 1

:: Product liability ::

_________ is the area of law in which manufacturers, distributors, suppliers, retailers, and others who make products available to the public are held responsible for the injuries those products cause. Although the word "product" has broad connotations, _________ as an area of law is traditionally limited to products in the form of tangible personal property.

Exam Probability: **Low**

26. *Answer choices:*
(see index for correct answer)

- a. Consumer Protection Act 1987
- b. Market share liability
- c. Product liability
- d. Chinese drywall

Guidance: level 1

:: Shareholders ::

A _________ is a payment made by a corporation to its shareholders, usually as a distribution of profits. When a corporation earns a profit or surplus, the corporation is able to re-invest the profit in the business and pay a proportion of the profit as a _________ to shareholders. Distribution to shareholders may be in cash or, if the corporation has a _________ reinvestment plan, the amount can be paid by the issue of further shares or share repurchase. When _________ s are paid, shareholders typically must pay income taxes, and the corporation does not receive a corporate income tax deduction for the _________ payments.

Exam Probability: **Medium**

27. *Answer choices:*
(see index for correct answer)

- a. Dividend
- b. Stock dilution
- c. Friedman doctrine
- d. Shareholder Rights Directive

Guidance: level 1

:: ::

The _________ is the central philosophical concept in the deontological moral philosophy of Immanuel Kant. Introduced in Kant's 1785 Groundwork of the Metaphysics of Morals, it may be defined as a way of evaluating motivations for action.

Exam Probability: **Medium**

28. *Answer choices:*
(see index for correct answer)

- a. deep-level diversity
- b. levels of analysis
- c. Categorical imperative
- d. Character

Guidance: level 1

:: Sexual harassment in the United States ::

In law, a _________ , reasonable man, or the man on the Clapham omnibus is a hypothetical person of legal fiction crafted by the courts and communicated through case law and jury instructions.

Exam Probability: **Low**

29. *Answer choices:*
(see index for correct answer)

- a. Sexual harassment in education in the United States
- b. Blakey v. Continental Airlines
- c. Alexander v. Yale
- d. Charol Shakeshaft

Guidance: level 1

:: ::

Industrial espionage, _________ , corporate spying or corporate espionage is a form of espionage conducted for commercial purposes instead of purely national security. While _________ is conducted or orchestrated by governments and is international in scope, industrial or corporate espionage is more often national and occurs between companies or corporations.

Exam Probability: **High**

30. *Answer choices:*

(see index for correct answer)

- a. co-culture
- b. similarity-attraction theory
- c. hierarchical perspective
- d. open system

Guidance: level 1

:: Contract law ::

An _________ , or simply option, is defined as "a promise which meets the requirements for the formation of a contract and limits the promisor`s power to revoke an offer."

Exam Probability: **Medium**

31. *Answer choices:*

(see index for correct answer)

- a. Option contract
- b. Posting rule
- c. Unjust enrichment
- d. Reciprocal obligation

Guidance: level 1

:: ::

Business is the activity of making one`s living or making money by producing or buying and selling products . Simply put, it is "any activity or enterprise entered into for profit. It does not mean it is a company, a corporation, partnership, or have any such formal organization, but it can range from a street peddler to General Motors."

Exam Probability: **Low**

32. *Answer choices:*
(see index for correct answer)

- a. imperative
- b. cultural
- c. Character
- d. Firm

Guidance: level 1

:: Legal procedure ::

__________ , adjective law, or rules of court comprises the rules by which a court hears and determines what happens in civil, lawsuit, criminal or administrative proceedings. The rules are designed to ensure a fair and consistent application of due process or fundamental justice to all cases that come before a court.

Exam Probability: **Medium**

33. *Answer choices:*
(see index for correct answer)

- a. appellate
- b. Closing argument
- c. Opening statement
- d. Procedural law

Guidance: level 1

:: Ethically disputed business practices ::

__________ is the trading of a public company`s stock or other securities by individuals with access to nonpublic information about the company. In various countries, some kinds of trading based on insider information is illegal. This is because it is seen as unfair to other investors who do not have access to the information, as the investor with insider information could potentially make larger profits than a typical investor could make. The rules governing __________ are complex and vary significantly from country to country. The extent of enforcement also varies from one country to another. The definition of insider in one jurisdiction can be broad, and may cover not only insiders themselves but also any persons related to them, such as brokers, associates and even family members. A person who becomes aware of non-public information and trades on that basis may be guilty of a crime.

Exam Probability: **High**

34. *Answer choices:*

(see index for correct answer)

- a. Anti-competitive practices
- b. anti-competitive
- c. Persuasive technology
- d. Insider trading

Guidance: level 1

:: ::

__________ is the act or practice of forbidding something by law; more particularly the term refers to the banning of the manufacture, storage , transportation, sale, possession, and consumption of alcoholic beverages. The word is also used to refer to a period of time during which such bans are enforced.

Exam Probability: **Low**

35. *Answer choices:*

(see index for correct answer)

- a. Prohibition
- b. similarity-attraction theory
- c. corporate values
- d. functional perspective

Guidance: level 1

:: Marketing ::

__________ or stock is the goods and materials that a business holds for the ultimate goal of resale .

Exam Probability: **High**

36. *Answer choices:*

(see index for correct answer)

- a. Cumulative prospect theory
- b. Inventory
- c. Effie Award
- d. Product category volume

Guidance: level 1

:: ::

The __________ of 1977 is a United States federal law known primarily for two of its main provisions: one that addresses accounting transparency requirements under the Securities Exchange Act of 1934 and another concerning bribery of foreign officials. The Act was amended in 1988 and in 1998, and has been subject to continued congressional concerns, namely whether its enforcement discourages U.S. companies from investing abroad.

Exam Probability: **Low**

37. *Answer choices:*

(see index for correct answer)

- a. open system
- b. functional perspective
- c. information systems assessment
- d. process perspective

Guidance: level 1

:: Euthenics ::

_________ is an ethical framework and suggests that an entity, be it an organization or individual, has an obligation to act for the benefit of society at large. _________ is a duty every individual has to perform so as to maintain a balance between the economy and the ecosystems. A trade-off may exist between economic development, in the material sense, and the welfare of the society and environment, though this has been challenged by many reports over the past decade. _________ means sustaining the equilibrium between the two. It pertains not only to business organizations but also to everyone whose any action impacts the environment. This responsibility can be passive, by avoiding engaging in socially harmful acts, or active, by performing activities that directly advance social goals. _________ must be intergenerational since the actions of one generation have consequences on those following.

Exam Probability: **Medium**

38. *Answer choices:*
(see index for correct answer)

- a. Home economics
- b. Euthenics
- c. Social responsibility
- d. Minnie Cumnock Blodgett

Guidance: level 1

:: ::

An _________ , for United States federal income tax, is a closely held corporation that makes a valid election to be taxed under Subchapter S of Chapter 1 of the Internal Revenue Code. In general, _________ s do not pay any income taxes. Instead, the corporation`s income or losses are divided among and passed through to its shareholders. The shareholders must then report the income or loss on their own individual income tax returns.

Exam Probability: **High**

39. *Answer choices:*
(see index for correct answer)

- a. process perspective
- b. levels of analysis
- c. similarity-attraction theory
- d. S corporation

Guidance: level 1

:: ::

A __________ is a law passed by a legislative body in a common law system to set the maximum time after an event within which legal proceedings may be initiated.

Exam Probability: **High**

40. *Answer choices:*

(see index for correct answer)

- a. deep-level diversity
- b. process perspective
- c. Statute of limitations
- d. Sarbanes-Oxley act of 2002

Guidance: level 1

:: Project management ::

__________ is the right to exercise power, which can be formalized by a state and exercised by way of judges, appointed executives of government, or the ecclesiastical or priestly appointed representatives of a God or other deities.

Exam Probability: **Low**

41. *Answer choices:*

(see index for correct answer)

- a. Management process
- b. System anatomy
- c. Deployment Plan
- d. Authority

Guidance: level 1

:: ::

A _________ is the party who initiates a lawsuit before a court. By doing so, the _________ seeks a legal remedy; if this search is successful, the court will issue judgment in favor of the _________ and make the appropriate court order . " _________ " is the term used in civil cases in most English-speaking jurisdictions, the notable exception being England and Wales, where a _________ has, since the introduction of the Civil Procedure Rules in 1999, been known as a "claimant", but that term also has other meanings. In criminal cases, the prosecutor brings the case against the defendant, but the key complaining party is often called the "complainant".

Exam Probability: **High**

42. *Answer choices:*

(see index for correct answer)

- a. levels of analysis
- b. Sarbanes-Oxley act of 2002
- c. surface-level diversity
- d. Plaintiff

Guidance: level 1

:: ::

The words " _________ " and "testify" both derive from the Latin word testis, referring to the notion of a disinterested third-party witness.

Exam Probability: **High**

43. *Answer choices:*

(see index for correct answer)

- a. Testimony
- b. empathy
- c. open system
- d. deep-level diversity

Guidance: level 1

:: Utilitarianism ::

_________ is a family of consequentialist ethical theories that promotes actions that maximize happiness and well-being for the majority of a population. Although different varieties of _________ admit different characterizations, the basic idea behind all of them is to in some sense maximize utility, which is often defined in terms of well-being or related concepts. For instance, Jeremy Bentham, the founder of _________ , described utility as

Exam Probability: **Medium**

44. *Answer choices:*

(see index for correct answer)

- a. Act utilitarianism
- b. Informed judge
- c. Utilitarianism
- d. Equal consideration of interests

Guidance: level 1

:: ::

An _________ is a contingent motivator. Traditional _________ s are extrinsic motivators which reward actions to yield a desired outcome. The effectiveness of traditional _________ s has changed as the needs of Western society have evolved. While the traditional _________ model is effective when there is a defined procedure and goal for a task, Western society started to require a higher volume of critical thinkers, so the traditional model became less effective. Institutions are now following a trend in implementing strategies that rely on intrinsic motivations rather than the extrinsic motivations that the traditional _________ s foster.

Exam Probability: **Low**

45. *Answer choices:*

(see index for correct answer)

- a. personal values
- b. Sarbanes-Oxley act of 2002
- c. similarity-attraction theory
- d. Incentive

Guidance: level 1

:: ::

An __________ is a written sworn statement of fact voluntarily made by an affiant or deponent under an oath or affirmation administered by a person authorized to do so by law. Such statement is witnessed as to the authenticity of the affiant's signature by a taker of oaths, such as a notary public or commissioner of oaths. An __________ is a type of verified statement or showing, or in other words, it contains a verification, meaning it is under oath or penalty of perjury, and this serves as evidence to its veracity and is required for court proceedings.

Exam Probability: **Medium**

46. *Answer choices:*

(see index for correct answer)

- a. empathy
- b. personal values
- c. Affidavit
- d. Character

Guidance: level 1

:: Debt ::

__________ is the trust which allows one party to provide money or resources to another party wherein the second party does not reimburse the first party immediately , but promises either to repay or return those resources at a later date. In other words, __________ is a method of making reciprocity formal, legally enforceable, and extensible to a large group of unrelated people.

Exam Probability: **Low**

47. *Answer choices:*

(see index for correct answer)

- a. Recourse debt
- b. Household debt
- c. Troubled Debt Restructuring
- d. Credit

Guidance: level 1

:: ::

__________ is a process under which executive or legislative actions are subject to review by the judiciary. A court with authority for __________ may invalidate laws, acts and governmental actions that are incompatible with a higher authority: an executive decision may be invalidated for being unlawful or a statute may be invalidated for violating the terms of a constitution. __________ is one of the checks and balances in the separation of powers: the power of the judiciary to supervise the legislative and executive branches when the latter exceed their authority. The doctrine varies between jurisdictions, so the procedure and scope of __________ may differ between and within countries.

Exam Probability: **Low**

48. *Answer choices:*

(see index for correct answer)

- a. process perspective
- b. Judicial review
- c. co-culture
- d. deep-level diversity

Guidance: level 1

:: Contract law ::

A __________ is an event or state of affairs that is required before something else will occur. In contract law, a __________ is an event which must occur, unless its non-occurrence is excused, before performance under a contract becomes due, i.e., before any contractual duty exists.

Exam Probability: **Low**

49. *Answer choices:*

(see index for correct answer)

- a. Reciprocal obligation
- b. Condition precedent
- c. Capacity
- d. Culpa in contrahendo

Guidance: level 1

:: Contract law ::

_________ is an equitable remedy in the law of contract, whereby a court issues an order requiring a party to perform a specific act, such as to complete performance of the contract. It is typically available in the sale of land, but otherwise is not generally available if damages are an appropriate alternative. _________ is almost never available for contracts of personal service, although performance may also be ensured through the threat of proceedings for contempt of court.

Exam Probability: **Low**

50. *Answer choices:*
(see index for correct answer)

- a. Non-repudiation
- b. Ticket cases
- c. Heads of Agreement
- d. Illegal agreement

Guidance: level 1

:: Majority–minority relations ::

_________ , also known as reservation in India and Nepal, positive discrimination / action in the United Kingdom, and employment equity in Canada and South Africa, is the policy of promoting the education and employment of members of groups that are known to have previously suffered from discrimination. Historically and internationally, support for _________ has sought to achieve goals such as bridging inequalities in employment and pay, increasing access to education, promoting diversity, and redressing apparent past wrongs, harms, or hindrances.

Exam Probability: **Medium**

51. *Answer choices:*
(see index for correct answer)

- a. cultural dissonance
- b. Affirmative action
- c. positive discrimination

Guidance: level 1

:: ::

Advertising is a marketing communication that employs an openly sponsored, non-personal message to promote or sell a product, service or idea. Sponsors of advertising are typically businesses wishing to promote their products or services. Advertising is differentiated from public relations in that an advertiser pays for and has control over the message. It differs from personal selling in that the message is non-personal, i.e., not directed to a particular individual.Advertising is communicated through various mass media, including traditional media such as newspapers, magazines, television, radio, outdoor advertising or direct mail; and new media such as search results, blogs, social media, websites or text messages. The actual presentation of the message in a medium is referred to as an _________ , or "ad" or advert for short.

Exam Probability: **Low**

52. *Answer choices:*

(see index for correct answer)

- a. imperative
- b. Advertisement
- c. deep-level diversity
- d. Character

Guidance: level 1

:: Contract law ::

An _________ is a contract that has not yet been fully performed or fully executed. It is a contract in which both sides still have important performance remaining. However, an obligation to pay money, even if such obligation is material, does not usually make a contract executory. An obligation is material if a breach of contract would result from the failure to satisfy the obligation. A contract that has been fully performed by one party but not by the other party is not an _________ .

Exam Probability: **High**

53. *Answer choices:*

(see index for correct answer)

- a. Executory contract
- b. Sweetheart deal

- c. Unenforceable
- d. Standard form contract

Guidance: level 1

:: ::

The __________ is an independent agency of the Federal government of the United States with responsibilities for enforcing U.S. labor law in relation to collective bargaining and unfair labor practices. Under the National Labor Relations Act of 1935 it supervises elections for labor union representation and can investigate and remedy unfair labor practices. Unfair labor practices may involve union-related situations or instances of protected concerted activity. The NLRB is governed by a five-person board and a General Counsel, all of whom are appointed by the President with the consent of the Senate. Board members are appointed to five-year terms and the General Counsel is appointed to a four-year term. The General Counsel acts as a prosecutor and the Board acts as an appellate quasi-judicial body from decisions of administrative law judges.

Exam Probability: **High**

54. *Answer choices:*

(see index for correct answer)

- a. National Labor Relations Board
- b. functional perspective
- c. empathy
- d. information systems assessment

Guidance: level 1

:: Labour relations ::

_________ is a field of study that can have different meanings depending on the context in which it is used. In an international context, it is a subfield of labor history that studies the human relations with regard to work – in its broadest sense – and how this connects to questions of social inequality. It explicitly encompasses unregulated, historical, and non-Western forms of labor. Here, _________ define "for or with whom one works and under what rules. These rules determine the type of work, type and amount of remuneration, working hours, degrees of physical and psychological strain, as well as the degree of freedom and autonomy associated with the work."

Exam Probability: **Low**

55. *Answer choices:*

(see index for correct answer)

- a. Labor relations
- b. Social dialogue
- c. Global union federation
- d. Passfield Memorandum

Guidance: level 1

:: Anti-competitive behaviour ::

Restraints of trade is a common law doctrine relating to the enforceability of contractual restrictions on freedom to conduct business. It is a precursor of modern competition law. In an old leading case of Mitchel v Reynolds Lord Smith LC said,

Exam Probability: **Medium**

56. *Answer choices:*

(see index for correct answer)

- a. Restraint of trade
- b. Conscious parallelism
- c. Ringfencing
- d. Suggested retail price

Guidance: level 1

:: Progressive Era in the United States ::

The Clayton Antitrust Act of 1914 , was a part of United States antitrust law with the goal of adding further substance to the U.S. antitrust law regime; the _________ sought to prevent anticompetitive practices in their incipiency. That regime started with the Sherman Antitrust Act of 1890, the first Federal law outlawing practices considered harmful to consumers . The _________ specified particular prohibited conduct, the three-level enforcement scheme, the exemptions, and the remedial measures.

Exam Probability: **Medium**

57. *Answer choices:*

(see index for correct answer)

- a. pragmatism
- b. Mann Act
- c. Clayton Antitrust Act

Guidance: level 1

:: ::

A concept of English law, a _________ is an untrue or misleading statement of fact made during negotiations by one party to another, the statement then inducing that other party into the contract. The misled party may normally rescind the contract, and sometimes may be awarded damages as well .

Exam Probability: **Medium**

58. *Answer choices:*

(see index for correct answer)

- a. empathy
- b. Misrepresentation
- c. deep-level diversity
- d. interpersonal communication

Guidance: level 1

:: Services management and marketing ::

A _________ or servicemark is a trademark used in the United States and several other countries to identify a service rather than a product.

Exam Probability: **Low**

59. *Answer choices:*

(see index for correct answer)

- a. Service mark
- b. Service delivery framework
- c. Integrated customer management
- d. Services marketing

Guidance: level 1

Finance

Finance is a field that is concerned with the allocation (investment) of assets and liabilities over space and time, often under conditions of risk or uncertainty. Finance can also be defined as the science of money management. Participants in the market aim to price assets based on their risk level, fundamental value, and their expected rate of return. Finance can be split into three sub-categories: public finance, corporate finance and personal finance.

:: ::

_________ focuses on ratios, equities and debts. It is useful for portfolio management,distribution of dividend,capital raising,hedging and looking after fluctuations in foreign currency and product cycles.Financial managers are the people who will do research and based on the research, decide what sort of capital to obtain in order to fund the company`s assets as well as maximizing the value of the firm for all the stakeholders. It also refers to the efficient and effective management of money in such a manner as to accomplish the objectives of the organization. It is the specialized function directly associated with the top management. The significance of this function is not seen in the `Line` but also in the capacity of the `Staff` in overall of a company. It has been defined differently by different experts in the field.

Exam Probability: **Low**

1. *Answer choices:*

(see index for correct answer)

- a. hierarchical perspective
- b. Financial management
- c. personal values
- d. interpersonal communication

Guidance: level 1

:: Financial crises ::

A _________ is any of a broad variety of situations in which some financial assets suddenly lose a large part of their nominal value. In the 19th and early 20th centuries, many financial crises were associated with banking panics, and many recessions coincided with these panics. Other situations that are often called financial crises include stock market crashes and the bursting of other financial bubbles, currency crises, and sovereign defaults. Financial crises directly result in a loss of paper wealth but do not necessarily result in significant changes in the real economy .

Exam Probability: **Low**

2. *Answer choices:*

(see index for correct answer)

- a. Biflation
- b. Kibbutz crisis
- c. Mexican peso crisis
- d. Panic of 1866

Guidance: level 1

:: Derivatives (finance) ::

_________ is any bodily activity that enhances or maintains physical fitness and overall health and wellness. It is performed for various reasons, to aid growth and improve strength, preventing aging, developing muscles and the cardiovascular system, honing athletic skills, weight loss or maintenance, improving health and also for enjoyment. Many individuals choose to _________ outdoors where they can congregate in groups, socialize, and enhance well-being.

Exam Probability: **Medium**

3. *Answer choices:*

(see index for correct answer)

- a. International Securities Lending Association
- b. Currency future
- c. Credit default swap index
- d. Exercise

Guidance: level 1

:: Commerce ::

A _________ , manufacturing plant or a production plant is an industrial site, usually consisting of buildings and machinery, or more commonly a complex having several buildings, where workers manufacture goods or operate machines processing one product into another.

Exam Probability: **High**

4. *Answer choices:*
(see index for correct answer)

- a. Fast track
- b. Statutory holdback
- c. Perfect tender rule
- d. Electronic article surveillance

Guidance: level 1

:: ::

_________ is the consumption and saving opportunity gained by an entity within a specified timeframe, which is generally expressed in monetary terms. For households and individuals, " _________ is the sum of all the wages, salaries, profits, interest payments, rents, and other forms of earnings received in a given period of time."

Exam Probability: **High**

5. *Answer choices:*
(see index for correct answer)

- a. hierarchical perspective
- b. process perspective
- c. Income
- d. deep-level diversity

Guidance: level 1

:: Investment ::

_________ , and investment appraisal, is the planning process used to determine whether an organization`s long term investments such as new machinery, replacement of machinery, new plants, new products, and research development projects are worth the funding of cash through the firm`s capitalization structure . It is the process of allocating resources for major capital, or investment, expenditures. One of the primary goals of _________ investments is to increase the value of the firm to the shareholders.

Exam Probability: **Low**

6. *Answer choices:*

(see index for correct answer)

- a. Equity repositioning
- b. Capital budgeting
- c. Tax transparent fund
- d. Price return

Guidance: level 1

:: Generally Accepted Accounting Principles ::

_________ is the accounting classification of an account. It is part of double-entry book-keeping technique.

Exam Probability: **Low**

7. *Answer choices:*

(see index for correct answer)

- a. Paid in capital
- b. Expense
- c. Earnings before interest, taxes, depreciation, and amortization
- d. Profit

Guidance: level 1

:: Asset ::

In accounting, a _________ is any asset which can reasonably be expected to be sold, consumed, or exhausted through the normal operations of a business within the current fiscal year or operating cycle . Typical _________ s include cash, cash equivalents, short-term investments , accounts receivable, stock inventory, supplies, and the portion of prepaid liabilities which will be paid within a year.In simple words, assets which are held for a short period are known as _________ s. Such assets are expected to be realised in cash or consumed during the normal operating cycle of the business.

Exam Probability: **Low**

8. *Answer choices:*

(see index for correct answer)

- a. Asset
- b. Fixed asset

Guidance: level 1

:: Financial markets ::

A _________ is a market in which people trade financial securities and derivatives such as futures and options at low transaction costs. Securities include stocks and bonds, and precious metals.

Exam Probability: **Medium**

9. *Answer choices:*

(see index for correct answer)

- a. Fourth market
- b. STAMP
- c. TradersStudio
- d. Financial market

Guidance: level 1

:: Capital (economics) ::

In Economics and Accounting, the _________ is the cost of a company`s funds , or, from an investor`s point of view "the required rate of return on a portfolio company`s existing securities". It is used to evaluate new projects of a company. It is the minimum return that investors expect for providing capital to the company, thus setting a benchmark that a new project has to meet.

Exam Probability: **Low**

10. *Answer choices:*

(see index for correct answer)

- a. operating capital
- b. Information capital
- c. patient capital
- d. required rate of return

Guidance: level 1

:: Financial markets ::

For an individual, a _________ is the minimum amount of money by which the expected return on a risky asset must exceed the known return on a risk-free asset in order to induce an individual to hold the risky asset rather than the risk-free asset. It is positive if the person is risk averse. Thus it is the minimum willingness to accept compensation for the risk.

Exam Probability: **High**

11. *Answer choices:*

(see index for correct answer)

- a. Financial market
- b. Hot equity periods
- c. Future Trading Act
- d. Risk premium

Guidance: level 1

:: International taxation ::

_________ is the levying of tax by two or more jurisdictions on the same declared income , asset , or financial transaction . Double liability is mitigated in a number of ways, for example.

Exam Probability: **Medium**

12. *Answer choices:*

(see index for correct answer)

- a. Double taxation
- b. Foreign personal holding company
- c. Withholding
- d. Withholding tax

Guidance: level 1

:: Financial accounting ::

In accounting, _________ is the value of an asset according to its balance sheet account balance. For assets, the value is based on the original cost of the asset less any depreciation, amortization or impairment costs made against the asset. Traditionally, a company`s _________ is its total assets minus intangible assets and liabilities. However, in practice, depending on the source of the calculation, _________ may variably include goodwill, intangible assets, or both. The value inherent in its workforce, part of the intellectual capital of a company, is always ignored. When intangible assets and goodwill are explicitly excluded, the metric is often specified to be "tangible _________ ".

Exam Probability: **Low**

13. *Answer choices:*

(see index for correct answer)

- a. SEC filing
- b. Hidden asset
- c. Exit rate
- d. Asset swap

Guidance: level 1

:: Generally Accepted Accounting Principles ::

An _________ or profit and loss account is one of the financial statements of a company and shows the company's revenues and expenses during a particular period.

Exam Probability: **High**

14. *Answer choices:*

(see index for correct answer)

- a. Income statement
- b. Goodwill
- c. Completed-contract method
- d. Cost pool

Guidance: level 1

:: Commerce ::

Continuation of an entity as a _________ is presumed as the basis for financial reporting unless and until the entity's liquidation becomes imminent. Preparation of financial statements under this presumption is commonly referred to as the _________ basis of accounting. If and when an entity's liquidation becomes imminent, financial statements are prepared under the liquidation basis of accounting .

Exam Probability: **High**

15. *Answer choices:*

(see index for correct answer)

- a. Car boot sale
- b. International Marketmakers Combination
- c. Going concern
- d. Retail loss prevention

Guidance: level 1

:: Generally Accepted Accounting Principles ::

In accounting, an economic item`s _________ is the original nominal monetary value of that item. _________ accounting involves reporting assets and liabilities at their _________ s, which are not updated for changes in the items` values. Consequently, the amounts reported for these balance sheet items often differ from their current economic or market values.

Exam Probability: **Medium**

16. *Answer choices:*

(see index for correct answer)

- a. Depreciation
- b. Historical cost
- c. Contributed capital
- d. Earnings before interest and taxes

Guidance: level 1

:: Expense ::

An _________ , operating expenditure, operational expense, operational expenditure or opex is an ongoing cost for running a product, business, or system. Its counterpart, a capital expenditure , is the cost of developing or providing non-consumable parts for the product or system. For example, the purchase of a photocopier involves capex, and the annual paper, toner, power and maintenance costs represents opex. For larger systems like businesses, opex may also include the cost of workers and facility expenses such as rent and utilities.

Exam Probability: **Low**

17. *Answer choices:*

(see index for correct answer)

- a. Operating expense
- b. Corporate travel
- c. Expense account
- d. Business overhead expense disability insurance

Guidance: level 1

:: Accounting terminology ::

Total _________ is a method of Accounting cost which entails the full cost of manufacturing or providing a service. TAC includes not just the costs of materials and labour, but also of all manufacturing overheads . The cost of each cost center can be direct or indirect. The direct cost can be easily identified with individual cost centers. Whereas indirect cost cannot be easily identified with the cost center. The distribution of overhead among the departments is called apportionment.

Exam Probability: **Medium**

18. *Answer choices:*

(see index for correct answer)

- a. Total absorption costing
- b. Enterprise liquidity
- c. Accounts payable
- d. Absorption costing

Guidance: level 1

:: ::

_________ involves decision making. It can include judging the merits of multiple options and selecting one or more of them. One can make a _________ between imagined options or between real options followed by the corresponding action. For example, a traveler might choose a route for a journey based on the preference of arriving at a given destination as soon as possible. The preferred route can then follow from information such as the length of each of the possible routes, traffic conditions, etc. The arrival at a _________ can include more complex motivators such as cognition, instinct, and feeling.

Exam Probability: **High**

19. *Answer choices:*

(see index for correct answer)

- a. similarity-attraction theory
- b. Choice
- c. imperative
- d. open system

Guidance: level 1

:: Investment ::

In finance, the benefit from an _________ is called a return. The return may consist of a gain realised from the sale of property or an _________ , unrealised capital appreciation , or _________ income such as dividends, interest, rental income etc., or a combination of capital gain and income. The return may also include currency gains or losses due to changes in foreign currency exchange rates.

Exam Probability: **Medium**

20. *Answer choices:*

(see index for correct answer)

- a. Asian option
- b. Investment
- c. Tax transparent fund
- d. Stock market cycles

Guidance: level 1

:: Accounting terminology ::

In accounting/accountancy, _________ are journal entries usually made at the end of an accounting period to allocate income and expenditure to the period in which they actually occurred. The revenue recognition principle is the basis of making _________ that pertain to unearned and accrued revenues under accrual-basis accounting. They are sometimes called Balance Day adjustments because they are made on balance day.

Exam Probability: **Low**

21. *Answer choices:*

(see index for correct answer)

- a. Adjusting entries
- b. Absorption costing
- c. Mark-to-market
- d. Double-entry accounting

Guidance: level 1

:: Competition (economics) ::

_________ arises whenever at least two parties strive for a goal which cannot be shared: where one`s gain is the other`s loss .

Exam Probability: **High**

22. *Answer choices:*
(see index for correct answer)

- a. Competition
- b. Economic forces
- c. National Competitiveness Report of Armenia
- d. Self-competition

Guidance: level 1

:: Financial markets ::

_________ s are monetary contracts between parties. They can be created, traded, modified and settled. They can be cash , evidence of an ownership interest in an entity , or a contractual right to receive or deliver cash .

Exam Probability: **Medium**

23. *Answer choices:*
(see index for correct answer)

- a. Flight-to-quality
- b. Financial astrology
- c. Financial instrument
- d. Holy grail distribution

Guidance: level 1

:: Budgets ::

A _________ is a financial plan for a defined period, often one year. It may also include planned sales volumes and revenues, resource quantities, costs and expenses, assets, liabilities and cash flows. Companies, governments, families and other organizations use it to express strategic plans of activities or events in measurable terms.

Exam Probability: **Low**

24. *Answer choices:*
(see index for correct answer)

- a. Budget
- b. Marginal budgeting for bottlenecks
- c. Zero budget
- d. Black budget

Guidance: level 1

:: Land value taxation ::

_________ , sometimes referred to as dry _________ , is the solid surface of Earth that is not permanently covered by water. The vast majority of human activity throughout history has occurred in _________ areas that support agriculture, habitat, and various natural resources. Some life forms have developed from predecessor species that lived in bodies of water.

Exam Probability: **Medium**

25. *Answer choices:*
(see index for correct answer)

- a. Henry George
- b. Land
- c. Lands Valuation Appeal Court
- d. Land value tax

Guidance: level 1

:: Decision theory ::

Within economics the concept of _________ is used to model worth or value, but its usage has evolved significantly over time. The term was introduced initially as a measure of pleasure or satisfaction within the theory of utilitarianism by moral philosophers such as Jeremy Bentham and John Stuart Mill. But the term has been adapted and reapplied within neoclassical economics, which dominates modern economic theory, as a _________ function that represents a consumer`s preference ordering over a choice set. As such, it is devoid of its original interpretation as a measurement of the pleasure or satisfaction obtained by the consumer from that choice.

Exam Probability: **Medium**

26. *Answer choices:*

(see index for correct answer)

- a. Decision field theory
- b. Rational Focal Point
- c. Utility
- d. Rete algorithm

Guidance: level 1

:: Fixed income market ::

In finance, the _________ is a curve showing several yields or interest rates across different contract lengths for a similar debt contract. The curve shows the relation between the interest rate and the time to maturity, known as the "term", of the debt for a given borrower in a given currency. For example, the U.S. dollar interest rates paid on U.S. Treasury securities for various maturities are closely watched by many traders, and are commonly plotted on a graph such as the one on the right which is informally called "the _________ ". More formal mathematical descriptions of this relation are often called the term structure of interest rates.

Exam Probability: **High**

27. *Answer choices:*

(see index for correct answer)

- a. Fixed-income attribution
- b. Pool factor
- c. Fixed income
- d. Inter-dealer broker

Guidance: level 1

:: Stock market ::

A __________ , securities exchange or bourse, is a facility where stock brokers and traders can buy and sell securities, such as shares of stock and bonds and other financial instruments. __________ s may also provide for facilities the issue and redemption of such securities and instruments and capital events including the payment of income and dividends. Securities traded on a __________ include stock issued by listed companies, unit trusts, derivatives, pooled investment products and bonds. __________ s often function as "continuous auction" markets with buyers and sellers consummating transactions via open outcry at a central location such as the floor of the exchange or by using an electronic trading platform.

Exam Probability: **Medium**

28. *Answer choices:*
(see index for correct answer)

- a. S chip
- b. Stock exchange
- c. Monthly income preferred stock
- d. Gross dealer concession

Guidance: level 1

:: Basic financial concepts ::

In finance, maturity or __________ refers to the final payment date of a loan or other financial instrument, at which point the principal is due to be paid.

Exam Probability: **Low**

29. *Answer choices:*
(see index for correct answer)

- a. Present value of benefits
- b. balloon payment
- c. Financial transaction
- d. Deflation

Guidance: level 1

:: Institutional investors ::

A _________ is an investment fund that pools capital from accredited investors or institutional investors and invests in a variety of assets, often with complex portfolio-construction and risk management techniques. It is administered by a professional investment management firm, and often structured as a limited partnership, limited liability company, or similar vehicle. _________ s are generally distinct from mutual funds and regarded as alternative investments, as their use of leverage is not capped by regulators, and distinct from private equity funds, as the majority of _________ s invest in relatively liquid assets. However, funds which operate similarly to _________ s but are regulated similarly to mutual funds are available and known as liquid alternative investments.

Exam Probability: **Low**

30. *Answer choices:*
(see index for correct answer)

- a. Davidson Kempner Capital Management
- b. Hedge fund
- c. Admiral Administration
- d. Capital Introduction

Guidance: level 1

:: Business economics ::

In finance, _________ is the risk of losses caused by interest rate changes. The prices of most financial instruments, such as stocks and bonds move inversely with interest rates, so investors are subject to capital loss when rates rise.

Exam Probability: **High**

31. *Answer choices:*
(see index for correct answer)

- a. Financial risk modeling
- b. Cost object
- c. Service innovation
- d. Rate risk

Guidance: level 1

:: Insolvency ::

_________ is the process in accounting by which a company is brought to an end in the United Kingdom, Republic of Ireland and United States. The assets and property of the company are redistributed. _________ is also sometimes referred to as winding-up or dissolution, although dissolution technically refers to the last stage of _________ . The process of _________ also arises when customs, an authority or agency in a country responsible for collecting and safeguarding customs duties, determines the final computation or ascertainment of the duties or drawback accruing on an entry.

Exam Probability: **Low**

32. *Answer choices:*

(see index for correct answer)

- a. Debt consolidation
- b. Liquidation
- c. George Samuel Ford
- d. United Kingdom insolvency law

Guidance: level 1

:: Bonds (finance) ::

In finance, a _________ or convertible note or convertible debt is a type of bond that the holder can convert into a specified number of shares of common stock in the issuing company or cash of equal value. It is a hybrid security with debt- and equity-like features. It originated in the mid-19th century, and was used by early speculators such as Jacob Little and Daniel Drew to counter market cornering.

Exam Probability: **Low**

33. *Answer choices:*

(see index for correct answer)

- a. Convertible bond
- b. Reinsurance sidecar
- c. Land bonds
- d. Agency debt

Guidance: level 1

:: Costs ::

In economics, _________ is the total economic cost of production and is made up of variable cost, which varies according to the quantity of a good produced and includes inputs such as labour and raw materials, plus fixed cost, which is independent of the quantity of a good produced and includes inputs that cannot be varied in the short term: fixed costs such as buildings and machinery, including sunk costs if any. Since cost is measured per unit of time, it is a flow variable.

Exam Probability: **Medium**

34. *Answer choices:*

(see index for correct answer)

- a. Cost competitiveness of fuel sources
- b. Social cost
- c. Opportunity cost of capital
- d. Khozraschyot

Guidance: level 1

:: ::

A _________ is an organization, usually a group of people or a company, authorized to act as a single entity and recognized as such in law. Early incorporated entities were established by charter . Most jurisdictions now allow the creation of new _________ s through registration.

Exam Probability: **Low**

35. *Answer choices:*

(see index for correct answer)

- a. Corporation
- b. imperative
- c. interpersonal communication
- d. process perspective

Guidance: level 1

:: Management accounting ::

_________ are costs that are not directly accountable to a cost object . _________ may be either fixed or variable. _________ include administration, personnel and security costs. These are those costs which are not directly related to production. Some _________ may be overhead. But some overhead costs can be directly attributed to a project and are direct costs.

Exam Probability: **Medium**

36. *Answer choices:*

(see index for correct answer)

- a. Relevant cost
- b. Institute of Cost and Management Accountants of Bangladesh
- c. Resource consumption accounting
- d. Indirect costs

Guidance: level 1

:: Commerce ::

A _________ , is a document acknowledging that a person has received money or property in payment following a sale or other transfer of goods or provision of a service. All _________ s must have the date of purchase on them. If the recipient of the payment is legally required to collect sales tax or VAT from the customer, the amount would be added to the _________ and the collection would be deemed to have been on behalf of the relevant tax authority. In many countries, a retailer is required to include the sales tax or VAT in the displayed price of goods sold, from which the tax amount would be calculated at point of sale and remitted to the tax authorities in due course. Similarly, amounts may be deducted from amounts payable, as in the case of wage withholding taxes. On the other hand, tips or other gratuities given by a customer, for example in a restaurant, would not form part of the payment amount or appear on the _________ .

Exam Probability: **High**

37. *Answer choices:*

(see index for correct answer)

- a. Retail loss prevention
- b. White Elephant Sale
- c. Sell-side analyst
- d. Receipt

Guidance: level 1

:: Inventory ::

Costs are associated with particular goods using one of the several formulas, including specific identification, first-in first-out , or average cost. Costs include all costs of purchase, costs of conversion and other costs that are incurred in bringing the inventories to their present location and condition. Costs of goods made by the businesses include material, labor, and allocated overhead. The costs of those goods which are not yet sold are deferred as costs of inventory until the inventory is sold or written down in value.

Exam Probability: **High**

38. *Answer choices:*

(see index for correct answer)

- a. Phantom inventory
- b. Cost of goods sold
- c. Order fulfillment
- d. New old stock

Guidance: level 1

:: Financial risk ::

The __________ on a financial investment is the expected value of its return . It is a measure of the center of the distribution of the random variable that is the return.

Exam Probability: **Medium**

39. *Answer choices:*

(see index for correct answer)

- a. Risk-free interest rate
- b. Tracking error
- c. Time consistency
- d. ORRF Risk Research Forum

Guidance: level 1

:: Global systemically important banks ::

The _________ Corporation is an American multinational investment bank and financial services company based in Charlotte, North Carolina with central hubs in New York City, London, Hong Kong, Minneapolis, and Toronto. _________ was formed through NationsBank`s acquisition of BankAmerica in 1998. It is the second largest banking institution in the United States, after JP Morgan Chase. As a part of the Big Four, it services approximately 10.73% of all American bank deposits, in direct competition with Citigroup, Wells Fargo, and JPMorgan Chase. Its primary financial services revolve around commercial banking, wealth management, and investment banking.

Exam Probability: **Low**

40. *Answer choices:*

(see index for correct answer)

- a. UniCredit
- b. Groupe BPCE
- c. The Bank of New York Mellon
- d. Morgan Stanley

Guidance: level 1

:: Accounting ::

_________ is a process of providing relief to shared service organization`s cost centers that provide a product or service. In turn, the associated expense is assigned to internal clients` cost centers that consume the products and services. For example, the CIO may provide all IT services within the company and assign the costs back to the business units that consume each offering.

Exam Probability: **Low**

41. *Answer choices:*

(see index for correct answer)

- a. Voluntary disclosure
- b. Accounting records
- c. Della mercatura e del mercante perfetto
- d. AICPA Code of Professional Conduct

Guidance: level 1

:: Income taxes ::

An _________ is a tax imposed on individuals or entities that varies with respective income or profits . _________ generally is computed as the product of a tax rate times taxable income. Taxation rates may vary by type or characteristics of the taxpayer.

Exam Probability: **Medium**

42. *Answer choices:*

(see index for correct answer)

- a. Income tax
- b. Income and Corporation Taxes Act 1970
- c. Income Tax Act 2007
- d. Income tax in Australia

Guidance: level 1

:: Goods ::

In most contexts, the concept of _________ denotes the conduct that should be preferred when posed with a choice between possible actions. _________ is generally considered to be the opposite of evil, and is of interest in the study of morality, ethics, religion and philosophy. The specific meaning and etymology of the term and its associated translations among ancient and contemporary languages show substantial variation in its inflection and meaning depending on circumstances of place, history, religious, or philosophical context.

Exam Probability: **Medium**

43. *Answer choices:*

(see index for correct answer)

- a. Composite good
- b. Positional good
- c. Club good
- d. Credence good

Guidance: level 1

:: Business law ::

A _________ is a group of people who jointly supervise the activities of an organization, which can be either a for-profit business, nonprofit organization, or a government agency. Such a board`s powers, duties, and responsibilities are determined by government regulations and the organization`s own constitution and bylaws. These authorities may specify the number of members of the board, how they are to be chosen, and how often they are to meet.

Exam Probability: **Low**

44. *Answer choices:*

(see index for correct answer)

- a. Hundi
- b. Doing business as
- c. Board of directors
- d. Interest of the company

Guidance: level 1

:: ::

An _________ is an asset that lacks physical substance. It is defined in opposition to physical assets such as machinery and buildings. An _________ is usually very hard to evaluate. Patents, copyrights, franchises, goodwill, trademarks, and trade names. The general interpretation also includes software and other intangible computer based assets are all examples of _________ s. _________ s generally—though not necessarily—suffer from typical market failures of non-rivalry and non-excludability.

Exam Probability: **High**

45. *Answer choices:*

(see index for correct answer)

- a. imperative
- b. functional perspective
- c. interpersonal communication
- d. Intangible asset

Guidance: level 1

:: Social security ::

__________ is "any government system that provides monetary assistance to people with an inadequate or no income." In the United States, this is usually called welfare or a social safety net, especially when talking about Canada and European countries.

Exam Probability: **High**

46. *Answer choices:*

(see index for correct answer)

- a. Gosselin v. Quebec
- b. Baby bonus
- c. Intergenerational struggle
- d. South African Social Security Agency

Guidance: level 1

:: ::

A __________ is an entity that owes a debt to another entity. The entity may be an individual, a firm, a government, a company or other legal person. The counterparty is called a creditor. When the counterpart of this debt arrangement is a bank, the __________ is more often referred to as a borrower.

Exam Probability: **Medium**

47. *Answer choices:*

(see index for correct answer)

- a. Debtor
- b. co-culture
- c. process perspective
- d. empathy

Guidance: level 1

:: ::

_________ is a political and social philosophy promoting traditional social institutions in the context of culture and civilization. The central tenets of _________ include tradition, human imperfection, organic society, hierarchy, authority, and property rights. Conservatives seek to preserve a range of institutions such as religion, parliamentary government, and property rights, with the aim of emphasizing social stability and continuity. The more traditional elements—reactionaries—oppose modernism and seek a return to "the way things were".

Exam Probability: **Low**

48. *Answer choices:*
(see index for correct answer)

- a. functional perspective
- b. Conservatism
- c. interpersonal communication
- d. information systems assessment

Guidance: level 1

:: Marketing ::

_________ or stock is the goods and materials that a business holds for the ultimate goal of resale .

Exam Probability: **Low**

49. *Answer choices:*
(see index for correct answer)

- a. Packshot
- b. LIDA
- c. Purchase funnel
- d. Party plan

Guidance: level 1

:: Debt ::

_________ is the trust which allows one party to provide money or resources to another party wherein the second party does not reimburse the first party immediately , but promises either to repay or return those resources at a later date. In other words, _________ is a method of making reciprocity formal, legally enforceable, and extensible to a large group of unrelated people.

Exam Probability: **Low**

50. *Answer choices:*

(see index for correct answer)

- a. Credit
- b. Financial assistance
- c. Christians Against Poverty
- d. Debt adjustment

Guidance: level 1

:: Options (finance) ::

A _________ , often simply labeled a "call", is a financial contract between two parties, the buyer and the seller of this type of option. The buyer of the _________ has the right, but not the obligation, to buy an agreed quantity of a particular commodity or financial instrument from the seller of the option at a certain time for a certain price . The seller is obligated to sell the commodity or financial instrument to the buyer if the buyer so decides. The buyer pays a fee for this right. The term "call" comes from the fact that the owner has the right to "call the stock away" from the seller.

Exam Probability: **High**

51. *Answer choices:*

(see index for correct answer)

- a. callable
- b. Call option
- c. Credit default option
- d. Straddle

Guidance: level 1

:: International trade ::

In finance, an _________ is the rate at which one currency will be exchanged for another. It is also regarded as the value of one country's currency in relation to another currency. For example, an interbank _________ of 114 Japanese yen to the United States dollar means that ¥114 will be exchanged for each US$1 or that US$1 will be exchanged for each ¥114. In this case it is said that the price of a dollar in relation to yen is ¥114, or equivalently that the price of a yen in relation to dollars is $1/114.

Exam Probability: **Low**

52. *Answer choices:*

(see index for correct answer)

- a. Harberger-Laursen-Metzler effect
- b. Reimportation
- c. Exchange rate
- d. International commodity agreement

Guidance: level 1

:: ::

An _________ is a contingent motivator. Traditional _________ s are extrinsic motivators which reward actions to yield a desired outcome. The effectiveness of traditional _________ s has changed as the needs of Western society have evolved. While the traditional _________ model is effective when there is a defined procedure and goal for a task, Western society started to require a higher volume of critical thinkers, so the traditional model became less effective. Institutions are now following a trend in implementing strategies that rely on intrinsic motivations rather than the extrinsic motivations that the traditional _________ s foster.

Exam Probability: **High**

53. *Answer choices:*

(see index for correct answer)

- a. personal values
- b. open system
- c. levels of analysis
- d. Incentive

Guidance: level 1

:: Money ::

Cash and _________ s are the most liquid current assets found on a business`s balance sheet. _________ s are short-term commitments "with temporarily idle cash and easily convertible into a known cash amount". An investment normally counts to be a _________ when it has a short maturity period of 90 days or less, and can be included in the cash and _________ s balance from the date of acquisition when it carries an insignificant risk of changes in the asset value; with more than 90 days maturity, the asset is not considered as cash and _________ s. Equity investments mostly are excluded from _________ s, unless they are essentially _________ s, for instance, if the preferred shares acquired within a short maturity period and with specified recovery date.

Exam Probability: **Low**

54. *Answer choices:*

(see index for correct answer)

- a. Cash equivalent
- b. Key money
- c. Spondulix
- d. Fungibility

Guidance: level 1

:: Money market instruments ::

_________ , in the global financial market, is an unsecured promissory note with a fixed maturity of not more than 270 days.

Exam Probability: **Medium**

55. *Answer choices:*

(see index for correct answer)

- a. Banker's acceptance
- b. Commercial paper in India

Guidance: level 1

:: Generally Accepted Accounting Principles ::

A __________ , in accrual accounting, is any account where the asset or liability is not realized until a future date , e.g. annuities, charges, taxes, income, etc. The deferred item may be carried, dependent on type of __________ , as either an asset or liability. See also accrual.

Exam Probability: **Medium**

56. *Answer choices:*

(see index for correct answer)

- a. Long-term liabilities
- b. Deferred income
- c. Deferral
- d. net realisable value

Guidance: level 1

:: Mathematical finance ::

In economics and finance, __________ , also known as present discounted value, is the value of an expected income stream determined as of the date of valuation. The __________ is always less than or equal to the future value because money has interest-earning potential, a characteristic referred to as the time value of money, except during times of negative interest rates, when the __________ will be more than the future value. Time value can be described with the simplified phrase, "A dollar today is worth more than a dollar tomorrow". Here, `worth more` means that its value is greater. A dollar today is worth more than a dollar tomorrow because the dollar can be invested and earn a day`s worth of interest, making the total accumulate to a value more than a dollar by tomorrow. Interest can be compared to rent. Just as rent is paid to a landlord by a tenant without the ownership of the asset being transferred, interest is paid to a lender by a borrower who gains access to the money for a time before paying it back. By letting the borrower have access to the money, the lender has sacrificed the exchange value of this money, and is compensated for it in the form of interest. The initial amount of the borrowed funds is less than the total amount of money paid to the lender.

Exam Probability: **High**

57. *Answer choices:*

(see index for correct answer)

- a. Finite difference methods for option pricing
- b. Constant elasticity of variance model
- c. Earnings response coefficient
- d. Present value

Guidance: level 1

:: Government bonds ::

A _________ , commonly known as a Muni Bond, is a bond issued by a local government or territory, or one of their agencies. It is generally used to finance public projects such as roads, schools, airports and seaports, and infrastructure-related repairs. The term _________ is commonly used in the United States, which has the largest market of such trade-able securities in the world. As of 2011, the _________ market was valued at $3.7 trillion. Potential issuers of _________ s include states, cities, counties, redevelopment agencies, special-purpose districts, school districts, public utility districts, publicly owned airports and seaports, and other governmental entities at or below the state level having more than a de minimis amount of one of the three sovereign powers: the power of taxation, the power of eminent domain or the police power.

Exam Probability: **Low**

58. *Answer choices:*

(see index for correct answer)

- a. Texas v. White
- b. Risk-free bond
- c. Municipal bond
- d. War bond

Guidance: level 1

:: Mathematical finance ::

_________ is the value of an asset at a specific date. It measures the nominal future sum of money that a given sum of money is "worth" at a specified time in the future assuming a certain interest rate, or more generally, rate of return; it is the present value multiplied by the accumulation function.The value does not include corrections for inflation or other factors that affect the true value of money in the future. This is used in time value of money calculations.

Exam Probability: **Medium**

59. *Answer choices:*

(see index for correct answer)

- a. Holding period return
- b. Snell envelope
- c. Inverse demand function
- d. Black model

Guidance: level 1

Human resource management

Human resource (HR) management is the strategic approach to the effective management of organization workers so that they help the business gain a competitive advantage. It is designed to maximize employee performance in service of an employer's strategic objectives. HR is primarily concerned with the management of people within organizations, focusing on policies and on systems. HR departments are responsible for overseeing employee-benefits design, employee recruitment, training and development, performance appraisal, and rewarding (e.g., managing pay and benefit systems). HR also concerns itself with organizational change and industrial relations, that is, the balancing of organizational practices with requirements arising from collective bargaining and from governmental laws.

:: ::

_________ is a form of government characterized by strong central power and limited political freedoms. Individual freedoms are subordinate to the state and there is no constitutional accountability and rule of law under an authoritarian regime. Authoritarian regimes can be autocratic with power concentrated in one person or it can be more spread out between multiple officials and government institutions. Juan Linz's influential 1964 description of _________ characterized authoritarian political systems by four qualities.

Exam Probability: **High**

1. *Answer choices:*

(see index for correct answer)

- a. corporate values
- b. empathy
- c. Authoritarianism
- d. functional perspective

Guidance: level 1

:: Legal terms ::

_________ , a form of alternative dispute resolution , is a way to resolve disputes outside the courts. The dispute will be decided by one or more persons , which renders the " _________ award". An _________ award is legally binding on both sides and enforceable in the courts.

Exam Probability: **Medium**

2. *Answer choices:*

(see index for correct answer)

- a. Legal benefit
- b. Commanding precedent
- c. Arbitration
- d. Financing statement

Guidance: level 1

:: Labour relations ::

An _________ is a place of employment at which one is not required to join or financially support a union as a condition of hiring or continued employment. _________ is also known as a merit shop.

Exam Probability: **Low**

3. *Answer choices:*

(see index for correct answer)

- a. Acas
- b. Open shop
- c. Disciplinary counseling
- d. Scranton Declaration

Guidance: level 1

:: ::

_________ is the administration of an organization, whether it is a business, a not-for-profit organization, or government body. _________ includes the activities of setting the strategy of an organization and coordinating the efforts of its employees to accomplish its objectives through the application of available resources, such as financial, natural, technological, and human resources. The term " _________ " may also refer to those people who manage an organization.

Exam Probability: **High**

4. *Answer choices:*

(see index for correct answer)

- a. hierarchical
- b. surface-level diversity
- c. personal values
- d. functional perspective

Guidance: level 1

:: Human resource management ::

_________ encompasses values and behaviors that contribute to the unique social and psychological environment of a business. The _________ influences the way people interact, the context within which knowledge is created, the resistance they will have towards certain changes, and ultimately the way they share knowledge. _________ represents the collective values, beliefs and principles of organizational members and is a product of factors such as history, product, market, technology, strategy, type of employees, management style, and national culture; culture includes the organization`s vision, values, norms, systems, symbols, language, assumptions, environment, location, beliefs and habits.

Exam Probability: **High**

5. *Answer choices:*

(see index for correct answer)

- a. Cross-functional team
- b. Organizational culture
- c. Open plan
- d. Human relations movement

Guidance: level 1

:: Problem solving ::

In other words, _________ is a situation where a group of people meet to generate new ideas and solutions around a specific domain of interest by removing inhibitions. People are able to think more freely and they suggest as many spontaneous new ideas as possible. All the ideas are noted down and those ideas are not criticized and after _________ session the ideas are evaluated.The term was popularized by Alex Faickney Osborn in the 1953 book Applied Imagination.

Exam Probability: **High**

6. *Answer choices:*

(see index for correct answer)

- a. Convergent and divergent production
- b. Objective approach
- c. Creative problem-solving
- d. Brainstorming

Guidance: level 1

:: ::

A _________ , medical practitioner, medical doctor, or simply doctor, is a professional who practises medicine, which is concerned with promoting, maintaining, or restoring health through the study, diagnosis, prognosis and treatment of disease, injury, and other physical and mental impairments. _________ s may focus their practice on certain disease categories, types of patients, and methods of treatment—known as specialities—or they may assume responsibility for the provision of continuing and comprehensive medical care to individuals, families, and communities—known as general practice. Medical practice properly requires both a detailed knowledge of the academic disciplines, such as anatomy and physiology, underlying diseases and their treatment—the science of medicine—and also a decent competence in its applied practice—the art or craft of medicine.

Exam Probability: **Low**

7. *Answer choices:*

(see index for correct answer)

- a. hierarchical perspective
- b. information systems assessment
- c. Physician
- d. cultural

Guidance: level 1

:: Human resource management ::

__________ are transactions in which the ownership of companies, other business organizations, or their operating units are transferred or consolidated with other entities. As an aspect of strategic management, M&A can allow enterprises to grow or downsize, and change the nature of their business or competitive position.

Exam Probability: **High**

8. *Answer choices:*

(see index for correct answer)

- a. human resource
- b. Training and development
- c. Mergers and acquisitions
- d. T-shaped skills

Guidance: level 1

:: ::

__________ is the process of two or more people or organizations working together to complete a task or achieve a goal. __________ is similar to cooperation. Most __________ requires leadership, although the form of leadership can be social within a decentralized and egalitarian group. Teams that work collaboratively often access greater resources, recognition and rewards when facing competition for finite resources.

Exam Probability: **Low**

9. *Answer choices:*

(see index for correct answer)

- a. Collaboration
- b. Character
- c. cultural
- d. open system

Guidance: level 1

:: United States employment discrimination case law ::

_________ , 411 U.S. 792 , is a US employment law case by the United States Supreme Court regarding the burdens and nature of proof in proving a Title VII case and the order in which plaintiffs and defendants present proof. It was the seminal case in the McDonnell Douglas burden-shifting framework.

Exam Probability: **Medium**

10. *Answer choices:*

(see index for correct answer)

- a. Price Waterhouse v. Hopkins
- b. New York City Transit Authority v. Beazer
- c. McDonnell Douglas Corp. v. Green
- d. Reeves v. Sanderson Plumbing Products, Inc.

Guidance: level 1

:: Human resource management ::

_________ means increasing the scope of a job through extending the range of its job duties and responsibilities generally within the same level and periphery. _________ involves combining various activities at the same level in the organization and adding them to the existing job. It is also called the horizontal expansion of job activities. This contradicts the principles of specialisation and the division of labour whereby work is divided into small units, each of which is performed repetitively by an individual worker and the responsibilities are always clear. Some motivational theories suggest that the boredom and alienation caused by the division of labour can actually cause efficiency to fall. Thus, _________ seeks to motivate workers through reversing the process of specialisation. A typical approach might be to replace assembly lines with modular work; instead of an employee repeating the same step on each product, they perform several tasks on a single item. In order for employees to be provided with _________ they will need to be retrained in new fields to understand how each field works.

Exam Probability: **Low**

11. *Answer choices:*

(see index for correct answer)

- a. Appreciative inquiry
- b. Cross-training
- c. human resource
- d. Job enlargement

Guidance: level 1

:: Labour relations ::

__________ is a form of protest in which people congregate outside a place of work or location where an event is taking place. Often, this is done in an attempt to dissuade others from going in , but it can also be done to draw public attention to a cause. Picketers normally endeavor to be non-violent. It can have a number of aims, but is generally to put pressure on the party targeted to meet particular demands or cease operations. This pressure is achieved by harming the business through loss of customers and negative publicity, or by discouraging or preventing workers or customers from entering the site and thereby preventing the business from operating normally.

Exam Probability: **Low**

12. *Answer choices:*

(see index for correct answer)

- a. Boulwarism
- b. Union shop
- c. Picketing
- d. Passfield Memorandum

Guidance: level 1

:: Business ::

__________ is a trade policy that does not restrict imports or exports; it can also be understood as the free market idea applied to international trade. In government, __________ is predominantly advocated by political parties that hold liberal economic positions while economically left-wing and nationalist political parties generally support protectionism, the opposite of __________ .

Exam Probability: **High**

13. *Answer choices:*

(see index for correct answer)

- a. Serviced office broker
- b. Customer experience
- c. Free Trade
- d. Disappointment

Guidance: level 1

:: Offshoring ::

Outsourcing is an agreement in which one company hires another company to be responsible for a planned or existing activity that is or could be done internally,and sometimes involves transferring employees and assets from one firm to another.

Exam Probability: **High**

14. *Answer choices:*

(see index for correct answer)

- a. Programmers Guild
- b. Offshore company
- c. American Jobs
- d. Nearshoring

Guidance: level 1

:: ::

__________ is a labor union representing almost 1.9 million workers in over 100 occupations in the United States and Canada. SEIU is focused on organizing workers in three sectors: health care , including hospital, home care and nursing home workers; public services ; and property services .

Exam Probability: **High**

15. *Answer choices:*

(see index for correct answer)

- a. interpersonal communication
- b. co-culture
- c. Service Employees International Union
- d. personal values

Guidance: level 1

:: ::

__________ consists of using generic or ad hoc methods in an orderly manner to find solutions to problems. Some of the problem-solving techniques developed and used in philosophy, artificial intelligence, computer science, engineering, mathematics, or medicine are related to mental problem-solving techniques studied in psychology.

Exam Probability: **Low**

16. *Answer choices:*
(see index for correct answer)

- a. functional perspective
- b. imperative
- c. Problem solving
- d. Character

Guidance: level 1

:: Industrial agreements ::

__________ is a process in labour relations, where a trade union gains a new and superior entitlement from one employer and then uses that agreement as a precedent to demand the same entitlement or a superior one from other employers.

Exam Probability: **Medium**

17. *Answer choices:*
(see index for correct answer)

- a. WorkChoices
- b. In Place of Strife
- c. Enterprise bargaining agreement
- d. Industrial Disputes Act 1947

Guidance: level 1

:: Recruitment ::

_________ is a specialized recruitment service which organizations pay to seek out and recruit highly qualified candidates for senior-level and executive jobs . Headhunters may also seek out and recruit other highly specialized and/or skilled positions in organizations for which there is strong competition in the job market for the top talent, such as senior data analysts or computer programmers. The method usually involves commissioning a third-party organization, typically an _________ firm, but possibly a standalone consultant or consulting firm, to research the availability of suitable qualified candidates working for competitors or related businesses or organizations. Having identified a shortlist of qualified candidates who match the client`s requirements, the _________ firm may act as an intermediary to contact the individual and see if they might be interested in moving to a new employer. The _________ firm may also carry out initial screening of the candidate, negotiations on remuneration and benefits, and preparing the employment contract. In some markets there has been a move towards using _________ for lower positions driven by the fact that there are less candidates for some positions even on lower levels than executive.

Exam Probability: **Low**

18. *Answer choices:*

(see index for correct answer)

- a. Europass
- b. Versatilist
- c. Candidate submittal
- d. Probation

Guidance: level 1

:: Labour law ::

In law, _________ is to give an immediately secured right of present or future deployment. One has a vested right to an asset that cannot be taken away by any third party, even though one may not yet possess the asset. When the right, interest, or title to the present or future possession of a legal estate can be transferred to any other party, it is termed a vested interest.

Exam Probability: **Medium**

19. *Answer choices:*

(see index for correct answer)

- a. Michele Tiraboschi
- b. Core Labor Standards
- c. Vesting
- d. Positive action

Guidance: level 1

:: Employment compensation ::

A _________ is pay and benefits employees receive when they leave employment at a company unwillfully. In addition to their remaining regular pay, it may include some of the following.

Exam Probability: **High**

20. *Answer choices:*

(see index for correct answer)

- a. Wages for housework
- b. Federal Wage System
- c. Performance-related pay
- d. Labour law

Guidance: level 1

:: ::

From an accounting perspective, _________ is crucial because _________ and _________ taxes considerably affect the net income of most companies and because they are subject to laws and regulations .

Exam Probability: **Low**

21. *Answer choices:*

(see index for correct answer)

- a. functional perspective
- b. interpersonal communication
- c. Payroll
- d. surface-level diversity

Guidance: level 1

:: Employment discrimination ::

A __________ is a metaphor used to represent an invisible barrier that keeps a given demographic from rising beyond a certain level in a hierarchy.

Exam Probability: **Low**

22. *Answer choices:*

(see index for correct answer)

- a. Employment discrimination law in the European Union
- b. Glass ceiling
- c. LGBT employment discrimination in the United States
- d. Glass cliff

Guidance: level 1

:: Business law ::

A __________ is an arrangement where parties, known as partners, agree to cooperate to advance their mutual interests. The partners in a __________ may be individuals, businesses, interest-based organizations, schools, governments or combinations. Organizations may partner to increase the likelihood of each achieving their mission and to amplify their reach. A __________ may result in issuing and holding equity or may be only governed by a contract.

Exam Probability: **Medium**

23. *Answer choices:*

(see index for correct answer)

- a. Power harassment
- b. Partnership
- c. Recharacterisation
- d. Complex structured finance transactions

Guidance: level 1

:: ::

A __________ is monetary compensation paid by an employer to an employee in exchange for work done. Payment may be calculated as a fixed amount for each task completed , or at an hourly or daily rate , or based on an easily measured quantity of work done.

Exam Probability: **Medium**

24. *Answer choices:*

(see index for correct answer)

- a. interpersonal communication
- b. hierarchical perspective
- c. Wage
- d. deep-level diversity

Guidance: level 1

:: ::

_________ is defined by sociologist John R. Schermerhorn as the "...degree to which the people affected by decision are treated by dignity and respect. The theory focuses on the interpersonal treatment people receive when procedures are implemented.

Exam Probability: **Medium**

25. *Answer choices:*

(see index for correct answer)

- a. Interactional justice
- b. hierarchical perspective
- c. co-culture
- d. interpersonal communication

Guidance: level 1

:: Income ::

A _________ is a unit in systems of monetary compensation for employment. It is commonly used in public service, both civil and military, but also for companies of the private sector. _________ s facilitate the employment process by providing a fixed framework of salary ranges, as opposed to a free negotiation. Typically, _________ s encompass two dimensions: a "vertical" range where each level corresponds to the responsibility of, and requirements needed for a certain position; and a "horizontal" range within this scale to allow for monetary incentives rewarding the employee`s quality of performance or length of service. Thus, an employee progresses within the horizontal and vertical ranges upon achieving positive appraisal on a regular basis. In most cases, evaluation is done annually and encompasses more than one method.

Exam Probability: **Low**

26. *Answer choices:*

(see index for correct answer)

- a. Pay grade
- b. Imputed income
- c. National average salary
- d. Family income

Guidance: level 1

:: Business ethics ::

In United States labor law, a _________ exists when one`s behavior within a workplace creates an environment that is difficult or uncomfortable for another person to work in, due to discrimination. Common complaints in sexual harassment lawsuits include fondling, suggestive remarks, sexually-suggestive photos displayed in the workplace, use of sexual language, or off-color jokes. Small matters, annoyances, and isolated incidents are usually not considered to be statutory violations of the discrimination laws. For a violation to impose liability, the conduct must create a work environment that would be intimidating, hostile, or offensive to a reasonable person. An employer can be held liable for failing to prevent these workplace conditions, unless it can prove that it attempted to prevent the harassment and that the employee failed to take advantage of existing harassment counter-measures or tools provided by the employer.

Exam Probability: **Low**

27. *Answer choices:*

(see index for correct answer)

- a. Hostile work environment
- b. Third-party technique
- c. Accounting scandals
- d. Society for Business Ethics

Guidance: level 1

:: Employment compensation ::

A _________ is an agreement between a company and an employee specifying that the employee will receive certain significant benefits if employment is terminated. Most definitions specify the employment termination is as a result of a merger or takeover, also known as "Change-in-control benefits", but more recently the term has been used to describe perceived excessive CEO severance packages unrelated to change in ownership . The benefits may include severance pay, cash bonuses, stock options, or other benefits.

Exam Probability: **Low**

28. *Answer choices:*

(see index for correct answer)

- a. Spiff
- b. Golden parachute
- c. Compensation of employees
- d. Interactive accommodation process

Guidance: level 1

:: Human resource management ::

_________ , also known as organizational socialization, is management jargon first created in 1988 that refers to the mechanism through which new employees acquire the necessary knowledge, skills, and behaviors in order to become effective organizational members and insiders.

Exam Probability: **Low**

29. *Answer choices:*

(see index for correct answer)

- a. ROWE

- b. Onboarding
- c. Labour is not a commodity
- d. Person specification

Guidance: level 1

:: Information systems ::

__________ is the process of creating, sharing, using and managing the knowledge and information of an organisation. It refers to a multidisciplinary approach to achieving organisational objectives by making the best use of knowledge.

Exam Probability: **Medium**

30. *Answer choices:*
(see index for correct answer)

- a. Automated information system
- b. Decision support system
- c. Self-service software vendors
- d. DAD-IS

Guidance: level 1

:: Business process ::

Outsourcing is an agreement in which one company hires another company to be responsible for a planned or existing activity that is or could be done internally,and sometimes involves transferring employees and assets from one firm to another.

Exam Probability: **Low**

31. *Answer choices:*
(see index for correct answer)

- a. Business communication
- b. Closure by stealth
- c. Business process outsourcing
- d. Dynamic business process management

Guidance: level 1

:: Bankruptcy ::

_________ is the concept of a person or group of people taking precedence over another person or group because the former is either older than the latter or has occupied a particular position longer than the latter. _________ is present between parents and children and may be present in other common relationships, such as among siblings of different ages or between workers and their managers.

Exam Probability: **Medium**

32. *Answer choices:*

(see index for correct answer)

- a. Peter S. Kaufman
- b. Seniority
- c. Deficiency judgment
- d. Tools of trade

Guidance: level 1

:: ::

_________ is a form of development in which a person called a coach supports a learner or client in achieving a specific personal or professional goal by providing training and guidance. The learner is sometimes called a coachee. Occasionally, _________ may mean an informal relationship between two people, of whom one has more experience and expertise than the other and offers advice and guidance as the latter learns; but _________ differs from mentoring in focusing on specific tasks or objectives, as opposed to more general goals or overall development.

Exam Probability: **High**

33. *Answer choices:*

(see index for correct answer)

- a. Coaching
- b. information systems assessment
- c. open system
- d. Sarbanes-Oxley act of 2002

Guidance: level 1

:: Telecommuting ::

__________ , also called telework, teleworking, working from home, mobile work, remote work, and flexible workplace, is a work arrangement in which employees do not commute or travel to a central place of work, such as an office building, warehouse, or store. Teleworkers in the 21st century often use mobile telecommunications technology such as Wi-Fi-equipped laptop or tablet computers and smartphones to work from coffee shops; others may use a desktop computer and a landline phone at their home. According to a Reuters poll, approximately "one in five workers around the globe, particularly employees in the Middle East, Latin America and Asia, telecommute frequently and nearly 10 percent work from home every day." In the 2000s, annual leave or vacation in some organizations was seen as absence from the workplace rather than ceasing work, and some office employees used telework to continue to check work e-mails while on vacation.

Exam Probability: **Medium**

34. *Answer choices:*

(see index for correct answer)

- a. Home Work Convention, 1996
- b. Telecommuting
- c. IvanAnywhere
- d. VenueGen

Guidance: level 1

:: ::

_________ is a method for employees to organize into a labor union in which a majority of employees in a bargaining unit sign authorization forms, or "cards", stating they wish to be represented by the union. Since the National Labor Relations Act became law in 1935, _________ has been an alternative to the National Labor Relations Board`s election process. _________ and election are both overseen by the National Labor Relations Board. The difference is that with card sign-up, employees sign authorization cards stating they want a union, the cards are submitted to the NLRB and if more than 50% of the employees submitted cards, the NLRB requires the employer to recognize the union. The NLRA election process is an additional step with the NLRB conducting a secret ballot election after authorization cards are submitted. In both cases the employer never sees the authorization cards or any information that would disclose how individual employees voted.

Exam Probability: **High**

35. *Answer choices:*

(see index for correct answer)

- a. hierarchical perspective
- b. Card check
- c. personal values
- d. process perspective

Guidance: level 1

:: Industrial engineering ::

_________ is the formal process that sits alongside Requirements analysis and focuses on the human elements of the requirements.

Exam Probability: **High**

36. *Answer choices:*

(see index for correct answer)

- a. Work sampling
- b. Efficiency factor
- c. Material flow
- d. Source reduction

Guidance: level 1

:: Human resource management ::

_________ involves improving the effectiveness of organizations and the individuals and teams within them. Training may be viewed as related to immediate changes in organizational effectiveness via organized instruction, while development is related to the progress of longer-term organizational and employee goals. While _________ technically have differing definitions, the two are oftentimes used interchangeably and/or together. _________ has historically been a topic within applied psychology but has within the last two decades become closely associated with human resources management, talent management, human resources development, instructional design, human factors, and knowledge management.

Exam Probability: **Low**

37. *Answer choices:*

(see index for correct answer)

- a. Training and development
- b. Co-determination
- c. Organizational orientations
- d. Formal organization

Guidance: level 1

:: Trade union legislation ::

The _________ of 1935 is a foundational statute of United States labor law which guarantees the right of private sector employees to organize into trade unions, engage in collective bargaining, and take collective action such as strikes. The act was written by Senator Robert F. Wagner, passed by the 74th United States Congress, and signed into law by President Franklin D. Roosevelt.

Exam Probability: **High**

38. *Answer choices:*

(see index for correct answer)

- a. Trade Union and Labour Relations Act 1974
- b. Labor Management Relations Act
- c. Trade Union Reform and Employment Rights Act 1993
- d. National Labor Relations Act

Guidance: level 1

:: Supply chain management terms ::

In business and finance, _________ is a system of organizations, people, activities, information, and resources involved inmoving a product or service from supplier to customer. _________ activities involve the transformation of natural resources, raw materials, and components into a finished product that is delivered to the end customer. In sophisticated _________ systems, used products may re-enter the _________ at any point where residual value is recyclable. _________ s link value chains.

Exam Probability: **Low**

39. *Answer choices:*

(see index for correct answer)

- a. Last mile
- b. Consumables
- c. Final assembly schedule
- d. Supply chain

Guidance: level 1

:: ::

In production, research, retail, and accounting, a _________ is the value of money that has been used up to produce something or deliver a service, and hence is not available for use anymore. In business, the _________ may be one of acquisition, in which case the amount of money expended to acquire it is counted as _________ . In this case, money is the input that is gone in order to acquire the thing. This acquisition _________ may be the sum of the _________ of production as incurred by the original producer, and further _________ s of transaction as incurred by the acquirer over and above the price paid to the producer. Usually, the price also includes a mark-up for profit over the _________ of production.

Exam Probability: **Medium**

40. *Answer choices:*

(see index for correct answer)

- a. deep-level diversity
- b. corporate values
- c. process perspective
- d. Cost

Guidance: level 1

:: Offshoring ::

A _________ is the temporary suspension or permanent termination of employment of an employee or, more commonly, a group of employees for business reasons, such as personnel management or downsizing an organization. Originally, _________ referred exclusively to a temporary interruption in work, or employment but this has evolved to a permanent elimination of a position in both British and US English, requiring the addition of "temporary" to specify the original meaning of the word. A _________ is not to be confused with wrongful termination. Laid off workers or displaced workers are workers who have lost or left their jobs because their employer has closed or moved, there was insufficient work for them to do, or their position or shift was abolished . Downsizing in a company is defined to involve the reduction of employees in a workforce. Downsizing in companies became a popular practice in the 1980s and early 1990s as it was seen as a way to deliver better shareholder value as it helps to reduce the costs of employers . Indeed, recent research on downsizing in the U.S., UK, and Japan suggests that downsizing is being regarded by management as one of the preferred routes to help declining organizations, cutting unnecessary costs, and improve organizational performance. Usually a _________ occurs as a cost cutting measure.

Exam Probability: **Low**

41. *Answer choices:*

(see index for correct answer)

- a. Antex
- b. Nearshoring
- c. Layoff
- d. Advanced Contact Solutions

Guidance: level 1

:: Training ::

_________ is action or inaction that is regulated to be in accordance with a particular system of governance. _________ is commonly applied to regulating human and animal behavior, and furthermore, it is applied to each activity-branch in all branches of organized activity, knowledge, and other fields of study and observation. _________ can be a set of expectations that are required by any governing entity including the self, groups, classes, fields, industries, or societies.

Exam Probability: **Medium**

42. *Answer choices:*
(see index for correct answer)

- a. Makers Academy
- b. Jeff Phillips
- c. Person Analysis
- d. Overlearning

Guidance: level 1

:: Recruitment ::

The _________ is an American nonprofit professional association established in 1956 in Bethlehem, Pennsylvania, for college career services, recruiting practitioners, and others who wish to hire the college educated.

Exam Probability: **Medium**

43. *Answer choices:*
(see index for correct answer)

- a. National Association of Colleges and Employers
- b. Social recruiting
- c. Job fair
- d. Haigui

Guidance: level 1

:: Teams ::

A _________ usually refers to a group of individuals who work together from different geographic locations and rely on communication technology such as email, FAX, and video or voice conferencing services in order to collaborate. The term can also refer to groups or teams that work together asynchronously or across organizational levels. Powell, Piccoli and Ives define _________ s as "groups of geographically, organizationally and/or time dispersed workers brought together by information and telecommunication technologies to accomplish one or more organizational tasks." According to Ale Ebrahim et. al. , _________ s can also be defined as "small temporary groups of geographically, organizationally and/or time dispersed knowledge workers who coordinate their work predominantly with electronic information and communication technologies in order to accomplish one or more organization tasks."

Exam Probability: **High**

44. *Answer choices:*
(see index for correct answer)

- a. Virtual team
- b. Team-building

Guidance: level 1

:: Trade unions in the United States ::

_________ is a labor union in the United States and Canada with roughly 300,000 active members. The union`s members work predominantly in the hotel, food service, laundry, warehouse, and casino gaming industries. The union was formed in 2004 by the merger of Union of Needletrades, Industrial, and Textile Employees and Hotel Employees and Restaurant Employees Union .

Exam Probability: **High**

45. *Answer choices:*
(see index for correct answer)

- a. Oregon Education Association
- b. Graphic Communications Conference
- c. American Train Dispatchers Association
- d. UNITE HERE

Guidance: level 1

:: United States federal labor legislation ::

The _________ of 1988 is a United States federal law that generally prevents employers from using polygraph tests, either for pre-employment screening or during the course of employment, with certain exemptions.

Exam Probability: **High**

46. *Answer choices:*

(see index for correct answer)

- a. Employee Polygraph Protection Act
- b. Anti-Pinkerton Act
- c. Railway Labor Act
- d. Adamson Act

Guidance: level 1

:: Human resource management ::

_________ are the people who make up the workforce of an organization, business sector, or economy. "Human capital" is sometimes used synonymously with " _________ ", although human capital typically refers to a narrower effect . Likewise, other terms sometimes used include manpower, talent, labor, personnel, or simply people.

Exam Probability: **High**

47. *Answer choices:*

(see index for correct answer)

- a. Employee retention
- b. Salary
- c. Corporate Equality Index
- d. Human resources

Guidance: level 1

:: ::

_________ is a common standard in United States labor law arbitration that is used in labor union contracts in the United States as a form of job security.

Exam Probability: **Medium**

48. *Answer choices:*

(see index for correct answer)

- a. co-culture
- b. Just cause
- c. process perspective
- d. similarity-attraction theory

Guidance: level 1

:: Industrial agreements ::

A _________, in labor relations, is a group of employees with a clear and identifiable community of interests who are represented by a single labor union in collective bargaining and other dealings with management. Examples would be non-management professors, law enforcement professionals, blue-collar workers, clerical and administrative employees, etc. Geographic location as well as the number of facilities included in _________ s can be at issue during representation cases.

Exam Probability: **High**

49. *Answer choices:*

(see index for correct answer)

- a. Bargaining unit
- b. Court of Arbitration
- c. Common rule awards
- d. Compromise agreement

Guidance: level 1

:: ::

__________ is an experience a person may have when one moves to a cultural environment which is different from one`s own; it is also the personal disorientation a person may feel when experiencing an unfamiliar way of life due to immigration or a visit to a new country, a move between social environments, or simply transition to another type of life. One of the most common causes of __________ involves individuals in a foreign environment. __________ can be described as consisting of at least one of four distinct phases: honeymoon, negotiation, adjustment, and adaptation.

Exam Probability: **High**

50. *Answer choices:*

(see index for correct answer)

- a. Culture shock
- b. Character
- c. surface-level diversity
- d. cultural

Guidance: level 1

:: Business ethics ::

A __________ is a person who exposes any kind of information or activity that is deemed illegal, unethical, or not correct within an organization that is either private or public. The information of alleged wrongdoing can be classified in many ways: violation of company policy/rules, law, regulation, or threat to public interest/national security, as well as fraud, and corruption. Those who become __________ s can choose to bring information or allegations to surface either internally or externally. Internally, a __________ can bring his/her accusations to the attention of other people within the accused organization such as an immediate supervisor. Externally, a __________ can bring allegations to light by contacting a third party outside of an accused organization such as the media, government, law enforcement, or those who are concerned. __________ s, however, take the risk of facing stiff reprisal and retaliation from those who are accused or alleged of wrongdoing.

Exam Probability: **Medium**

51. *Answer choices:*

(see index for correct answer)

- a. Whistleblower
- b. Business Ethics Quarterly
- c. MBA Oath
- d. FRISK Software International

Guidance: level 1

:: Employee relations ::

The _________ can be used to bring together employment and job-related information which employees need to know. It typically has three types of content.

Exam Probability: **Medium**

52. *Answer choices:*

(see index for correct answer)

- a. Employee motivation
- b. Industry Federation of the State of Rio de Janeiro
- c. Employee morale
- d. Employee stock

Guidance: level 1

:: Employee relations ::

_________ are tools used by organizational leadership to gain feedback on and measure employee engagement, employee morale, and performance. Usually answered anonymously, surveys are also used to gain a holistic picture of employees` feelings on such areas as working conditions, supervisory impact, and motivation that regular channels of communication may not. Surveys are considered effective in this regard provided they are well-designed, effectively administered, have validity, and evoke changes and improvements.

Exam Probability: **Low**

53. *Answer choices:*

(see index for correct answer)

- a. Employee stock
- b. Employee engagement
- c. Employee handbook
- d. Employee motivation

Guidance: level 1

:: Business terms ::

Centralisation or _________ is the process by which the activities of an organization, particularly those regarding planning and decision-making, framing strategy and policies become concentrated within a particular geographical location group. This moves the important decision-making and planning powers within the center of the organisation.

Exam Probability: **High**

54. *Answer choices:*

(see index for correct answer)

- a. customer base
- b. Centralization
- c. granular
- d. front office

Guidance: level 1

:: Psychometrics ::

_________ is a dynamic, structured, interactive process where a neutral third party assists disputing parties in resolving conflict through the use of specialized communication and negotiation techniques. All participants in _________ are encouraged to actively participate in the process. _________ is a "party-centered" process in that it is focused primarily upon the needs, rights, and interests of the parties. The mediator uses a wide variety of techniques to guide the process in a constructive direction and to help the parties find their optimal solution. A mediator is facilitative in that she/he manages the interaction between parties and facilitates open communication. _________ is also evaluative in that the mediator analyzes issues and relevant norms , while refraining from providing prescriptive advice to the parties .

Exam Probability: **High**

55. *Answer choices:*

(see index for correct answer)

- a. Visual analogue scale
- b. Torrance Tests of Creative Thinking

- c. Mediation
- d. IPPQ

Guidance: level 1

:: Occupations ::

__________ means a restricted practice or a restriction on the use of an occupational title, requiring a license. A license created under a "practice act" requires a license before performing a certain activity, such as driving a car on public roads. A license created under a "title act" restricts the use of a given occupational title to licensees, but anyone can perform the activity itself under a less restricted title. For example, in Oregon, anyone can practice counseling, but only licensees can call themselves "Licensed Professional Counselors." Thus depending on the type of law,practicing without a license may carry civil or criminal penalties or may be perfectly legal. For some occupations and professions, licensing is often granted through a professional body or a licensing board composed of practitioners who oversee the applications for licenses. This often involves accredited training and examinations, but varies a great deal for different activities and in different countries.

Exam Probability: **Low**

56. *Answer choices:*
(see index for correct answer)

- a. Environmentalist
- b. Occupational inequality
- c. Conveyancer
- d. Chief economist

Guidance: level 1

:: Occupational safety and health ::

__________ is a set of six naturally occurring silicate minerals, which all have in common their asbestiform habit: i.e., long , thin fibrous crystals, with each visible fiber composed of millions of microscopic "fibrils" that can be released by abrasion and other processes. The minerals are chrysotile, amosite, crocidolite, tremolite, anthophyllite, and actinolite.

Exam Probability: **Low**

57. *Answer choices:*

(see index for correct answer)

- a. Benzene
- b. Comcare
- c. PIACT
- d. Code of safe working practices

Guidance: level 1

:: Labour law ::

An _________ is special or specified circumstances that partially or fully exempt a person or organization from performance of a legal obligation so as to avoid an unreasonable or disproportionate burden or obstacle.

Exam Probability: **Medium**

58. *Answer choices:*

(see index for correct answer)

- a. Undue hardship
- b. Victimisation
- c. Unreported employment
- d. Bharat Forge Co Ltd v Uttam Manohar Nakate

Guidance: level 1

:: Sociological terminology ::

In moral and political philosophy, the _________ is a theory or model that originated during the Age of Enlightenment and usually concerns the legitimacy of the authority of the state over the individual. _________ arguments typically posit that individuals have consented, either explicitly or tacitly, to surrender some of their freedoms and submit to the authority in exchange for protection of their remaining rights or maintenance of the social order. The relation between natural and legal rights is often a topic of _________ theory. The term takes its name from The _________ , a 1762 book by Jean-Jacques Rousseau that discussed this concept. Although the antecedents of _________ theory are found in antiquity, in Greek and Stoic philosophy and Roman and Canon Law, the heyday of the _________ was the mid-17th to early 19th centuries, when it emerged as the leading doctrine of political legitimacy.

Exam Probability: **Low**

59. *Answer choices:*

(see index for correct answer)

- a. Internalized
- b. Social engagement
- c. Social fact
- d. McDonaldization

Guidance: level 1

Information systems

Information systems (IS) are formal, sociotechnical, organizational systems designed to collect, process, store, and distribute information. In a sociotechnical perspective Information Systems are composed by four components: technology, process, people and organizational structure.

:: Web analytics ::

A click path or _________ is the sequence of hyperlinks one or more website visitors follows on a given site, presented in the order viewed. A visitor's click path may start within the website or at a separate 3rd party website, often a search engine results page, and it continues as a sequence of successive webpages visited by the user. Click paths take call data and can match it to ad sources, keywords, and/or referring domains, in order to capture data.

Exam Probability: **High**

1. *Answer choices:*

(see index for correct answer)

- a. Apptegic
- b. Wikipedia article traffic
- c. SeeVolution
- d. Unica NetTracker

Guidance: level 1

:: Security compliance ::

A _________ is a communicated intent to inflict harm or loss on another person. A _________ is considered an act of coercion. _________ s are widely observed in animal behavior, particularly in a ritualized form, chiefly in order to avoid the unnecessary physical violence that can lead to physical damage or the death of both conflicting parties.

Exam Probability: **Low**

2. *Answer choices:*

(see index for correct answer)

- a. Month of bugs
- b. 201 CMR 17.00
- c. Vulnerability management
- d. Threat

Guidance: level 1

:: ::

In communications and information processing, _________ is a system of rules to convert information—such as a letter, word, sound, image, or gesture—into another form or representation, sometimes shortened or secret, for communication through a communication channel or storage in a storage medium. An early example is the invention of language, which enabled a person, through speech, to communicate what they saw, heard, felt, or thought to others. But speech limits the range of communication to the distance a voice can carry, and limits the audience to those present when the speech is uttered. The invention of writing, which converted spoken language into visual symbols, extended the range of communication across space and time.

Exam Probability: **Medium**

3. *Answer choices:*

(see index for correct answer)

- a. levels of analysis
- b. information systems assessment
- c. hierarchical perspective
- d. co-culture

Guidance: level 1

:: Information technology management ::

__________ s or pop-ups are forms of online advertising on the World Wide Web. A pop-up is a graphical user interface display area, usually a small window, that suddenly appears in the foreground of the visual interface. The pop-up window containing an advertisement is usually generated by JavaScript that uses cross-site scripting , sometimes with a secondary payload that uses Adobe Flash. They can also be generated by other vulnerabilities/security holes in browser security.

Exam Probability: **Medium**

4. *Answer choices:*

(see index for correct answer)

- a. ESCM-SP
- b. Pop-up ad
- c. SFIAPlus
- d. XML/EDIFACT

Guidance: level 1

:: Virtual reality ::

A __________ is a computer-based simulated environment which may be populated by many users who can create a personal avatar, and simultaneously and independently explore the __________ , participate in its activities and communicate with others. These avatars can be textual, two or three-dimensional graphical representations, or live video avatars with auditory and touch sensations. In general, __________ s allow for multiple users but single player computer games, such as Skyrim, can also be considered a type of __________ .

Exam Probability: **Low**

5. *Answer choices:*

(see index for correct answer)

- a. ST1080
- b. Virtual world
- c. Liquid Image
- d. NearGlobal

Guidance: level 1

:: SQL ::

SQL is a domain-specific language used in programming and designed for managing data held in a relational database management system , or for stream processing in a relational data stream management system . It is particularly useful in handling structured data where there are relations between different entities/variables of the data. SQL offers two main advantages over older read/write APIs like ISAM or VSAM. First, it introduced the concept of accessing many records with one single command; and second, it eliminates the need to specify how to reach a record, e.g. with or without an index.

Exam Probability: **Low**

6. *Answer choices:*

(see index for correct answer)

- a. Meta-SQL
- b. SQL Server Agent
- c. SQL/XML
- d. Structured query language

Guidance: level 1

:: Business process ::

__________ is a discipline in operations management in which people use various methods to discover, model, analyze, measure, improve, optimize, and automate business processes. BPM focuses on improving corporate performance by managing business processes. Any combination of methods used to manage a company`s business processes is BPM. Processes can be structured and repeatable or unstructured and variable. Though not required, enabling technologies are often used with BPM.

Exam Probability: **High**

7. *Answer choices:*

(see index for correct answer)

- a. IBM Blueworks Live
- b. Order processing
- c. Business process management
- d. ADONIS

Guidance: level 1

:: Management ::

A __________ describes the rationale of how an organization creates, delivers, and captures value, in economic, social, cultural or other contexts. The process of __________ construction and modification is also called __________ innovation and forms a part of business strategy.

Exam Probability: **Medium**

8. *Answer choices:*

(see index for correct answer)

- a. Business model
- b. Innovation management
- c. Integrative thinking
- d. Corporate recovery

Guidance: level 1

:: Supply chain management ::

ERP is usually referred to as a category of business management software — typically a suite of integrated applications—that an organization can use to collect, store, manage, and interpret data from these many business activities.

Exam Probability: **Low**

9. *Answer choices:*

(see index for correct answer)

- a. Supply Chain Management Review
- b. Confirmed line item performance
- c. Scan-based trading
- d. Enterprise resource planning

Guidance: level 1

:: Product testing ::

__________ is a characteristic of a product or system, whose interfaces are completely understood, to work with other products or systems, at present or in the future, in either implementation or access, without any restrictions.

Exam Probability: **Low**

10. *Answer choices:*

(see index for correct answer)

- a. Destructive testing
- b. Testing reliability
- c. Conformance testing
- d. Wine tasting

Guidance: level 1

:: Data transmission ::

In telecommunication a _________ is the means of connecting one location to another for the purpose of transmitting and receiving digital information. It can also refer to a set of electronics assemblies, consisting of a transmitter and a receiver and the interconnecting data telecommunication circuit. These are governed by a link protocol enabling digital data to be transferred from a data source to a data sink.

Exam Probability: **High**

11. *Answer choices:*

(see index for correct answer)

- a. Digital call quality
- b. Data Radio Channel
- c. Data link
- d. Channel Division Multiple Access

Guidance: level 1

:: Identity management ::

_________ is the ability of an individual or group to seclude themselves, or information about themselves, and thereby express themselves selectively. The boundaries and content of what is considered private differ among cultures and individuals, but share common themes. When something is private to a person, it usually means that something is inherently special or sensitive to them. The domain of _________ partially overlaps with security , which can include the concepts of appropriate use, as well as protection of information. _________ may also take the form of bodily integrity.

Exam Probability: **Medium**

12. *Answer choices:*

(see index for correct answer)

- a. Privacy
- b. Common Indexing Protocol
- c. Trombinoscope
- d. Identity verification service

Guidance: level 1

:: ::

_________ are interactive computer-mediated technologies that facilitate the creation and sharing of information, ideas, career interests and other forms of expression via virtual communities and networks. The variety of stand-alone and built-in _________ services currently available introduces challenges of definition; however, there are some common features.

Exam Probability: **Medium**

13. *Answer choices:*

(see index for correct answer)

- a. Social media
- b. open system
- c. empathy
- d. surface-level diversity

Guidance: level 1

:: Data ::

_________ is a branch of mathematics working with data collection, organization, analysis, interpretation and presentation. In applying _________ to, for example, a scientific, industrial, or social problem, it is conventional to begin with a statistical population or a statistical model process to be studied. Populations can be diverse topics such as "all people living in a country" or "every atom composing a crystal". _________ deals with every aspect of data, including the planning of data collection in terms of the design of surveys and experiments.See glossary of probability and _________ .

Exam Probability: **Medium**

14. *Answer choices:*

(see index for correct answer)

- a. Data acquisition
- b. Serial concatenated convolutional codes
- c. Statistics
- d. Dummy data

Guidance: level 1

:: Data management ::

" __________ " is a field that treats ways to analyze, systematically extract information from, or otherwise deal with data sets that are too large or complex to be dealt with by traditional data-processing application software. Data with many cases offer greater statistical power, while data with higher complexity may lead to a higher false discovery rate. __________ challenges include capturing data, data storage, data analysis, search, sharing, transfer, visualization, querying, updating, information privacy and data source. __________ was originally associated with three key concepts: volume, variety, and velocity. Other concepts later attributed with __________ are veracity and value.

Exam Probability: **Medium**

15. *Answer choices:*

(see index for correct answer)

- a. Content inventory
- b. SQL/PSM
- c. Versomatic
- d. PureXML

Guidance: level 1

:: Ergonomics ::

__________ is the design of products, devices, services, or environments for people with disabilities. The concept of accessible design and practice of accessible development ensures both "direct access" and "indirect access" meaning compatibility with a person's assistive technology .

Exam Probability: **High**

16. *Answer choices:*

(see index for correct answer)

- a. Dvorak Simplified Keyboard
- b. StickyKeys
- c. International Ergonomics Association
- d. Riding-like sitting

Guidance: level 1

:: ::

A _________ is a discussion or informational website published on the World Wide Web consisting of discrete, often informal diary-style text entries . Posts are typically displayed in reverse chronological order, so that the most recent post appears first, at the top of the web page. Until 2009, _________ s were usually the work of a single individual, occasionally of a small group, and often covered a single subject or topic. In the 2010s, "multi-author _________ s" emerged, featuring the writing of multiple authors and sometimes professionally edited. MABs from newspapers, other media outlets, universities, think tanks, advocacy groups, and similar institutions account for an increasing quantity of _________ traffic. The rise of Twitter and other "micro _________ ging" systems helps integrate MABs and single-author _________ s into the news media. _________ can also be used as a verb, meaning to maintain or add content to a _________ .

Exam Probability: **High**

17. *Answer choices:*

(see index for correct answer)

- a. hierarchical perspective
- b. similarity-attraction theory
- c. Blog
- d. surface-level diversity

Guidance: level 1

:: Monopoly (economics) ::

A _________ exists when a specific person or enterprise is the only supplier of a particular commodity. This contrasts with a monopsony which relates to a single entity`s control of a market to purchase a good or service, and with oligopoly which consists of a few sellers dominating a market. Monopolies are thus characterized by a lack of economic competition to produce the good or service, a lack of viable substitute goods, and the possibility of a high _________ price well above the seller`s marginal cost that leads to a high _________ profit. The verb monopolise or monopolize refers to the process by which a company gains the ability to raise prices or exclude competitors. In economics, a _________ is a single seller. In law, a _________ is a business entity that has significant market power, that is, the power to charge overly high prices. Although monopolies may be big businesses, size is not a characteristic of a _________ . A small business may still have the power to raise prices in a small industry .

Exam Probability: **Medium**

18. *Answer choices:*

(see index for correct answer)

- a. Monopoly
- b. National Competition Policy
- c. De facto monopoly
- d. Government-granted monopoly

Guidance: level 1

:: ::

The _________ , commonly known as the Web, is an information system where documents and other web resources are identified by Uniform Resource Locators , which may be interlinked by hypertext, and are accessible over the Internet. The resources of the WWW may be accessed by users by a software application called a web browser.

Exam Probability: **Low**

19. *Answer choices:*

(see index for correct answer)

- a. World Wide Web
- b. cultural
- c. hierarchical

- d. surface-level diversity

Guidance: level 1

:: Information systems ::

_________ is the process of creating, sharing, using and managing the knowledge and information of an organisation. It refers to a multidisciplinary approach to achieving organisational objectives by making the best use of knowledge.

Exam Probability: **Medium**

20. *Answer choices:*

(see index for correct answer)

- a. Expert systems for mortgages
- b. Intelligent decision support system
- c. LabLynx, Inc.
- d. Knowledge management

Guidance: level 1

:: Multi-agent systems ::

A _________ is a number of Internet-connected devices, each of which is running one or more bots. _________ s can be used to perform distributed denial-of-service attack , steal data, send spam, and allows the attacker to access the device and its connection. The owner can control the _________ using command and control software. The word " _________ " is a combination of the words "robot" and "network". The term is usually used with a negative or malicious connotation.

Exam Probability: **Medium**

21. *Answer choices:*

(see index for correct answer)

- a. Botnet
- b. Monitoring and Surveillance Agents
- c. Zabbix
- d. BredoLab botnet

Guidance: level 1

:: Global Positioning System ::

A _________ is a mechanism for determining the location of an object in space. Technologies for this task exist ranging from worldwide coverage with meter accuracy to workspace coverage with sub-millimetre accuracy.

Exam Probability: **High**

22. *Answer choices:*

(see index for correct answer)

- a. Positioning system
- b. SailTimer
- c. SiReNT
- d. Spartan Packet Radio Experiment

Guidance: level 1

:: ::

_________ LLC is an American multinational technology company that specializes in Internet-related services and products, which include online advertising technologies, search engine, cloud computing, software, and hardware. It is considered one of the Big Four technology companies, alongside Amazon, Apple and Facebook.

Exam Probability: **Low**

23. *Answer choices:*

(see index for correct answer)

- a. hierarchical
- b. corporate values
- c. Sarbanes-Oxley act of 2002
- d. functional perspective

Guidance: level 1

:: ::

Collaborative software or _________ is application software designed to help people involved in a common task to achieve their goals. One of the earliest definitions of collaborative software is "intentional group processes plus software to support them".

Exam Probability: **High**

24. *Answer choices:*

(see index for correct answer)

- a. Groupware
- b. empathy
- c. hierarchical perspective
- d. cultural

Guidance: level 1

:: Process management ::

When used in the context of communication networks, such as Ethernet or packet radio, _________ or network _________ is the rate of successful message delivery over a communication channel. The data these messages belong to may be delivered over a physical or logical link, or it can pass through a certain network node. _________ is usually measured in bits per second , and sometimes in data packets per second or data packets per time slot.

Exam Probability: **Low**

25. *Answer choices:*

(see index for correct answer)

- a. Hazard analysis and critical control points
- b. Business process orientation
- c. Planning horizon
- d. Business process modeling

Guidance: level 1

:: Enterprise modelling ::

_________ are large-scale application software packages that support business processes, information flows, reporting, and data analytics in complex organizations. While ES are generally packaged enterprise application software systems they can also be bespoke, custom developed systems created to support a specific organization`s needs.

Exam Probability: **High**

26. *Answer choices:*

(see index for correct answer)

- a. Business reference model
- b. Enterprise systems
- c. Enterprise engineering
- d. Business engineering

Guidance: level 1

:: ::

A database is an organized collection of data, generally stored and accessed electronically from a computer system. Where databases are more complex they are often developed using formal design and modeling techniques.

Exam Probability: **Low**

27. *Answer choices:*

(see index for correct answer)

- a. process perspective
- b. cultural
- c. corporate values
- d. Database management system

Guidance: level 1

:: Data management ::

In business, _________ is a method used to define and manage the critical data of an organization to provide, with data integration, a single point of reference. The data that is mastered may include reference data- the set of permissible values, and the analytical data that supports decision making.

Exam Probability: **High**

28. *Answer choices:*

(see index for correct answer)

- a. Master data management
- b. PureXML
- c. Content repository
- d. National Information Governance Board for Health and Social Care

Guidance: level 1

:: Network management ::

__________ is the process of administering and managing computer networks. Services provided by this discipline include fault analysis, performance management, provisioning of networks and maintaining the quality of service. Software that enables network administrators to perform their functions is called __________ software.

Exam Probability: **Low**

29. *Answer choices:*

(see index for correct answer)

- a. Baselining
- b. Management agent
- c. Network management
- d. RRDtool

Guidance: level 1

:: Computer networking ::

__________ is a method of grouping data that is transmitted over a digital network into packets. Packets are made of a header and a payload. Data in the header are used by networking hardware to direct the packet to its destination where the payload is extracted and used by application software. __________ is the primary basis for data communications in computer networks worldwide.

Exam Probability: **Medium**

30. *Answer choices:*

(see index for correct answer)

- a. Switch virtual interface
- b. Windows domain
- c. HPM.1
- d. Packet switching

Guidance: level 1

:: ::

A _________ is the event in which two or more bodies exert forces on each other in about a relatively short time. Although the most common use of the word _________ refers to incidents in which two or more objects collide with great force, the scientific use of the term implies nothing about the magnitude of the force.

Exam Probability: **Medium**

31. *Answer choices:*
(see index for correct answer)

- a. hierarchical perspective
- b. Collision
- c. Character
- d. open system

Guidance: level 1

:: Commerce ::

_________ , Inc. is an American media-services provider headquartered in Los Gatos, California, founded in 1997 by Reed Hastings and Marc Randolph in Scotts Valley, California. The company`s primary business is its subscription-based streaming OTT service which offers online streaming of a library of films and television programs, including those produced in-house. As of April 2019, _________ had over 148 million paid subscriptions worldwide, including 60 million in the United States, and over 154 million subscriptions total including free trials. It is available almost worldwide except in mainland China as well as Syria, North Korea, and Crimea . The company also has offices in the Netherlands, Brazil, India, Japan, and South Korea. _________ is a member of the Motion Picture Association of America .

Exam Probability: **High**

32. *Answer choices:*

(see index for correct answer)

- a. Netflix
- b. Export restriction
- c. Weight
- d. Defective on arrival

Guidance: level 1

:: Data management ::

__________ s or data __________ s are computer languages used to make queries in databases and information systems.

Exam Probability: **Low**

33. *Answer choices:*

(see index for correct answer)

- a. Computer-aided software engineering
- b. Semantic warehousing
- c. Query language
- d. Data management plan

Guidance: level 1

:: Data collection ::

__________ is information that either does not have a pre-defined data model or is not organized in a pre-defined manner. Unstructured information is typically text-heavy, but may contain data such as dates, numbers, and facts as well. This results in irregularities and ambiguities that make it difficult to understand using traditional programs as compared to data stored in fielded form in databases or annotated in documents.

Exam Probability: **Medium**

34. *Answer choices:*

(see index for correct answer)

- a. Human-based computation game
- b. Dye tracing
- c. Unstructured data
- d. Question

Guidance: level 1

:: E-commerce ::

Electronic governance or e-governance is the application of information and communication technology for delivering government services, exchange of information, communication transactions, integration of various stand-alone systems and services between government-to-citizen , _________ , government-to-government , government-to-employees as well as back-office processes and interactions within the entire government framework. Through e-governance, government services are made available to citizens in a convenient, efficient, and transparent manner. The three main target groups that can be distinguished in governance concepts are government, citizens, andbusinesses/interest groups. In e-governance, there are no distinct boundaries.

Exam Probability: **Medium**

35. *Answer choices:*

(see index for correct answer)

- a. Government-to-business
- b. Associate-O-Matic
- c. Digital ticket
- d. Onbuy

Guidance: level 1

:: Domain name system ::

_________ , Inc. is an American company based in Reston, Virginia, United States that operates a diverse array of network infrastructure, including two of the Internet`s thirteen root nameservers, the authoritative registry for the .com, .net, and .name generic top-level domains and the .cc and .tv country-code top-level domains, and the back-end systems for the .jobs, .gov, and .edu top-level domains. _________ also offers a range of security services, including managed DNS, distributed denial-of-service attack mitigation and cyber-threat reporting.

Exam Probability: **High**

36. *Answer choices:*

(see index for correct answer)

- a. IDN.IDN
- b. DNS zone
- c. Verisign
- d. Domain hijacking

Guidance: level 1

:: Procurement practices ::

_________ or commercially available off-the-shelf products are packaged solutions which are then adapted to satisfy the needs of the purchasing organization, rather than the commissioning of custom-made, or bespoke, solutions. A related term, Mil-COTS, refers to COTS products for use by the U.S. military.

Exam Probability: **Low**

37. *Answer choices:*
(see index for correct answer)

- a. Commercial off-the-shelf
- b. Syndicated procurement

Guidance: level 1

:: Business process ::

Business process re-engineering is a business management strategy, originally pioneered in the early 1990s, focusing on the analysis and design of workflows and business processes within an organization. BPR aimed to help organizations fundamentally rethink how they do their work in order to improve customer service, cut operational costs, and become world-class competitors.

Exam Probability: **Low**

38. *Answer choices:*
(see index for correct answer)

- a. Information technology outsourcing
- b. Business process reengineering
- c. Bonita BPM
- d. Process capital

Guidance: level 1

:: Information science ::

__________ has been defined as "the branch of ethics that focuses on the relationship between the creation, organization, dissemination, and use of information, and the ethical standards and moral codes governing human conduct in society". It examines the morality that comes from information as a resource, a product, or as a target. It provides a critical framework for considering moral issues concerning informational privacy, moral agency , new environmental issues , problems arising from the life-cycle of information . It is very vital to understand that librarians, archivists, information professionals among others, really understand the importance of knowing how to disseminate proper information as well as being responsible with their actions when addressing information.

Exam Probability: **Low**

39. *Answer choices:*

(see index for correct answer)

- a. Information ethics
- b. World Congress of Universal Documentation
- c. Taxonomic database
- d. Web Feature Service

Guidance: level 1

:: Business models ::

__________ , or The Computer Utility, is a service provisioning model in which a service provider makes computing resources and infrastructure management available to the customer as needed, and charges them for specific usage rather than a flat rate. Like other types of on-demand computing , the utility model seeks to maximize the efficient use of resources and/or minimize associated costs. Utility is the packaging of system resources, such as computation, storage and services, as a metered service. This model has the advantage of a low or no initial cost to acquire computer resources; instead, resources are essentially rented.

Exam Probability: **Medium**

40. *Answer choices:*

(see index for correct answer)

- a. Technology push
- b. Business Model Canvas
- c. Utility computing
- d. Free-to-play

Guidance: level 1

:: Data quality ::

__________ is the maintenance of, and the assurance of the accuracy and consistency of, data over its entire life-cycle, and is a critical aspect to the design, implementation and usage of any system which stores, processes, or retrieves data. The term is broad in scope and may have widely different meanings depending on the specific context even under the same general umbrella of computing. It is at times used as a proxy term for data quality, while data validation is a pre-requisite for __________ . __________ is the opposite of data corruption. The overall intent of any __________ technique is the same: ensure data is recorded exactly as intended and upon later retrieval, ensure the data is the same as it was when it was originally recorded. In short, __________ aims to prevent unintentional changes to information. __________ is not to be confused with data security, the discipline of protecting data from unauthorized parties.

Exam Probability: **High**

41. *Answer choices:*

(see index for correct answer)

- a. Data Quality Campaign
- b. Referential integrity
- c. Data corruption
- d. Input mask

Guidance: level 1

:: Information systems ::

In artificial intelligence, an _________ is a computer system that emulates the decision-making ability of a human expert. _________ s are designed to solve complex problems by reasoning through bodies of knowledge, represented mainly as if–then rules rather than through conventional procedural code. The first _________ s were created in the 1970s and then proliferated in the 1980s. _________ s were among the first truly successful forms of artificial intelligence software. However, some experts point out that _________ s were not part of true artificial intelligence since they lack the ability to learn autonomously from external data.An _________ is divided into two subsystems: the inference engine and the knowledge base. The knowledge base represents facts and rules. The inference engine applies the rules to the known facts to deduce new facts. Inference engines can also include explanation and debugging abilities.

Exam Probability: **Medium**

42. *Answer choices:*

(see index for correct answer)

- a. Geographical Operations System
- b. ISCRAM
- c. Expert system
- d. Virtual information services

Guidance: level 1

:: Credit cards ::

The _________ Company, also known as Amex, is an American multinational financial services corporation headquartered in Three World Financial Center in New York City. The company was founded in 1850 and is one of the 30 components of the Dow Jones Industrial Average. The company is best known for its charge card, credit card, and traveler`s cheque businesses.

Exam Probability: **Medium**

43. *Answer choices:*

(see index for correct answer)

- a. American Express
- b. Japan Credit Bureau
- c. North American Bancard
- d. Credit card debt

Guidance: level 1

:: Tag editors ::

_________ is a media player, media library, Internet radio broadcaster, and mobile device management application developed by Apple Inc. It was announced on January 9, 2001. It is used to play, download, and organize digital multimedia files, including music and video, on personal computers running the macOS and Windows operating systems. Content must be purchased through the _________ Store, whereas _________ is the software letting users manage their purchases.

Exam Probability: **High**

44. *Answer choices:*

(see index for correct answer)

- a. CD Player
- b. Kid3
- c. Puddletag
- d. ITunes

Guidance: level 1

:: Data quality ::

_________ or data cleaning is the process of detecting and correcting corrupt or inaccurate records from a record set, table, or database and refers to identifying incomplete, incorrect, inaccurate or irrelevant parts of the data and then replacing, modifying, or deleting the dirty or coarse data. _________ may be performed interactively with data wrangling tools, or as batch processing through scripting.

Exam Probability: **Medium**

45. *Answer choices:*

(see index for correct answer)

- a. Data validation
- b. Data degradation
- c. Data cleansing
- d. Data quality assessment

Guidance: level 1

:: Service-oriented (business computing) ::

__________ is a style of software design where services are provided to the other components by application components, through a communication protocol over a network. The basic principles of __________ are independent of vendors, products and technologies.A service is a discrete unit of functionality that can be accessed remotely and acted upon and updated independently, such as retrieving a credit card statement online.

Exam Probability: **High**

46. *Answer choices:*

(see index for correct answer)

- a. Mushroom Networks
- b. SEMCI
- c. Service-oriented architecture
- d. Multitenancy

Guidance: level 1

:: Production and manufacturing ::

__________ is the manufacturing approach of using computers to control entire production process. This integration allows individual processes to exchange information with each other and initiate actions. Although manufacturing can be faster and less error-prone by the integration of computers, the main advantage is the ability to create automated manufacturing processes. Typically CIM relies of closed-loop control processes, based on real-time input from sensors. It is also known as flexible design and manufacturing.

Exam Probability: **Low**

47. *Answer choices:*

(see index for correct answer)

- a. Computer-integrated manufacturing
- b. BOMtracker
- c. Economic dispatch
- d. Piece work

Guidance: level 1

:: ::

Within the Internet, _________ s are formed by the rules and procedures of the _________ System . Any name registered in the DNS is a _________ . _________ s are used in various networking contexts and for application-specific naming and addressing purposes. In general, a _________ represents an Internet Protocol resource, such as a personal computer used to access the Internet, a server computer hosting a web site, or the web site itself or any other service communicated via the Internet. In 2017, 330.6 million _________ s had been registered.

Exam Probability: **Low**

48. *Answer choices:*

(see index for correct answer)

- a. Domain name
- b. information systems assessment
- c. personal values
- d. Character

Guidance: level 1

:: Stochastic processes ::

_________ in its modern meaning is a "new idea, creative thoughts, new imaginations in form of device or method". _________ is often also viewed as the application of better solutions that meet new requirements, unarticulated needs, or existing market needs. Such _________ takes place through the provision of more-effective products, processes, services, technologies, or business models that are made available to markets, governments and society. An _________ is something original and more effective and, as a consequence, new, that "breaks into" the market or society. _________ is related to, but not the same as, invention, as _________ is more apt to involve the practical implementation of an invention to make a meaningful impact in the market or society, and not all _________ s require an invention. _________ often manifests itself via the engineering process, when the problem being solved is of a technical or scientific nature. The opposite of _________ is exnovation.

Exam Probability: **Medium**

49. *Answer choices:*

(see index for correct answer)

- a. Innovation
- b. Brownian excursion
- c. Telegraph process
- d. Random dynamical system

Guidance: level 1

:: ::

__________ , Inc. was a company that provided human resource management systems , Financial Management Solutions , supply chain management , customer relationship management , and enterprise performance management software, as well as software for manufacturing, and student administration to large corporations, governments, and organizations. It existed as an independent corporation until its acquisition by Oracle Corporation in 2005. The __________ name and product line are now marketed by Oracle.

Exam Probability: **Medium**

50. *Answer choices:*

(see index for correct answer)

- a. PeopleSoft
- b. functional perspective
- c. deep-level diversity
- d. process perspective

Guidance: level 1

:: Production economics ::

__________ is a way of producing goods and services that relies on self-organizing communities of individuals. In such communities, the labor of a large number of people is coordinated towards a shared outcome.

Exam Probability: **Low**

51. *Answer choices:*

(see index for correct answer)

- a. Marginal product
- b. Peer production
- c. Production theory

- d. Isoquant

Guidance: level 1

:: Asset ::

In financial accounting, an _________ is any resource owned by the business. Anything tangible or intangible that can be owned or controlled to produce value and that is held by a company to produce positive economic value is an _________ . Simply stated, _________ s represent value of ownership that can be converted into cash . The balance sheet of a firm records the monetary value of the _________ s owned by that firm. It covers money and other valuables belonging to an individual or to a business.

Exam Probability: **Low**

52. *Answer choices:*

(see index for correct answer)

- a. Asset
- b. Fixed asset

Guidance: level 1

:: Information technology management ::

_________ concerns a cycle of organizational activity: the acquisition of information from one or more sources, the custodianship and the distribution of that information to those who need it, and its ultimate disposition through archiving or deletion.

Exam Probability: **High**

53. *Answer choices:*

(see index for correct answer)

- a. Information management
- b. Microsoft Operations Framework
- c. Digital asset management
- d. Spreadmart

Guidance: level 1

:: ::

_________ is a set of documents provided on paper, or online, or on digital or analog media, such as audio tape or CDs. Examples are user guides, white papers, on-line help, quick-reference guides. It is becoming less common to see paper _________ . _________ is distributed via websites, software products, and other on-line applications.

Exam Probability: **Medium**

54. *Answer choices:*

(see index for correct answer)

- a. similarity-attraction theory
- b. process perspective
- c. co-culture
- d. surface-level diversity

Guidance: level 1

:: Infographics ::

A _________ is a symbolic representation of information according to visualization technique. _________ s have been used since ancient times, but became more prevalent during the Enlightenment. Sometimes, the technique uses a three-dimensional visualization which is then projected onto a two-dimensional surface. The word graph is sometimes used as a synonym for _________ .

Exam Probability: **High**

55. *Answer choices:*

(see index for correct answer)

- a. Diagram
- b. Print reading
- c. Motion chart
- d. Graphic organizer

Guidance: level 1

:: Computer access control protocols ::

An _________ is a type of computer communications protocol or cryptographic protocol specifically designed for transfer of authentication data between two entities. It allows the receiving entity to authenticate the connecting entity as well as authenticate itself to the connecting entity by declaring the type of information needed for authentication as well as syntax. It is the most important layer of protection needed for secure communication within computer networks.

Exam Probability: **Medium**

56. *Answer choices:*

(see index for correct answer)

- a. Bcrypt
- b. Authentication protocol
- c. Simple Authentication and Security Layer
- d. LAN Manager

Guidance: level 1

:: Data management ::

_________ is a set of processes and technologies that supports the collection, managing, and publishing of information in any form or medium. When stored and accessed via computers, this information may be more specifically referred to as digital content, or simply as content.

Exam Probability: **Medium**

57. *Answer choices:*

(see index for correct answer)

- a. Data architect
- b. Content management
- c. Government Performance Management
- d. Cognos ReportNet

Guidance: level 1

:: Data management ::

_________ is a form of intellectual property that grants the creator of an original creative work an exclusive legal right to determine whether and under what conditions this original work may be copied and used by others, usually for a limited term of years. The exclusive rights are not absolute but limited by limitations and exceptions to _________ law, including fair use. A major limitation on _________ on ideas is that _________ protects only the original expression of ideas, and not the underlying ideas themselves.

Exam Probability: **Low**

58. *Answer choices:*

(see index for correct answer)

- a. PureXML
- b. Query language
- c. Chunked transfer encoding
- d. Copyright

Guidance: level 1

:: ::

A _________ is an organized collection of data, generally stored and accessed electronically from a computer system. Where _________ s are more complex they are often developed using formal design and modeling techniques.

Exam Probability: **Medium**

59. *Answer choices:*

(see index for correct answer)

- a. Database
- b. cultural
- c. surface-level diversity
- d. Character

Guidance: level 1

Marketing

Marketing is the study and management of exchange relationships. Marketing is the business process of creating relationships with and satisfying customers. With its focus on the customer, marketing is one of the premier components of business management.
Marketing is defined by the American Marketing Association as "the activity, set of institutions, and processes for creating, communicating, delivering, and exchanging offerings that have value for customers, clients, partners, and society at large."

:: Survey methodology ::

An _________ is a conversation where questions are asked and answers are given. In common parlance, the word " _________ " refers to a one-on-one conversation between an _________ er and an _________ ee. The _________ er asks questions to which the _________ ee responds, usually so information may be transferred from _________ ee to _________ er . Sometimes, information can be transferred in both directions. It is a communication, unlike a speech, which produces a one-way flow of information.

Exam Probability: **High**

1. *Answer choices:*

(see index for correct answer)

- a. Interview
- b. Total survey error
- c. Survey research
- d. National Health Interview Survey

Guidance: level 1

:: ::

An __________ , often referred to as a creative agency or an ad agency, is a business dedicated to creating, planning, and handling advertising and sometimes other forms of promotion and marketing for its clients. An ad agency is generally independent from the client; it may be an internal department or agency that provides an outside point of view to the effort of selling the client`s products or services, or an outside firm. An agency can also handle overall marketing and branding strategies promotions for its clients, which may include sales as well.

Exam Probability: **Medium**

2. *Answer choices:*

(see index for correct answer)

- a. Advertising agency
- b. levels of analysis
- c. interpersonal communication
- d. Character

Guidance: level 1

:: Data analysis ::

__________ is a process of inspecting, cleansing, transforming, and modeling data with the goal of discovering useful information, informing conclusions, and supporting decision-making. __________ has multiple facets and approaches, encompassing diverse techniques under a variety of names, and is used in different business, science, and social science domains. In today`s business world, __________ plays a role in making decisions more scientific and helping businesses operate more effectively.

Exam Probability: **Medium**

3. *Answer choices:*

(see index for correct answer)

- a. Data analysis
- b. Experimental uncertainty analysis
- c. Variance-stabilizing transformation
- d. Data definition specification

Guidance: level 1

:: Services management and marketing ::

_________ is a specialised branch of marketing. _________ emerged as a separate field of study in the early 1980s, following the recognition that the unique characteristics of services required different strategies compared with the marketing of physical goods.

Exam Probability: **Low**

4. *Answer choices:*

(see index for correct answer)

- a. Industrialization of services business model
- b. Automated attendant
- c. Service climate
- d. Night service

Guidance: level 1

:: Progressive Era in the United States ::

The Clayton Antitrust Act of 1914 , was a part of United States antitrust law with the goal of adding further substance to the U.S. antitrust law regime; the _________ sought to prevent anticompetitive practices in their incipiency. That regime started with the Sherman Antitrust Act of 1890, the first Federal law outlawing practices considered harmful to consumers . The _________ specified particular prohibited conduct, the three-level enforcement scheme, the exemptions, and the remedial measures.

Exam Probability: **Medium**

5. *Answer choices:*

(see index for correct answer)

- a. Mann Act
- b. Clayton Antitrust Act
- c. pragmatism

Guidance: level 1

:: Commercial item transport and distribution ::

Wholesaling or distributing is the sale of goods or merchandise to retailers; to industrial, commercial, institutional, or other professional business users; or to other _________ rs and related subordinated services. In general, it is the sale of goods to anyone other than a standard consumer.

Exam Probability: **Low**

6. *Answer choices:*

(see index for correct answer)

- a. Wholesale fashion distribution
- b. Wholesale
- c. Distribution deal
- d. Automated Export System

Guidance: level 1

:: ::

_________ or commercialisation is the process of introducing a new product or production method into commerce—making it available on the market. The term often connotes especially entry into the mass market , but it also includes a move from the laboratory into commerce. Many technologies begin in a research and development laboratory or in an inventor's workshop and may not be practical for commercial use in their infancy . The "development" segment of the "research and development" spectrum requires time and money as systems are engineered with a view to making the product or method a paying commercial proposition. The product launch of a new product is the final stage of new product development - at this point advertising, sales promotion, and other marketing efforts encourage commercial adoption of the product or method. Beyond _________ can lie consumerization .

Exam Probability: **High**

7. *Answer choices:*

(see index for correct answer)

- a. process perspective
- b. levels of analysis
- c. Commercialization
- d. functional perspective

Guidance: level 1

:: ::

_________ , or auditory perception, is the ability to perceive sounds by detecting vibrations, changes in the pressure of the surrounding medium through time, through an organ such as the ear. The academic field concerned with _________ is auditory science.

Exam Probability: **Medium**

8. *Answer choices:*
(see index for correct answer)

- a. Hearing
- b. deep-level diversity
- c. surface-level diversity
- d. levels of analysis

Guidance: level 1

:: Marketing ::

A _________ is an overall experience of a customer that distinguishes an organization or product from its rivals in the eyes of the customer. _________ s are used in business, marketing, and advertising. Name _________ s are sometimes distinguished from generic or store _________ s.

Exam Probability: **Medium**

9. *Answer choices:*
(see index for correct answer)

- a. Customer acquisition management
- b. Marketing myopia
- c. Adobe Marketing Cloud
- d. Brand

Guidance: level 1

:: ::

_________ are interactive computer-mediated technologies that facilitate the creation and sharing of information, ideas, career interests and other forms of expression via virtual communities and networks. The variety of stand-alone and built-in _________ services currently available introduces challenges of definition; however, there are some common features.

Exam Probability: **Low**

10. *Answer choices:*

(see index for correct answer)

- a. similarity-attraction theory
- b. Social media
- c. levels of analysis
- d. personal values

Guidance: level 1

:: Management ::

_________ is the organizational discipline which focuses on the practical application of marketing orientation, techniques and methods inside enterprises and organizations and on the management of a firm`s marketing resources and activities.

Exam Probability: **High**

11. *Answer choices:*

(see index for correct answer)

- a. Line manager
- b. Project management
- c. Marketing management
- d. Core competency

Guidance: level 1

:: Data management ::

__________ is a form of intellectual property that grants the creator of an original creative work an exclusive legal right to determine whether and under what conditions this original work may be copied and used by others, usually for a limited term of years. The exclusive rights are not absolute but limited by limitations and exceptions to __________ law, including fair use. A major limitation on __________ on ideas is that __________ protects only the original expression of ideas, and not the underlying ideas themselves.

Exam Probability: **Low**

12. *Answer choices:*

(see index for correct answer)

- a. Versomatic
- b. Enterprise manufacturing intelligence
- c. Cloud Data Management Interface
- d. Content format

Guidance: level 1

:: ::

__________ is the process of making predictions of the future based on past and present data and most commonly by analysis of trends. A commonplace example might be estimation of some variable of interest at some specified future date. Prediction is a similar, but more general term. Both might refer to formal statistical methods employing time series, cross-sectional or longitudinal data, or alternatively to less formal judgmental methods. Usage can differ between areas of application: for example, in hydrology the terms "forecast" and " __________ " are sometimes reserved for estimates of values at certain specific future times, while the term "prediction" is used for more general estimates, such as the number of times floods will occur over a long period.

Exam Probability: **Medium**

13. *Answer choices:*

(see index for correct answer)

- a. similarity-attraction theory
- b. Forecasting
- c. functional perspective
- d. levels of analysis

Guidance: level 1

:: Workplace ::

__________ is asystematic determination of a subject`s merit, worth and significance, using criteria governed by a set of standards. It can assist an organization, program, design, project or any other intervention or initiative to assess any aim, realisable concept/proposal, or any alternative, to help in decision-making; or to ascertain the degree of achievement or value in regard to the aim and objectives and results of any such action that has been completed. The primary purpose of __________ , in addition to gaining insight into prior or existing initiatives, is to enable reflection and assist in the identification of future change.

Exam Probability: **Low**

14. *Answer choices:*

(see index for correct answer)

- a. Evaluation
- b. Control freak
- c. Hostile environment sexual harassment
- d. Staff turnover

Guidance: level 1

:: Competition (economics) ::

__________ arises whenever at least two parties strive for a goal which cannot be shared: where one`s gain is the other`s loss .

Exam Probability: **Low**

15. *Answer choices:*

(see index for correct answer)

- a. National Competitiveness Report of Armenia
- b. Regulatory competition
- c. Competition
- d. Leapfrogging

Guidance: level 1

:: ::

_________ is a process whereby a person assumes the parenting of another, usually a child, from that person`s biological or legal parent or parents. Legal _________ s permanently transfers all rights and responsibilities, along with filiation, from the biological parent or parents.

Exam Probability: **High**

16. *Answer choices:*

(see index for correct answer)

- a. Adoption
- b. functional perspective
- c. interpersonal communication
- d. similarity-attraction theory

Guidance: level 1

:: ::

A _________ is an organized collection of data, generally stored and accessed electronically from a computer system. Where _________ s are more complex they are often developed using formal design and modeling techniques.

Exam Probability: **Medium**

17. *Answer choices:*

(see index for correct answer)

- a. functional perspective
- b. cultural
- c. process perspective
- d. empathy

Guidance: level 1

:: Generally Accepted Accounting Principles ::

Expenditure is an outflow of money to another person or group to pay for an item or service, or for a category of costs. For a tenant, rent is an _________ . For students or parents, tuition is an _________ . Buying food, clothing, furniture or an automobile is often referred to as an _________ . An _________ is a cost that is "paid" or "remitted", usually in exchange for something of value. Something that seems to cost a great deal is "expensive". Something that seems to cost little is "inexpensive". " _________ s of the table" are _________ s of dining, refreshments, a feast, etc.

Exam Probability: **High**

18. *Answer choices:*
(see index for correct answer)

- a. Indian Accounting Standards
- b. Gross sales
- c. Expense
- d. Pro forma

Guidance: level 1

:: Supply chain management terms ::

In business and finance, _________ is a system of organizations, people, activities, information, and resources involved inmoving a product or service from supplier to customer. _________ activities involve the transformation of natural resources, raw materials, and components into a finished product that is delivered to the end customer. In sophisticated _________ systems, used products may re-enter the _________ at any point where residual value is recyclable. _________ s link value chains.

Exam Probability: **Medium**

19. *Answer choices:*
(see index for correct answer)

- a. Capital spare
- b. Widget
- c. Direct shipment
- d. Supply chain

Guidance: level 1

:: ::

A _________ service is an online platform which people use to build social networks or social relationship with other people who share similar personal or career interests, activities, backgrounds or real-life connections.

Exam Probability: **High**

20. *Answer choices:*

(see index for correct answer)

- a. surface-level diversity
- b. information systems assessment
- c. interpersonal communication
- d. Social networking

Guidance: level 1

:: Management ::

In business, a _________ is the attribute that allows an organization to outperform its competitors. A _________ may include access to natural resources, such as high-grade ores or a low-cost power source, highly skilled labor, geographic location, high entry barriers, and access to new technology.

Exam Probability: **Medium**

21. *Answer choices:*

(see index for correct answer)

- a. Business value
- b. Competitive advantage
- c. Process capability
- d. Fleet management

Guidance: level 1

:: E-commerce ::

_________ is the activity of buying or selling of products on online services or over the Internet. Electronic commerce draws on technologies such as mobile commerce, electronic funds transfer, supply chain management, Internet marketing, online transaction processing, electronic data interchange , inventory management systems, and automated data collection systems.

Exam Probability: **Medium**

22. *Answer choices:*
(see index for correct answer)

- a. Mobilpenge
- b. E-commerce
- c. Public key certificate
- d. Virtual goods

Guidance: level 1

:: ::

_________ is the collection of techniques, skills, methods, and processes used in the production of goods or services or in the accomplishment of objectives, such as scientific investigation. _________ can be the knowledge of techniques, processes, and the like, or it can be embedded in machines to allow for operation without detailed knowledge of their workings. Systems applying _________ by taking an input, changing it according to the system`s use, and then producing an outcome are referred to as _________ systems or technological systems.

Exam Probability: **Medium**

23. *Answer choices:*
(see index for correct answer)

- a. Technology
- b. interpersonal communication
- c. corporate values
- d. personal values

Guidance: level 1

:: Marketing ::

_________ is a growth strategy that identifies and develops new market segments for current products. A _________ strategy targets non-buying customers in currently targeted segments. It also targets new customers in new segments.

Exam Probability: **Medium**

24. *Answer choices:*

(see index for correct answer)

- a. Product
- b. Movie gimmick
- c. Market development
- d. Content creation

Guidance: level 1

:: Meetings ::

A _________ is a body of one or more persons that is subordinate to a deliberative assembly. Usually, the assembly sends matters into a _________ as a way to explore them more fully than would be possible if the assembly itself were considering them. _________ s may have different functions and their type of work differ depending on the type of the organization and its needs.

Exam Probability: **Low**

25. *Answer choices:*

(see index for correct answer)

- a. Committee
- b. Staging area
- c. Popular assembly
- d. Convention

Guidance: level 1

:: Product management ::

A _________ , trade mark, or trade-mark is a recognizable sign, design, or expression which identifies products or services of a particular source from those of others, although _________ s used to identify services are usually called service marks. The _________ owner can be an individual, business organization, or any legal entity. A _________ may be located on a package, a label, a voucher, or on the product itself. For the sake of corporate identity, _________ s are often displayed on company buildings. It is legally recognized as a type of intellectual property.

Exam Probability: **High**

26. *Answer choices:*

(see index for correct answer)

- a. Trademark
- b. Technology acceptance model
- c. Obsolescence
- d. Brand extension

Guidance: level 1

:: Brand management ::

Marketing communications uses different marketing channels and tools in combination: Marketing communication channels focus on any way a business communicates a message to its desired market, or the market in general. A marketing communication tool can be anything from: advertising, personal selling, direct marketing, sponsorship, communication, and promotion to public relations.

Exam Probability: **Low**

27. *Answer choices:*

(see index for correct answer)

- a. MoonScoop Group
- b. Luxury goods
- c. Brandchannel
- d. Trade symbols

Guidance: level 1

:: ::

_________ is a concept of English common law and is a necessity for simple contracts but not for special contracts . The concept has been adopted by other common law jurisdictions, including the US.

Exam Probability: **High**

28. *Answer choices:*
(see index for correct answer)

- a. levels of analysis
- b. deep-level diversity
- c. imperative
- d. Consideration

Guidance: level 1

:: Graphic design ::

An _________ is an artifact that depicts visual perception, such as a photograph or other two-dimensional picture, that resembles a subject—usually a physical object—and thus provides a depiction of it. In the context of signal processing, an _________ is a distributed amplitude of color.

Exam Probability: **Medium**

29. *Answer choices:*
(see index for correct answer)

- a. Ikarus
- b. Ascender Corporation
- c. Variation diminishing property
- d. Interesource

Guidance: level 1

:: ::

In sales, commerce and economics, a _________ is the recipient of a good, service, product or an idea - obtained from a seller, vendor, or supplier via a financial transaction or exchange for money or some other valuable consideration.

Exam Probability: **Low**

30. *Answer choices:*

(see index for correct answer)

- a. corporate values
- b. Character
- c. interpersonal communication
- d. Customer

Guidance: level 1

:: Business ::

The seller, or the provider of the goods or services, completes a sale in response to an acquisition, appropriation, requisition or a direct interaction with the buyer at the point of sale. There is a passing of title of the item, and the settlement of a price, in which agreement is reached on a price for which transfer of ownership of the item will occur. The seller, not the purchaser typically executes the sale and it may be completed prior to the obligation of payment. In the case of indirect interaction, a person who sells goods or service on behalf of the owner is known as a _________ man or _________ woman or _________ person, but this often refers to someone selling goods in a store/shop, in which case other terms are also common, including _________ clerk, shop assistant, and retail clerk.

Exam Probability: **Low**

31. *Answer choices:*

(see index for correct answer)

- a. Corporate social media
- b. Business development
- c. Business directory
- d. Sales

Guidance: level 1

:: Marketing analytics ::

__________ is a long-term, forward-looking approach to planning with the fundamental goal of achieving a sustainable competitive advantage. Strategic planning involves an analysis of the company`s strategic initial situation prior to the formulation, evaluation and selection of market-oriented competitive position that contributes to the company`s goals and marketing objectives.

Exam Probability: **Medium**

32. *Answer choices:*

(see index for correct answer)

- a. Marketing strategy
- b. marketing dashboard
- c. Perceptual map
- d. Sumall

Guidance: level 1

:: Costs ::

In economics, __________ is the total economic cost of production and is made up of variable cost, which varies according to the quantity of a good produced and includes inputs such as labour and raw materials, plus fixed cost, which is independent of the quantity of a good produced and includes inputs that cannot be varied in the short term: fixed costs such as buildings and machinery, including sunk costs if any. Since cost is measured per unit of time, it is a flow variable.

Exam Probability: **High**

33. *Answer choices:*

(see index for correct answer)

- a. Cost curve
- b. Average cost
- c. Further processing cost
- d. Total cost

Guidance: level 1

:: ::

_________ s are formal, sociotechnical, organizational systems designed to collect, process, store, and distribute information. In a sociotechnical perspective, _________ s are composed by four components: task, people, structure , and technology.

Exam Probability: **Low**

34. *Answer choices:*

(see index for correct answer)

- a. functional perspective
- b. hierarchical
- c. surface-level diversity
- d. Sarbanes-Oxley act of 2002

Guidance: level 1

:: Business models ::

A _________ , _________ company or daughter company is a company that is owned or controlled by another company, which is called the parent company, parent, or holding company. The _________ can be a company, corporation, or limited liability company. In some cases it is a government or state-owned enterprise. In some cases, particularly in the music and book publishing industries, subsidiaries are referred to as imprints.

Exam Probability: **Low**

35. *Answer choices:*

(see index for correct answer)

- a. Open Music Model
- b. Business model pattern
- c. Strategy map
- d. Microfranchising

Guidance: level 1

:: Strategic alliances ::

A _________ is an agreement between two or more parties to pursue a set of agreed upon objectives needed while remaining independent organizations. A _________ will usually fall short of a legal partnership entity, agency, or corporate affiliate relationship. Typically, two companies form a _________ when each possesses one or more business assets or have expertise that will help the other by enhancing their businesses. _________ s can develop in outsourcing relationships where the parties desire to achieve long-term win-win benefits and innovation based on mutually desired outcomes.

Exam Probability: **Medium**

36. *Answer choices:*

(see index for correct answer)

- a. International joint venture
- b. Defensive termination
- c. Bridge Alliance
- d. Strategic alliance

Guidance: level 1

:: Income ::

_________ is a ratio between the net profit and cost of investment resulting from an investment of some resources. A high ROI means the investment's gains favorably to its cost. As a performance measure, ROI is used to evaluate the efficiency of an investment or to compare the efficiencies of several different investments. In purely economic terms, it is one way of relating profits to capital invested. _________ is a performance measure used by businesses to identify the efficiency of an investment or number of different investments.

Exam Probability: **High**

37. *Answer choices:*

(see index for correct answer)

- a. Property investment calculator
- b. Private income
- c. Independent income
- d. Gratuity

Guidance: level 1

:: ::

Advertising is a marketing communication that employs an openly sponsored, non-personal message to promote or sell a product, service or idea. Sponsors of advertising are typically businesses wishing to promote their products or services. Advertising is differentiated from public relations in that an advertiser pays for and has control over the message. It differs from personal selling in that the message is non-personal, i.e., not directed to a particular individual.Advertising is communicated through various mass media, including traditional media such as newspapers, magazines, television, radio, outdoor advertising or direct mail; and new media such as search results, blogs, social media, websites or text messages. The actual presentation of the message in a medium is referred to as an _________ , or "ad" or advert for short.

Exam Probability: **Medium**

38. *Answer choices:*

(see index for correct answer)

- a. interpersonal communication
- b. deep-level diversity
- c. similarity-attraction theory
- d. open system

Guidance: level 1

:: Consumer behaviour ::

_________ is an activity in which a customer browses the available goods or services presented by one or more retailers with the potential intent to purchase a suitable selection of them. A typology of shopper types has been developed by scholars which identifies one group of shoppers as recreational shoppers, that is, those who enjoy _________ and view it as a leisure activity.

Exam Probability: **High**

39. *Answer choices:*

(see index for correct answer)

- a. Customer analytics
- b. Cocooning
- c. Opinion leadership
- d. Shopping

Guidance: level 1

:: Market research ::

An _________ or lighthouse customer is an early customer of a given company, product, or technology. The term originates from Everett M. Rogers` Diffusion of Innovations .

Exam Probability: **High**

40. *Answer choices:*

(see index for correct answer)

- a. 6-3-5 Brainwriting
- b. Zeitgeist Research
- c. Firmographics
- d. Respondent error

Guidance: level 1

:: Production economics ::

In microeconomics, _________ are the cost advantages that enterprises obtain due to their scale of operation , with cost per unit of output decreasing with increasing scale.

Exam Probability: **High**

41. *Answer choices:*

(see index for correct answer)

- a. Marginal product
- b. Economies of scale
- c. Partial productivity
- d. The labor problem

Guidance: level 1

:: Marketing ::

The _________ is a foundation model for businesses. The _________ has been defined as the "set of marketing tools that the firm uses to pursue its marketing objectives in the target market". Thus the _________ refers to four broad levels of marketing decision, namely: product, price, place, and promotion. Marketing practice has been occurring for millennia, but marketing theory emerged in the early twentieth century. The contemporary _________ , or the 4 Ps, which has become the dominant framework for marketing management decisions, was first published in 1960. In services marketing, an extended _________ is used, typically comprising 7 Ps, made up of the original 4 Ps extended by process, people, and physical evidence. Occasionally service marketers will refer to 8 Ps, comprising these 7 Ps plus performance.

Exam Probability: **Medium**

42. *Answer choices:*

(see index for correct answer)

- a. Marketing mix
- b. Pitching engine
- c. Active adult retail
- d. Brand content management

Guidance: level 1

:: Evaluation methods ::

_________ is a scientific method of observation to gather non-numerical data. This type of research "refers to the meanings, concepts definitions, characteristics, metaphors, symbols, and description of things" and not to their "counts or measures." This research answers why and how a certain phenomenon may occur rather than how often. _________ approaches are employed across many academic disciplines, focusing particularly on the human elements of the social and natural sciences; in less academic contexts, areas of application include qualitative market research, business, service demonstrations by non-profits, and journalism.

Exam Probability: **Low**

43. *Answer choices:*

(see index for correct answer)

- a. Poll average
- b. Case series

- c. Qualitative research
- d. Participant observation

Guidance: level 1

:: Marketing ::

__________ , sometimes called trigger-based or event-driven marketing, is a marketing strategy that uses two-way communication channels to allow consumers to connect with a company directly. Although this exchange can take place in person, in the last decade it has increasingly taken place almost exclusively online through email, social media, and blogs.

Exam Probability: **Medium**

44. *Answer choices:*
(see index for correct answer)

- a. Interactive marketing
- b. Mass marketing
- c. Bluetooth advertising
- d. Double bottom line

Guidance: level 1

:: ::

Competition arises whenever at least two parties strive for a goal which cannot be shared: where one`s gain is the other`s loss .

Exam Probability: **Medium**

45. *Answer choices:*
(see index for correct answer)

- a. levels of analysis
- b. Competitor
- c. cultural
- d. personal values

Guidance: level 1

:: Commodities ::

In economics, a _________ is an economic good or service that has full or substantial fungibility: that is, the market treats instances of the good as equivalent or nearly so with no regard to who produced them. Most commodities are raw materials, basic resources, agricultural, or mining products, such as iron ore, sugar, or grains like rice and wheat. Commodities can also be mass-produced unspecialized products such as chemicals and computer memory.

Exam Probability: **High**

46. *Answer choices:*

(see index for correct answer)

- a. IRely
- b. Sample grade
- c. Commoditization
- d. Commodity

Guidance: level 1

:: Pricing ::

_________ is a pricing strategy in which the selling price is determined by adding a specific amount markup to a product`s unit cost. An alternative pricing method is value-based pricing.

Exam Probability: **Low**

47. *Answer choices:*

(see index for correct answer)

- a. Arbitrage pricing theory
- b. Nonlinear pricing
- c. Cost-plus pricing
- d. Price signal

Guidance: level 1

:: Monopoly (economics) ::

__________ is a category of property that includes intangible creations of the human intellect. __________ encompasses two types of rights: industrial property rights and copyright. It was not until the 19th century that the term " __________ " began to be used, and not until the late 20th century that it became commonplace in the majority of the world.

Exam Probability: **Low**

48. *Answer choices:*

(see index for correct answer)

- a. Intellectual property
- b. Quasi-rent
- c. Rate-of-return regulation
- d. Legal monopoly

Guidance: level 1

:: Marketing ::

__________ is a marketing practice of individuals or organizations . It allows them to sell products or services to other companies or organizations that resell them, use them in their products or services or use them to support their works.

Exam Probability: **High**

49. *Answer choices:*

(see index for correct answer)

- a. Medical science liaison
- b. Call centre
- c. Customer value proposition
- d. Business marketing

Guidance: level 1

:: Organizational structure ::

An __________ defines how activities such as task allocation, coordination, and supervision are directed toward the achievement of organizational aims.

Exam Probability: **Low**

50. *Answer choices:*

(see index for correct answer)

- a. Automated Bureaucracy
- b. Organizational structure
- c. Blessed Unrest
- d. Followership

Guidance: level 1

:: Advertising by type ::

__________ or advertising war is an advertisement in which a particular product, or service, specifically mentions a competitor by name for the express purpose of showing why the competitor is inferior to the product naming it. Also referred to as "knocking copy", it is loosely defined as advertising where "the advertised brand is explicitly compared with one or more competing brands and the comparison is obvious to the audience."

Exam Probability: **High**

51. *Answer choices:*

(see index for correct answer)

- a. Local advertising
- b. Aerial advertising
- c. Out-of-home advertising
- d. Forehead advertising

Guidance: level 1

:: Brokered programming ::

An _________ is a form of television commercial, which generally includes a toll-free telephone number or website. Most often used as a form of direct response television , long-form _________ s are typically 28:30 or 58:30 minutes in length. _________ s are also known as paid programming . This phenomenon started in the United States, where _________ s were typically shown overnight , outside peak prime time hours for commercial broadcasters. Some television stations chose to air _________ s as an alternative to the former practice of signing off. Some channels air _________ s 24 hours. Some stations also choose to air _________ s during the daytime hours mostly on weekends to fill in for unscheduled network or syndicated programming. By 2009, most _________ spending in the U.S. occurred during the early morning, daytime and evening hours, or in the afternoon. Stations in most countries around the world have instituted similar media structures. The _________ industry is worth over $200 billion.

Exam Probability: **High**

52. *Answer choices:*

(see index for correct answer)

- a. One Magnificent Morning
- b. Brokered programming
- c. Leased access
- d. Infomercial

Guidance: level 1

:: Marketing techniques ::

_________ , also known as embedded marketing, is a marketing technique where references to specific brands or products are incorporated into another work, such as a film or television program, with specific promotional intent.

Exam Probability: **High**

53. *Answer choices:*

(see index for correct answer)

- a. Product placement
- b. Locals casino
- c. Intermarket segmentation
- d. Virtual event

Guidance: level 1

:: International trade ::

In finance, an _________ is the rate at which one currency will be exchanged for another. It is also regarded as the value of one country's currency in relation to another currency. For example, an interbank _________ of 114 Japanese yen to the United States dollar means that ¥114 will be exchanged for each US$1 or that US$1 will be exchanged for each ¥114. In this case it is said that the price of a dollar in relation to yen is ¥114, or equivalently that the price of a yen in relation to dollars is $1/114.

Exam Probability: **High**

54. *Answer choices:*

(see index for correct answer)

- a. Exchange rate
- b. Transfer problem
- c. Trade mandate
- d. Strong dollar policy

Guidance: level 1

:: Supply chain management ::

_________ is the removal of intermediaries in economics from a supply chain, or cutting out the middlemen in connection with a transaction or a series of transactions. Instead of going through traditional distribution channels, which had some type of intermediary , companies may now deal with customers directly, for example via the Internet. Hence, the use of factory direct and direct from the factory to mean the same thing.

Exam Probability: **High**

55. *Answer choices:*

(see index for correct answer)

- a. Mobile asset management
- b. Demand sensing
- c. Disintermediation
- d. Yield management

Guidance: level 1

:: Marketing ::

__________ uses different marketing channels and tools in combination: Marketing communication channels focus on any way a business communicates a message to its desired market, or the market in general. A marketing communication tool can be anything from: advertising, personal selling, direct marketing, sponsorship, communication, and promotion to public relations.

Exam Probability: **Low**

56. *Answer choices:*

(see index for correct answer)

- a. Pitching engine
- b. Outsourcing relationship management
- c. Next-best-action marketing
- d. Consumer culture theory

Guidance: level 1

:: Public relations ::

__________ is the public visibility or awareness for any product, service or company. It may also refer to the movement of information from its source to the general public, often but not always via the media. The subjects of __________ include people , goods and services, organizations, and works of art or entertainment.

Exam Probability: **High**

57. *Answer choices:*

(see index for correct answer)

- a. Publicity
- b. Zakazukha
- c. Excellence theory
- d. Information subsidy

Guidance: level 1

:: Marketing ::

A _________ is the people, organizations, and activities necessary to transfer the ownership of goods from the point of production to the point of consumption. It is the way products get to the end-user, the consumer; and is also known as a distribution channel. A _________ is a useful tool for management, and is crucial to creating an effective and well-planned marketing strategy.

Exam Probability: **Medium**

58. *Answer choices:*

(see index for correct answer)

- a. Marketing channel
- b. Online lead generation
- c. Corporate anniversary
- d. Customer interaction tracker

Guidance: level 1

:: ::

Distribution is one of the four elements of the marketing mix. Distribution is the process of making a product or service available for the consumer or business user who needs it. This can be done directly by the producer or service provider, or using indirect channels with distributors or intermediaries. The other three elements of the marketing mix are product, pricing, and promotion.

Exam Probability: **Low**

59. *Answer choices:*

(see index for correct answer)

- a. open system
- b. Sarbanes-Oxley act of 2002
- c. Distribution channel
- d. cultural

Guidance: level 1

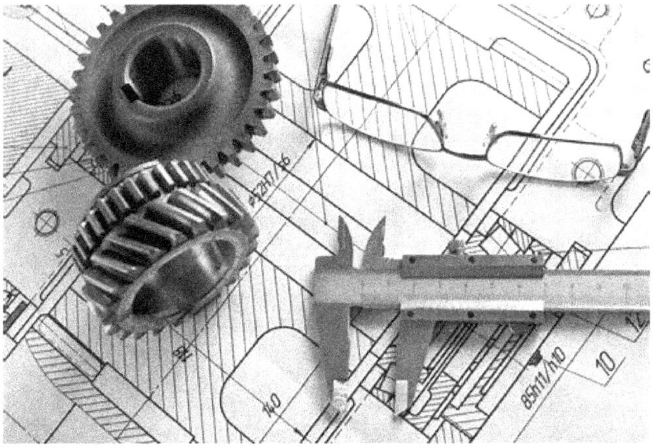

Manufacturing

Manufacturing is the production of merchandise for use or sale using labor and machines, tools, chemical and biological processing, or formulation. The term may refer to a range of human activity, from handicraft to high tech, but is most commonly applied to industrial design , in which raw materials are transformed into finished goods on a large scale. Such finished goods may be sold to other manufacturers for the production of other, more complex products, such as aircraft, household appliances, furniture, sports equipment or automobiles, or sold to wholesalers, who in turn sell them to retailers, who then sell them to end users and consumers.

:: Commercial item transport and distribution ::

__________ in logistics and supply chain management is an organization's use of third-party businesses to outsource elements of its distribution, warehousing, and fulfillment services.

Exam Probability: **High**

1. *Answer choices:*

(see index for correct answer)

- a. Steam wagon
- b. Toll Specialised and Domestic Freight
- c. Port of entry
- d. Third-party logistics

Guidance: level 1

:: Packaging materials ::

_________ is a thin material produced by pressing together moist fibres of cellulose pulp derived from wood, rags or grasses, and drying them into flexible sheets.It is a versatile material with many uses, including writing, printing, packaging, cleaning, decorating, and a number of industrial and construction processes. _________ s are essential in legal or non-legal documentation.

Exam Probability: **High**

2. *Answer choices:*
(see index for correct answer)

- a. Polyethylene
- b. Paper
- c. Polystyrene
- d. Jute

Guidance: level 1

:: Help desk ::

Data center management is the collection of tasks performed by those responsible for managing ongoing operation of a data center This includes Business service management and planning for the future.

Exam Probability: **Low**

3. *Answer choices:*
(see index for correct answer)

- a. SysAid Technologies
- b. KnowledgeBase Manager Pro
- c. Technical support
- d. Virtual help desk

Guidance: level 1

:: Industrial engineering ::

__________ , in its contemporary conceptualisation, is a comparison of perceived expectations of a service with perceived performance , giving rise to the equation SQ=P-E. This conceptualistion of __________ has its origins in the expectancy-disconfirmation paradigm.

Exam Probability: **Medium**

4. *Answer choices:*
(see index for correct answer)

- a. Package testing
- b. Efficiency factor
- c. Ergonomic
- d. Work Measurement

Guidance: level 1

:: Occupational safety and health ::

__________ is a chemical element with symbol Pb and atomic number 82. It is a heavy metal that is denser than most common materials. __________ is soft and malleable, and also has a relatively low melting point. When freshly cut, __________ is silvery with a hint of blue; it tarnishes to a dull gray color when exposed to air. __________ has the highest atomic number of any stable element and three of its isotopes are endpoints of major nuclear decay chains of heavier elements.

Exam Probability: **Low**

5. *Answer choices:*
(see index for correct answer)

- a. Indoor air quality
- b. Lead
- c. Hazard analysis
- d. Jury stress

Guidance: level 1

:: ::

_________ is the process of making predictions of the future based on past and present data and most commonly by analysis of trends. A commonplace example might be estimation of some variable of interest at some specified future date. Prediction is a similar, but more general term. Both might refer to formal statistical methods employing time series, cross-sectional or longitudinal data, or alternatively to less formal judgmental methods. Usage can differ between areas of application: for example, in hydrology the terms "forecast" and " _________ " are sometimes reserved for estimates of values at certain specific future times, while the term "prediction" is used for more general estimates, such as the number of times floods will occur over a long period.

Exam Probability: **Low**

6. *Answer choices:*

(see index for correct answer)

- a. interpersonal communication
- b. Forecasting
- c. surface-level diversity
- d. levels of analysis

Guidance: level 1

:: Production and manufacturing ::

In industry, _________ is a system of maintaining and improving the integrity of production and quality systems through the machines, equipment, processes, and employees that add business value to an organization.

Exam Probability: **Medium**

7. *Answer choices:*

(see index for correct answer)

- a. Low rate initial production
- b. Managed services
- c. DeviceNet
- d. Bill of resources

Guidance: level 1

:: ::

A _________ is a covering that is applied to the surface of an object, usually referred to as the substrate. The purpose of applying the _________ may be decorative, functional, or both. The _________ itself may be an all-over _________ , completely covering the substrate, or it may only cover parts of the substrate. An example of all of these types of _________ is a product label on many drinks bottles- one side has an all-over functional _________ and the other side has one or more decorative _________ s in an appropriate pattern to form the words and images.

Exam Probability: **High**

8. *Answer choices:*

(see index for correct answer)

- a. Sarbanes-Oxley act of 2002
- b. Coating
- c. functional perspective
- d. levels of analysis

Guidance: level 1

:: Information technology management ::

_________ concerns a cycle of organizational activity: the acquisition of information from one or more sources, the custodianship and the distribution of that information to those who need it, and its ultimate disposition through archiving or deletion.

Exam Probability: **Medium**

9. *Answer choices:*

(see index for correct answer)

- a. Information management
- b. Digital continuity
- c. Intelligent workload management
- d. Infra Corporation

Guidance: level 1

:: Industrial engineering ::

The _________ is the design of any task that aims to describe or explain the variation of information under conditions that are hypothesized to reflect the variation. The term is generally associated with experiments in which the design introduces conditions that directly affect the variation, but may also refer to the design of quasi-experiments, in which natural conditions that influence the variation are selected for observation.

Exam Probability: **High**

10. *Answer choices:*

(see index for correct answer)

- a. Defect concentration diagram
- b. Human factors and ergonomics
- c. Worker-machine activity chart
- d. Design of experiments

Guidance: level 1

:: Consortia ::

A _________ is an association of two or more individuals, companies, organizations or governments with the objective of participating in a common activity or pooling their resources for achieving a common goal.

Exam Probability: **High**

11. *Answer choices:*

(see index for correct answer)

- a. Serial Port Memory Technology
- b. Consortium
- c. World Wide Web Consortium
- d. Southern New Jersey Rail Group

Guidance: level 1

:: Management ::

__________ is a category of business activity made possible by software tools that aim to provide customers with both independence from vendors and better means for engaging with vendors. These same tools can also apply to individuals` relations with other institutions and organizations.

Exam Probability: **Low**

12. *Answer choices:*
(see index for correct answer)

- a. Vendor relationship management
- b. Intelligent customer
- c. Professional performances
- d. Completed Staff Work

Guidance: level 1

:: Data interchange standards ::

__________ is the concept of businesses electronically communicating information that was traditionally communicated on paper, such as purchase orders and invoices. Technical standards for EDI exist to facilitate parties transacting such instruments without having to make special arrangements.

Exam Probability: **Medium**

13. *Answer choices:*
(see index for correct answer)

- a. Domain Application Protocol
- b. ASC X12
- c. Data Interchange Standards Association
- d. Interaction protocol

Guidance: level 1

:: Management ::

An _________ is a loosely coupled, self-organizing network of firms that combine their economic output to provide products and services offerings to the market. Firms in the _________ may operate independently, for example, through market mechanisms, or cooperatively through agreements and contracts. They provide value added service or product to the OEM .

Exam Probability: **Medium**

14. *Answer choices:*

(see index for correct answer)

- a. Project management information system
- b. Peer pressure
- c. Unified interoperability
- d. Linear scheduling method

Guidance: level 1

:: Lean manufacturing ::

_________ is a scheduling system for lean manufacturing and just-in-time manufacturing . Taiichi Ohno, an industrial engineer at Toyota, developed _________ to improve manufacturing efficiency. _________ is one method to achieve JIT. The system takes its name from the cards that track production within a factory. For many in the automotive sector, _________ is known as the "Toyota nameplate system" and as such the term is not used by some other automakers.

Exam Probability: **Medium**

15. *Answer choices:*

(see index for correct answer)

- a. Oobeya
- b. Computer-aided lean management
- c. Lean product development
- d. Continuous improvement

Guidance: level 1

:: ::

An _________ is a company that produces parts and equipment that may be marketed by another manufacturer. For example, Foxconn, a Taiwanese electronics contract manufacturing company, which produces a variety of parts and equipment for companies such as Apple Inc., Dell, Google, Huawei, Nintendo, etc., is the largest OEM company in the world by both scale and revenue.

Exam Probability: **Medium**

16. *Answer choices:*

(see index for correct answer)

- a. process perspective
- b. levels of analysis
- c. information systems assessment
- d. hierarchical

Guidance: level 1

:: Unit operations ::

_________ is a discipline of thermal engineering that concerns the generation, use, conversion, and exchange of thermal energy between physical systems. _________ is classified into various mechanisms, such as thermal conduction, thermal convection, thermal radiation, and transfer of energy by phase changes. Engineers also consider the transfer of mass of differing chemical species, either cold or hot, to achieve _________ . While these mechanisms have distinct characteristics, they often occur simultaneously in the same system.

Exam Probability: **Low**

17. *Answer choices:*

(see index for correct answer)

- a. Heat transfer
- b. Homogenization
- c. Theoretical plate
- d. Unit Operations of Chemical Engineering

Guidance: level 1

:: ::

Catalysis is the process of increasing the rate of a chemical reaction by adding a substance known as a _________ , which is not consumed in the catalyzed reaction and can continue to act repeatedly. Because of this, only very small amounts of _________ are required to alter the reaction rate in principle.

Exam Probability: **Medium**

18. *Answer choices:*
(see index for correct answer)

- a. Sarbanes-Oxley act of 2002
- b. interpersonal communication
- c. Character
- d. Catalyst

Guidance: level 1

:: Casting (manufacturing) ::

A _________ is a regularity in the world, man-made design, or abstract ideas. As such, the elements of a _________ repeat in a predictable manner. A geometric _________ is a kind of _________ formed of geometric shapes and typically repeated like a wallpaper design.

Exam Probability: **Low**

19. *Answer choices:*
(see index for correct answer)

- a. AutoCAST
- b. Porosity sealing
- c. Castability
- d. Pattern

Guidance: level 1

:: Production economics ::

_________ is the creation of a whole that is greater than the simple sum of its parts. The term _________ comes from the Attic Greek word sea synergia from synergos, , meaning "working together".

Exam Probability: **High**

20. *Answer choices:*

(see index for correct answer)

- a. Foundations of Economic Analysis
- b. Capacity utilization
- c. Synergy
- d. Marginal cost of capital schedule

Guidance: level 1

:: Supply chain management ::

A __________ is a type of auction in which the traditional roles of buyer and seller are reversed. Thus, there is one buyer and many potential sellers. In an ordinary auction , buyers compete to obtain goods or services by offering increasingly higher prices. In contrast, in a __________ , the sellers compete to obtain business from the buyer and prices will typically decrease as the sellers underbid each other.

Exam Probability: **Low**

21. *Answer choices:*

(see index for correct answer)

- a. ICON-SCM
- b. Scan-based trading
- c. Blinco Systems Inc.
- d. Reverse auction

Guidance: level 1

:: Insulators ::

A __________ is a piece of soft cloth large enough either to cover or to enfold a great portion of the user's body, usually when sleeping or otherwise at rest, thereby trapping radiant bodily heat that otherwise would be lost through convection, and so keeping the body warm.

Exam Probability: **High**

22. *Answer choices:*

(see index for correct answer)

- a. Mechanical insulation
- b. R-value
- c. Dynamic insulation
- d. Fill power

Guidance: level 1

:: Management ::

__________ is a formal technique useful where many possible courses of action are competing for attention. In essence, the problem-solver estimates the benefit delivered by each action, then selects a number of the most effective actions that deliver a total benefit reasonably close to the maximal possible one.

Exam Probability: **Medium**

23. *Answer choices:*
(see index for correct answer)

- a. Overtime rate
- b. Reval
- c. Force-field analysis
- d. Process-based management

Guidance: level 1

:: Fault-tolerant computer systems ::

__________ decision-making is a group decision-making process in which group members develop, and agree to support a decision in the best interest of the whole group or common goal. __________ may be defined professionally as an acceptable resolution, one that can be supported, even if not the "favourite" of each individual. It has its origin in the Latin word consensus , which is from consentio meaning literally feel together. It is used to describe both the decision and the process of reaching a decision. __________ decision-making is thus concerned with the process of deliberating and finalizing a decision, and the social, economic, legal, environmental and political effects of applying this process.

Exam Probability: **Medium**

24. *Answer choices:*
(see index for correct answer)

- a. Fencing
- b. Toric code
- c. Virtual Link Trunking
- d. Consensus

Guidance: level 1

:: Lean manufacturing ::

_________ is a Japanese term that means "mistake-proofing" or "inadvertent error prevention". A _________ is any mechanism in any process that helps an equipment operator avoid mistakes . Its purpose is to eliminate product defects by preventing, correcting, or drawing attention to human errors as they occur. The concept was formalised, and the term adopted, by Shigeo Shingo as part of the Toyota Production System. It was originally described as baka-yoke, but as this means "fool-proofing" the name was changed to the milder _________ .

Exam Probability: **Medium**

25. *Answer choices:*
(see index for correct answer)

- a. Kaizen
- b. No value added
- c. Poka-yoke
- d. Lean accounting

Guidance: level 1

:: E-commerce ::

_________ is the business-to-business or business-to-consumer or business-to-government purchase and sale of supplies, work, and services through the Internet as well as other information and networking systems, such as electronic data interchange and enterprise resource planning.

Exam Probability: **Medium**

26. *Answer choices:*
(see index for correct answer)

- a. EatOye
- b. E-procurement

- c. Virtual goods
- d. EFaktura

Guidance: level 1

:: Management ::

A supply-chain network is an evolution of the basic supply chain. Due to rapid technological advancement, organisations with a basic supply chain can develop this chain into a more complex structure involving a higher level of interdependence and connectivity between more organisations, this constitutes a supply-chain network.

Exam Probability: **Low**

27. *Answer choices:*

(see index for correct answer)

- a. Supply chain network
- b. Business process interoperability
- c. Tacit knowledge
- d. Event management

Guidance: level 1

:: Production and manufacturing ::

Automatic _________ in continuous production processes is a combination of control engineering and chemical engineering disciplines that uses industrial control systems to achieve a production level of consistency, economy and safety which could not be achieved purely by human manual control. It is implemented widely in industries such as oil refining, pulp and paper manufacturing, chemical processing and power generating plants.

Exam Probability: **Low**

28. *Answer choices:*

(see index for correct answer)

- a. Process control
- b. First pass yield
- c. Production
- d. Original design manufacturer

Guidance: level 1

:: Data management ::

__________ is the ability of a physical product to remain functional, without requiring excessive maintenance or repair, when faced with the challenges of normal operation over its design lifetime. There are several measures of __________ in use, including years of life, hours of use, and number of operational cycles. In economics, goods with a long usable life are referred to as durable goods.

Exam Probability: **Medium**

29. *Answer choices:*

(see index for correct answer)

- a. Data profiling
- b. Inverted index
- c. Durability
- d. Holistic Data Management

Guidance: level 1

:: Management ::

A process is a unique combination of tools, materials, methods, and people engaged in producing a measurable output; for example a manufacturing line for machine parts. All processes have inherent statistical variability which can be evaluated by statistical methods.

Exam Probability: **Low**

30. *Answer choices:*

(see index for correct answer)

- a. Process capability
- b. Communications management
- c. Shrinkage
- d. Outrage constraint

Guidance: level 1

:: Information technology management ::

__________ is a collective term for all approaches to prepare , support and help individuals, teams, and organizations in making organizational change. The most common change drivers include: technological evolution, process reviews, crisis, and consumer habit changes; pressure from new business entrants, acquisitions, mergers, and organizational restructuring. It includes methods that redirect or redefine the use of resources, business process, budget allocations, or other modes of operation that significantly change a company or organization. Organizational __________ considers the full organization and what needs to change, while __________ may be used solely to refer to how people and teams are affected by such organizational transition. It deals with many different disciplines, from behavioral and social sciences to information technology and business solutions.

Exam Probability: **Medium**

31. *Answer choices:*

(see index for correct answer)

- a. Business transaction performance
- b. Change management
- c. ESCM-SP
- d. Storage virtualization

Guidance: level 1

:: Procurement ::

A __________ is a standard business process whose purpose is to invite suppliers into a bidding process to bid on specific products or services. RfQ generally means the same thing as Call for bids and Invitation for bid .

Exam Probability: **Medium**

32. *Answer choices:*

(see index for correct answer)

- a. Request for quotation
- b. Best value procurement
- c. Procure-to-pay
- d. Basware

Guidance: level 1

:: Promotion and marketing communications ::

The _________ of American Manufacturers, now ThomasNet, is an online platform for supplier discovery and product sourcing in the US and Canada. It was once known as the "big green books" and "Thomas Registry", and was a multi-volume directory of industrial product information covering 650,000 distributors, manufacturers and service companies within 67,000-plus industrial categories that is now published on ThomasNet.

Exam Probability: **Low**

33. *Answer choices:*

(see index for correct answer)

- a. Open2save
- b. PR NewsChannel
- c. Sales letter
- d. Reich Publishing and Marketing

Guidance: level 1

:: Process management ::

When used in the context of communication networks, such as Ethernet or packet radio, _________ or network _________ is the rate of successful message delivery over a communication channel. The data these messages belong to may be delivered over a physical or logical link, or it can pass through a certain network node. _________ is usually measured in bits per second , and sometimes in data packets per second or data packets per time slot.

Exam Probability: **Low**

34. *Answer choices:*

(see index for correct answer)

- a. Throughput
- b. Business process discovery
- c. Process modeling
- d. Chemical plant cost indexes

Guidance: level 1

:: Business ::

The seller, or the provider of the goods or services, completes a sale in response to an acquisition, appropriation, requisition or a direct interaction with the buyer at the point of sale. There is a passing of title of the item, and the settlement of a price, in which agreement is reached on a price for which transfer of ownership of the item will occur. The seller, not the purchaser typically executes the sale and it may be completed prior to the obligation of payment. In the case of indirect interaction, a person who sells goods or service on behalf of the owner is known as a _________ man or _________ woman or _________ person, but this often refers to someone selling goods in a store/shop, in which case other terms are also common, including _________ clerk, shop assistant, and retail clerk.

Exam Probability: **Low**

35. *Answer choices:*

(see index for correct answer)

- a. Equality impact assessment
- b. Business analysis
- c. Sales
- d. Winklevoss Capital Management

Guidance: level 1

:: ::

_________ refers to a business or organization attempting to acquire goods or services to accomplish its goals. Although there are several organizations that attempt to set standards in the _________ process, processes can vary greatly between organizations. Typically the word " _________ " is not used interchangeably with the word "procurement", since procurement typically includes expediting, supplier quality, and transportation and logistics in addition to _________ .

Exam Probability: **High**

36. *Answer choices:*

(see index for correct answer)

- a. hierarchical
- b. process perspective
- c. empathy
- d. hierarchical perspective

Guidance: level 1

:: Project management ::

Some scenarios associate "this kind of planning" with learning "life skills". _________ s are necessary, or at least useful, in situations where individuals need to know what time they must be at a specific location to receive a specific service, and where people need to accomplish a set of goals within a set time period.

Exam Probability: **Medium**

37. *Answer choices:*

(see index for correct answer)

- a. Cone of Uncertainty
- b. Schedule
- c. Project engineering
- d. Alexander Laufer

Guidance: level 1

:: Metalworking ::

A _________ is a round object with various uses. It is used in _________ games, where the play of the game follows the state of the _________ as it is hit, kicked or thrown by players. _________ s can also be used for simpler activities, such as catch or juggling. _________ s made from hard-wearing materials are used in engineering applications to provide very low friction bearings, known as _________ bearings. Black-powder weapons use stone and metal _________ s as projectiles.

Exam Probability: **High**

38. *Answer choices:*

(see index for correct answer)

- a. Ball
- b. Pig iron
- c. Peening
- d. Decambering

Guidance: level 1

:: Supply chain management ::

__________ is a core supply chain function and includes supply chain planning and supply chain execution capabilities. Specifically, __________ is the capability firms use to plan total material requirements. The material requirements are communicated to procurement and other functions for sourcing. __________ is also responsible for determining the amount of material to be deployed at each stocking location across the supply chain, establishing material replenishment plans, determining inventory levels to hold for each type of inventory , and communicating information regarding material needs throughout the extended supply chain.

Exam Probability: **High**

39. *Answer choices:*

(see index for correct answer)

- a. Spend analysis
- b. Supply Chain Management Review
- c. Transportation management system
- d. Pacific Access

Guidance: level 1

:: Gas technologies ::

A __________ is a rotary mechanical device that extracts energy from a fluid flow and converts it into useful work. The work produced by a __________ can be used for generating electrical power when combined with a generator. A __________ is a turbomachine with at least one moving part called a rotor assembly, which is a shaft or drum with blades attached. Moving fluid acts on the blades so that they move and impart rotational energy to the rotor. Early __________ examples are windmills and waterwheels.

Exam Probability: **Low**

40. *Answer choices:*

(see index for correct answer)

- a. Gas cylinder
- b. Hydrogen purifier
- c. Mass flow sensor
- d. Turbine

Guidance: level 1

:: Manufacturing ::

A _________ is an object used to extend the ability of an individual to modify features of the surrounding environment. Although many animals use simple _________ s, only human beings, whose use of stone _________ s dates back hundreds of millennia, use _________ s to make other _________ s. The set of _________ s needed to perform different tasks that are part of the same activity is called gear or equipment.

Exam Probability: **Medium**

41. *Answer choices:*

(see index for correct answer)

- a. Microfactory
- b. Can seamer
- c. Tool
- d. Greatpac

Guidance: level 1

:: Software testing ::

_________ 1 was the first artificial Earth satellite. The Soviet Union launched it into an elliptical low Earth orbit on 4 October 1957, orbiting for three weeks before its batteries died, then silently for two more months before falling back into the atmosphere. It was a 58 cm diameter polished metal sphere, with four external radio antennas to broadcast radio pulses. Its radio signal was easily detectable even by radio amateurs, and the 65° inclination and duration of its orbit made its flight path cover virtually the entire inhabited Earth. This surprise success precipitated the American _________ crisis and triggered the Space Race, a part of the Cold War. The launch was the beginning of a new era of political, military, technological, and scientific developments.

Exam Probability: **Low**

42. *Answer choices:*

(see index for correct answer)

- a. Pseudolocalization

- b. Conference room pilot
- c. Design predicates
- d. Robot Framework

Guidance: level 1

:: Production and manufacturing ::

__________ is a systematic method to improve the "value" of goods or products and services by using an examination of function. Value, as defined, is the ratio of function to cost. Value can therefore be manipulated by either improving the function or reducing the cost. It is a primary tenet of __________ that basic functions be preserved and not be reduced as a consequence of pursuing value improvements.

Exam Probability: **Low**

43. *Answer choices:*

(see index for correct answer)

- a. Equipment service management and rental
- b. Piece work
- c. Value engineering
- d. Economic dispatch

Guidance: level 1

:: Sensitivity analysis ::

__________ is the study of how the uncertainty in the output of a mathematical model or system can be divided and allocated to different sources of uncertainty in its inputs. A related practice is uncertainty analysis, which has a greater focus on uncertainty quantification and propagation of uncertainty; ideally, uncertainty and __________ should be run in tandem.

Exam Probability: **High**

44. *Answer choices:*

(see index for correct answer)

- a. Sensitivity analysis
- b. Variance-based sensitivity analysis
- c. Fourier amplitude sensitivity testing
- d. Tornado diagram

Guidance: level 1

:: Goods ::

In most contexts, the concept of _________ denotes the conduct that should be preferred when posed with a choice between possible actions. _________ is generally considered to be the opposite of evil, and is of interest in the study of morality, ethics, religion and philosophy. The specific meaning and etymology of the term and its associated translations among ancient and contemporary languages show substantial variation in its inflection and meaning depending on circumstances of place, history, religious, or philosophical context.

Exam Probability: **Low**

45. *Answer choices:*

(see index for correct answer)

- a. Designer label
- b. Good
- c. Normal good
- d. Common good

Guidance: level 1

:: Semiconductor companies ::

_________ Corporation is a Japanese multinational conglomerate corporation headquartered in Konan, Minato, Tokyo. Its diversified business includes consumer and professional electronics, gaming, entertainment and financial services. The company owns the largest music entertainment business in the world, the largest video game console business and one of the largest video game publishing businesses, and is one of the leading manufacturers of electronic products for the consumer and professional markets, and a leading player in the film and television entertainment industry. _________ was ranked 97th on the 2018 Fortune Global 500 list.

Exam Probability: **Medium**

46. *Answer choices:*

(see index for correct answer)

- a. NXP Semiconductors

- b. GainSpan
- c. Semitool
- d. Reading Works

Guidance: level 1

:: ::

__________ is the quantity of three-dimensional space enclosed by a closed surface, for example, the space that a substance or shape occupies or contains. __________ is often quantified numerically using the SI derived unit, the cubic metre. The __________ of a container is generally understood to be the capacity of the container; i. e., the amount of fluid that the container could hold, rather than the amount of space the container itself displaces.Three dimensional mathematical shapes are also assigned __________ s. __________ s of some simple shapes, such as regular, straight-edged, and circular shapes can be easily calculated using arithmetic formulas. __________ s of complicated shapes can be calculated with integral calculus if a formula exists for the shape`s boundary. One-dimensional figures and two-dimensional shapes are assigned zero __________ in the three-dimensional space.

Exam Probability: **High**

47. *Answer choices:*
(see index for correct answer)

- a. cultural
- b. surface-level diversity
- c. interpersonal communication
- d. deep-level diversity

Guidance: level 1

:: Supply chain management ::

__________ is the process of finding and agreeing to terms, and acquiring goods, services, or works from an external source, often via a tendering or competitive bidding process. __________ is used to ensure the buyer receives goods, services, or works at the best possible price when aspects such as quality, quantity, time, and location are compared. Corporations and public bodies often define processes intended to promote fair and open competition for their business while minimizing risks such as exposure to fraud and collusion.

Exam Probability: **Low**

48. *Answer choices:*

(see index for correct answer)

- a. Procurement
- b. Symphony EYC
- c. Service parts pricing
- d. Enterprise carbon accounting

Guidance: level 1

:: Time management ::

__________ is the process of planning and exercising conscious control of time spent on specific activities, especially to increase effectiveness, efficiency, and productivity. It involves a juggling act of various demands upon a person relating to work, social life, family, hobbies, personal interests and commitments with the finiteness of time. Using time effectively gives the person "choice" on spending/managing activities at their own time and expediency.

Exam Probability: **Low**

49. *Answer choices:*

(see index for correct answer)

- a. waiting room
- b. Sufficient unto the day is the evil thereof
- c. HabitRPG
- d. Time Trek

Guidance: level 1

:: Evaluation ::

__________ is a way of preventing mistakes and defects in manufactured products and avoiding problems when delivering products or services to customers; which ISO 9000 defines as "part of quality management focused on providing confidence that quality requirements will be fulfilled". This defect prevention in __________ differs subtly from defect detection and rejection in quality control and has been referred to as a shift left since it focuses on quality earlier in the process .

Exam Probability: **Low**

50. *Answer choices:*

(see index for correct answer)

- a. Scale of one to ten
- b. Transferable skills analysis
- c. SPECpower
- d. Quality assurance

Guidance: level 1

:: Lean manufacturing ::

__________ is the Sino-Japanese word for "improvement". In business, __________ refers to activities that continuously improve all functions and involve all employees from the CEO to the assembly line workers. It also applies to processes, such as purchasing and logistics, that cross organizational boundaries into the supply chain. It has been applied in healthcare, psychotherapy, life-coaching, government, and banking.

Exam Probability: **High**

51. *Answer choices:*

(see index for correct answer)

- a. Kaizen
- b. Lean services
- c. Lean Six Sigma
- d. Kanban board

Guidance: level 1

:: Water ::

__________ is a transparent, tasteless, odorless, and nearly colorless chemical substance, which is the main constituent of Earth`s streams, lakes, and oceans, and the fluids of most living organisms. It is vital for all known forms of life, even though it provides no calories or organic nutrients. Its chemical formula is H2O, meaning that each of its molecules contains one oxygen and two hydrogen atoms, connected by covalent bonds. __________ is the name of the liquid state of H2O at standard ambient temperature and pressure. It forms precipitation in the form of rain and aerosols in the form of fog. Clouds are formed from suspended droplets of __________ and ice, its solid state. When finely divided, crystalline ice may precipitate in the form of snow. The gaseous state of __________ is steam or __________ vapor. __________ moves continually through the __________ cycle of evaporation, transpiration , condensation, precipitation, and runoff, usually reaching the sea.

Exam Probability: **High**

52. *Answer choices:*
(see index for correct answer)

- a. Water resource policy
- b. Groundwater recharge
- c. Aqueduct
- d. Water

Guidance: level 1

:: Direct marketing ::

__________ Inc. is an American privately owned multi-level marketing company. According to Direct Selling News, __________ was the sixth largest network marketing company in the world in 2018, with a wholesale volume of US$3.25 billion. __________ is based in Addison, Texas, outside Dallas. The company was founded by __________ Ash in 1963. Richard Rogers, __________ `s son, is the chairman, and David Holl is president and was named CEO in 2006.

Exam Probability: **Low**

53. *Answer choices:*
(see index for correct answer)

- a. Mary Kay
- b. Arthur Schiff
- c. Multi-level marketing

- d. Wisconsin Cheeseman

Guidance: level 1

:: Planning ::

__________ is a high level plan to achieve one or more goals under conditions of uncertainty. In the sense of the "art of the general," which included several subsets of skills including tactics, siegecraft, logistics etc., the term came into use in the 6th century C.E. in East Roman terminology, and was translated into Western vernacular languages only in the 18th century. From then until the 20th century, the word " __________ " came to denote "a comprehensive way to try to pursue political ends, including the threat or actual use of force, in a dialectic of wills" in a military conflict, in which both adversaries interact.

Exam Probability: **High**

54. *Answer choices:*

(see index for correct answer)

- a. Resource-Task Network
- b. Strategy
- c. Plano Trienal
- d. Interactive planning

Guidance: level 1

:: Project management ::

__________ is a work methodology emphasizing the parallelisation of tasks , which is sometimes called simultaneous engineering or integrated product development using an integrated product team approach. It refers to an approach used in product development in which functions of design engineering, manufacturing engineering, and other functions are integrated to reduce the time required to bring a new product to market.

Exam Probability: **Medium**

55. *Answer choices:*

(see index for correct answer)

- a. project triangle

- b. Aggregate project plan
- c. Confluence Project Management
- d. Changes clause

Guidance: level 1

:: Management ::

__________ is a term used in business and Information Technology to describe the in-depth process of capturing customer`s expectations, preferences and aversions. Specifically, the __________ is a market research technique that produces a detailed set of customer wants and needs, organized into a hierarchical structure, and then prioritized in terms of relative importance and satisfaction with current alternatives. __________ studies typically consist of both qualitative and quantitative research steps. They are generally conducted at the start of any new product, process, or service design initiative in order to better understand the customer`s wants and needs, and as the key input for new product definition, Quality Function Deployment , and the setting of detailed design specifications.

Exam Probability: **Low**

56. *Answer choices:*

(see index for correct answer)

- a. Evidence-based management
- b. middle manager
- c. Voice of the customer
- d. Balanced scorecard

Guidance: level 1

:: Production and manufacturing ::

__________ was a management-led program to eliminate defects in industrial production that enjoyed brief popularity in American industry from 1964 to the early 1970s. Quality expert Philip Crosby later incorporated it into his "Absolutes of Quality Management" and it enjoyed a renaissance in the American automobile industry—as a performance goal more than as a program—in the 1990s. Although applicable to any type of enterprise, it has been primarily adopted within supply chains wherever large volumes of components are being purchased .

Exam Probability: **High**

57. *Answer choices:*

(see index for correct answer)

- a. Critical chain project management
- b. Zero Defects
- c. Computer-aided process planning
- d. International MTM Directorate

Guidance: level 1

:: Industrial processes ::

__________ is a technique involving the condensation of vapors and the return of this condensate to the system from which it originated. It is used in industrial and laboratory distillations. It is also used in chemistry to supply energy to reactions over a long period of time.

Exam Probability: **Medium**

58. *Answer choices:*

(see index for correct answer)

- a. Reflux
- b. Olive oil extraction
- c. Mechanical screening
- d. Czochralski process

Guidance: level 1

:: Building materials ::

__________ is an alloy of iron and carbon, and sometimes other elements. Because of its high tensile strength and low cost, it is a major component used in buildings, infrastructure, tools, ships, automobiles, machines, appliances, and weapons.

Exam Probability: **High**

59. *Answer choices:*

(see index for correct answer)

- a. Floating floor
- b. Enviroboard
- c. Opus albarium

- d. Steel

Guidance: level 1

Commerce

Commerce relates to "the exchange of goods and services, especially on a large scale." It includes legal, economic, political, social, cultural and technological systems that operate in any country or internationally.

:: ::

__________ s are formal, sociotechnical, organizational systems designed to collect, process, store, and distribute information. In a sociotechnical perspective, __________ s are composed by four components: task, people, structure , and technology.

Exam Probability: **Low**

1. *Answer choices:*

(see index for correct answer)

- a. Sarbanes-Oxley act of 2002
- b. functional perspective
- c. cultural
- d. process perspective

Guidance: level 1

:: E-commerce ::

__________ is the activity of buying or selling of products on online services or over the Internet. Electronic commerce draws on technologies such as mobile commerce, electronic funds transfer, supply chain management, Internet marketing, online transaction processing, electronic data interchange , inventory management systems, and automated data collection systems.

Exam Probability: **Low**

2. *Answer choices:*

(see index for correct answer)

- a. E-commerce
- b. Online auction tools
- c. Paywall
- d. Piano Media

Guidance: level 1

:: Decision theory ::

A _________ is a deliberate system of principles to guide decisions and achieve rational outcomes. A _________ is a statement of intent, and is implemented as a procedure or protocol. Policies are generally adopted by a governance body within an organization. Policies can assist in both subjective and objective decision making. Policies to assist in subjective decision making usually assist senior management with decisions that must be based on the relative merits of a number of factors, and as a result are often hard to test objectively, e.g. work-life balance _________ . In contrast policies to assist in objective decision making are usually operational in nature and can be objectively tested, e.g. password _________ .

Exam Probability: **High**

3. *Answer choices:*

(see index for correct answer)

- a. Policy
- b. Consensus-seeking decision-making
- c. Taleb distribution
- d. Probability matching

Guidance: level 1

:: ::

_________ is a process whereby a person assumes the parenting of another, usually a child, from that person`s biological or legal parent or parents. Legal _________ s permanently transfers all rights and responsibilities, along with filiation, from the biological parent or parents.

Exam Probability: **Low**

4. *Answer choices:*

(see index for correct answer)

- a. cultural
- b. personal values
- c. interpersonal communication
- d. surface-level diversity

Guidance: level 1

:: Mereology ::

__________ , in the abstract, is what belongs to or with something, whether as an attribute or as a component of said thing. In the context of this article, it is one or more components , whether physical or incorporeal, of a person's estate; or so belonging to, as in being owned by, a person or jointly a group of people or a legal entity like a corporation or even a society. Depending on the nature of the __________ , an owner of __________ has the right to consume, alter, share, redefine, rent, mortgage, pawn, sell, exchange, transfer, give away or destroy it, or to exclude others from doing these things, as well as to perhaps abandon it; whereas regardless of the nature of the __________ , the owner thereof has the right to properly use it , or at the very least exclusively keep it.

Exam Probability: **Medium**

5. *Answer choices:*

(see index for correct answer)

- a. Property
- b. Non-wellfounded mereology
- c. Gunk
- d. Mereology

Guidance: level 1

:: Generally Accepted Accounting Principles ::

In accounting, _________ is the income that a business have from its normal business activities, usually from the sale of goods and services to customers. _________ is also referred to as sales or turnover.Some companies receive _________ from interest, royalties, or other fees. _________ may refer to business income in general, or it may refer to the amount, in a monetary unit, earned during a period of time, as in "Last year, Company X had _________ of $42 million". Profits or net income generally imply total _________ minus total expenses in a given period. In accounting, in the balance statement it is a subsection of the Equity section and _________ increases equity, it is often referred to as the "top line" due to its position on the income statement at the very top. This is to be contrasted with the "bottom line" which denotes net income .

Exam Probability: **Medium**

6. *Answer choices:*
(see index for correct answer)

- a. Profit
- b. Completed-contract method
- c. Cash method of accounting
- d. Revenue

Guidance: level 1

:: Management occupations ::

_________ ship is the process of designing, launching and running a new business, which is often initially a small business. The people who create these businesses are called _________ s.

Exam Probability: **Medium**

7. *Answer choices:*
(see index for correct answer)

- a. Manager without portfolio
- b. Sport management
- c. General counsel
- d. Entrepreneur

Guidance: level 1

:: ::

_________ is a means of protection from financial loss. It is a form of risk management, primarily used to hedge against the risk of a contingent or uncertain loss

Exam Probability: **Medium**

8. *Answer choices:*

(see index for correct answer)

- a. Insurance
- b. open system
- c. surface-level diversity
- d. levels of analysis

Guidance: level 1

:: ::

_________ is the practical authority granted to a legal body to administer justice within a defined field of responsibility, e.g., Michigan tax law. In federations like the United States, areas of _________ apply to local, state, and federal levels; e.g. the court has _________ to apply federal law.

Exam Probability: **High**

9. *Answer choices:*

(see index for correct answer)

- a. process perspective
- b. Character
- c. Sarbanes-Oxley act of 2002
- d. hierarchical

Guidance: level 1

:: ::

The __________ or just chief executive , is the most senior corporate, executive, or administrative officer in charge of managing an organization especially an independent legal entity such as a company or nonprofit institution. CEOs lead a range of organizations, including public and private corporations, non-profit organizations and even some government organizations . The CEO of a corporation or company typically reports to the board of directors and is charged with maximizing the value of the entity, which may include maximizing the share price, market share, revenues or another element. In the non-profit and government sector, CEOs typically aim at achieving outcomes related to the organization's mission, such as reducing poverty, increasing literacy, etc.

Exam Probability: **Low**

10. *Answer choices:*
(see index for correct answer)

- a. similarity-attraction theory
- b. deep-level diversity
- c. Chief executive officer
- d. imperative

Guidance: level 1

:: E-commerce ::

__________ Inc. was an electronic money corporation founded by David Chaum in 1989. __________ transactions were unique in that they were anonymous due to a number of cryptographic protocols developed by its founder. __________ declared bankruptcy in 1998, and subsequently sold its assets to eCash Technologies, another digital currency company, which was acquired by InfoSpace on Feb. 19, 2002.

Exam Probability: **High**

11. *Answer choices:*
(see index for correct answer)

- a. DigiCash
- b. Interactive Financial Exchange
- c. UN/CEFACT
- d. SIE

Guidance: level 1

:: International trade ::

A __________ is a document issued by a carrier to acknowledge receipt of cargo for shipment. Although the term historically related only to carriage by sea, a __________ may today be used for any type of carriage of goods.

Exam Probability: **Medium**

12. *Answer choices:*

(see index for correct answer)

- a. Public international law
- b. State trading enterprises
- c. Trade office
- d. OPEC

Guidance: level 1

:: Commercial item transport and distribution ::

A __________, forwarder, or forwarding agent, also known as a non-vessel operating common carrier , is a person or company that organizes shipments for individuals or corporations to get goods from the manufacturer or producer to a market, customer or final point of distribution. Forwarders contract with a carrier or often multiple carriers to move the goods. A forwarder does not move the goods but acts as an expert in the logistics network. These carriers can use a variety of shipping modes, including ships, airplanes, trucks, and railroads, and often do utilize multiple modes for a single shipment. For example, the __________ may arrange to have cargo moved from a plant to an airport by truck, flown to the destination city, then moved from the airport to a customer`s building by another truck.

Exam Probability: **Medium**

13. *Answer choices:*

(see index for correct answer)

- a. Cross-docking
- b. Truck driver
- c. Backhaul
- d. Freight forwarder

Guidance: level 1

:: Production economics ::

In economics and related disciplines, a _________ is a cost in making any economic trade when participating in a market.

Exam Probability: **High**

14. *Answer choices:*

(see index for correct answer)

- a. Transaction cost
- b. short run
- c. Marginal product
- d. Limiting factor

Guidance: level 1

:: ::

The _________ is a U.S. business-focused, English-language international daily newspaper based in New York City. The Journal, along with its Asian and European editions, is published six days a week by Dow Jones & Company, a division of News Corp. The newspaper is published in the broadsheet format and online. The Journal has been printed continuously since its inception on July 8, 1889, by Charles Dow, Edward Jones, and Charles Bergstresser.

Exam Probability: **High**

15. *Answer choices:*

(see index for correct answer)

- a. surface-level diversity
- b. Wall Street Journal
- c. functional perspective
- d. levels of analysis

Guidance: level 1

:: Direct marketing ::

_________ is a form of advertising where organizations communicate directly to customers through a variety of media including cell phone text messaging, email, websites, online adverts, database marketing, fliers, catalog distribution, promotional letters, targeted television, newspapers, magazine advertisements, and outdoor advertising. Among practitioners, it is also known as direct response marketing.

Exam Probability: **Medium**

16. *Answer choices:*

(see index for correct answer)

- a. Solo Ads
- b. Direct marketing
- c. Forced Free Trial
- d. Database marketing

Guidance: level 1

:: Asset ::

In financial accounting, an _________ is any resource owned by the business. Anything tangible or intangible that can be owned or controlled to produce value and that is held by a company to produce positive economic value is an _________ . Simply stated, _________ s represent value of ownership that can be converted into cash . The balance sheet of a firm records the monetary value of the _________ s owned by that firm. It covers money and other valuables belonging to an individual or to a business.

Exam Probability: **Medium**

17. *Answer choices:*

(see index for correct answer)

- a. Fixed asset
- b. Current asset

Guidance: level 1

:: ::

_________ , also referred to as orthostasis, is a human position in which the body is held in an upright position and supported only by the feet.

Exam Probability: **Low**

18. *Answer choices:*

(see index for correct answer)

- a. Sarbanes-Oxley act of 2002
- b. imperative
- c. functional perspective
- d. Standing

Guidance: level 1

:: Business terms ::

The _________ or reception is an area where visitors arrive and first encounter a staff at a place of business. _________ staff will deal with whatever question the visitor has and put them in contact with a relevant person at the company. Broadly speaking, the _________ includes roles that affect the revenues of the business. The term _________ is in contrast to the term back office which refers to a company`s operations, personnel, accounting, payroll and financial departments which do not interact directly with customers.

Exam Probability: **Medium**

19. *Answer choices:*

(see index for correct answer)

- a. organic growth
- b. Front office
- c. churn rate
- d. operating cost

Guidance: level 1

:: Market structure and pricing ::

_________ has historically emerged in two separate types of discussions in economics, that of Adam Smith on the one hand, and that of Karl Marx on the other hand. Adam Smith in his writing on economics stressed the importance of laissez-faire principles outlining the operation of the market in the absence of dominant political mechanisms of control, while Karl Marx discussed the working of the market in the presence of a controlled economy sometimes referred to as a command economy in the literature. Both types of _________ have been in historical evidence throughout the twentieth century and twenty-first century.

Exam Probability: **Medium**

20. *Answer choices:*

(see index for correct answer)

- a. Market structure
- b. Open-source economics
- c. Liberalization
- d. Open source

Guidance: level 1

:: Monopoly (economics) ::

A _________ exists when a specific person or enterprise is the only supplier of a particular commodity. This contrasts with a monopsony which relates to a single entity`s control of a market to purchase a good or service, and with oligopoly which consists of a few sellers dominating a market. Monopolies are thus characterized by a lack of economic competition to produce the good or service, a lack of viable substitute goods, and the possibility of a high _________ price well above the seller`s marginal cost that leads to a high _________ profit. The verb monopolise or monopolize refers to the process by which a company gains the ability to raise prices or exclude competitors. In economics, a _________ is a single seller. In law, a _________ is a business entity that has significant market power, that is, the power to charge overly high prices. Although monopolies may be big businesses, size is not a characteristic of a _________ . A small business may still have the power to raise prices in a small industry .

Exam Probability: **Low**

21. *Answer choices:*
(see index for correct answer)

- a. Concentration ratio
- b. Bilateral monopoly
- c. Dominance
- d. Monopoly

Guidance: level 1

:: ::

A __________ is a graphic mark, emblem, or symbol used to aid and promote public identification and recognition. It may be of an abstract or figurative design or include the text of the name it represents as in a wordmark.

Exam Probability: **Low**

22. *Answer choices:*
(see index for correct answer)

- a. surface-level diversity
- b. co-culture
- c. Character
- d. personal values

Guidance: level 1

:: ::

__________ is a marketing communication that employs an openly sponsored, non-personal message to promote or sell a product, service or idea. Sponsors of __________ are typically businesses wishing to promote their products or services. __________ is differentiated from public relations in that an advertiser pays for and has control over the message. It differs from personal selling in that the message is non-personal, i.e., not directed to a particular individual. __________ is communicated through various mass media, including traditional media such as newspapers, magazines, television, radio, outdoor __________ or direct mail; and new media such as search results, blogs, social media, websites or text messages. The actual presentation of the message in a medium is referred to as an advertisement, or "ad" or advert for short.

Exam Probability: **High**

23. *Answer choices:*
(see index for correct answer)

- a. hierarchical perspective
- b. similarity-attraction theory
- c. imperative
- d. co-culture

Guidance: level 1

:: ::

__________ , in general use, is a devotion and faithfulness to a nation, cause, philosophy, country, group, or person. Philosophers disagree on what can be an object of __________ , as some argue that __________ is strictly interpersonal and only another human being can be the object of __________ . The definition of __________ in law and political science is the fidelity of an individual to a nation, either one`s nation of birth, or one`s declared home nation by oath .

Exam Probability: **Low**

24. *Answer choices:*
(see index for correct answer)

- a. functional perspective
- b. Loyalty
- c. surface-level diversity
- d. levels of analysis

Guidance: level 1

:: ::

__________ is a term frequently used in marketing. It is a measure of how products and services supplied by a company meet or surpass customer expectation. __________ is defined as "the number of customers, or percentage of total customers, whose reported experience with a firm, its products, or its services exceeds specified satisfaction goals."

Exam Probability: **High**

25. *Answer choices:*
(see index for correct answer)

- a. corporate values
- b. levels of analysis
- c. functional perspective
- d. Customer satisfaction

Guidance: level 1

:: Supply chain management ::

_________ is a variable pricing strategy, based on understanding, anticipating and influencing consumer behavior in order to maximize revenue or profits from a fixed, time-limited resource . As a specific, inventory-focused branch of revenue management, _________ involves strategic control of inventory to sell the right product to the right customer at the right time for the right price. This process can result in price discrimination, in which customers consuming identical goods or services are charged different prices. _________ is a large revenue generator for several major industries; Robert Crandall, former Chairman and CEO of American Airlines, gave _________ its name and has called it "the single most important technical development in transportation management since we entered deregulation."

Exam Probability: **Low**

26. *Answer choices:*

(see index for correct answer)

- a. Yield management
- b. Blinco Systems Inc.
- c. Service management
- d. Supplier enablement

Guidance: level 1

:: ::

_________ s is the linguistic and philosophical study of meaning, in language, programming languages, formal logics, and semiotics. It is concerned with the relationship between signifiers—like words, phrases, signs, and symbols—and what they stand for in reality, their denotation.

Exam Probability: **High**

27. *Answer choices:*

(see index for correct answer)

- a. Semantic
- b. open system
- c. information systems assessment
- d. surface-level diversity

Guidance: level 1

:: Project management ::

Contemporary business and science treat as a _________ any undertaking, carried out individually or collaboratively and possibly involving research or design, that is carefully planned to achieve a particular aim.

Exam Probability: **Medium**

28. *Answer choices:*

(see index for correct answer)

- a. Theory X and Theory Y
- b. Schedule
- c. Lean project management
- d. Project

Guidance: level 1

:: Management accounting ::

_________ , or dollar contribution per unit, is the selling price per unit minus the variable cost per unit. "Contribution" represents the portion of sales revenue that is not consumed by variable costs and so contributes to the coverage of fixed costs. This concept is one of the key building blocks of break-even analysis.

Exam Probability: **Medium**

29. *Answer choices:*

(see index for correct answer)

- a. Construction accounting
- b. Contribution margin
- c. Activity-based management
- d. Fixed assets management

Guidance: level 1

:: Commercial item transport and distribution ::

Wholesaling or distributing is the sale of goods or merchandise to retailers; to industrial, commercial, institutional, or other professional business users; or to other _________ rs and related subordinated services. In general, it is the sale of goods to anyone other than a standard consumer.

Exam Probability: **High**

30. *Answer choices:*

(see index for correct answer)

- a. Standard Carrier Alpha Code
- b. Wholesale
- c. Food distribution
- d. Shipbroking

Guidance: level 1

:: Auctioneering ::

A _________ is one of several similar kinds of auctions. Most commonly, it means an auction in which the auctioneer begins with a high asking price, and lowers it until some participant accepts the price, or it reaches a predetermined reserve price. This has also been called a clock auction or open-outcry descending-price auction. This type of auction is good for auctioning goods quickly, since a sale never requires more than one bid. Strategically, it`s similar to a first-price sealed-bid auction.

Exam Probability: **Low**

31. *Answer choices:*

(see index for correct answer)

- a. Virginity auction
- b. Dutch auction
- c. Demsetz auction
- d. Vehicle impoundment

Guidance: level 1

:: Industrial automation ::

__________ is the technology by which a process or procedure is performed with minimal human assistance. __________ or automatic control is the use of various control systems for operating equipment such as machinery, processes in factories, boilers and heat treating ovens, switching on telephone networks, steering and stabilization of ships, aircraft and other applications and vehicles with minimal or reduced human intervention.

Exam Probability: **Medium**

32. *Answer choices:*
(see index for correct answer)

- a. Collaborative process automation systems
- b. Distributed control system
- c. Automation
- d. Stack light

Guidance: level 1

:: ::

__________ is the social science that studies the production, distribution, and consumption of goods and services.

Exam Probability: **High**

33. *Answer choices:*
(see index for correct answer)

- a. empathy
- b. surface-level diversity
- c. levels of analysis
- d. information systems assessment

Guidance: level 1

:: ::

Business Model Canvas is a strategic management and lean startup template for developing new or documenting existing business models. It is a visual chart with elements describing a firm`s or product`s value proposition, infrastructure, customers, and finances. It assists firms in aligning their activities by illustrating potential trade-offs.

Exam Probability: **Low**

34. *Answer choices:*
(see index for correct answer)

- a. imperative
- b. surface-level diversity
- c. hierarchical perspective
- d. co-culture

Guidance: level 1

:: Budgets ::

A _________ is a financial plan for a defined period, often one year. It may also include planned sales volumes and revenues, resource quantities, costs and expenses, assets, liabilities and cash flows. Companies, governments, families and other organizations use it to express strategic plans of activities or events in measurable terms.

Exam Probability: **Medium**

35. *Answer choices:*
(see index for correct answer)

- a. Budget
- b. Operating budget
- c. Zero deficit budget
- d. Black budget

Guidance: level 1

:: Consumer theory ::

A __________ is a technical term in psychology, economics and philosophy usually used in relation to choosing between alternatives. For example, someone prefers A over B if they would rather choose A than B.

Exam Probability: **High**

36. *Answer choices:*
(see index for correct answer)

- a. Preference
- b. Cross elasticity of demand
- c. Expenditure function
- d. Hicksian demand function

Guidance: level 1

:: ::

__________ is the production of products for use or sale using labour and machines, tools, chemical and biological processing, or formulation. The term may refer to a range of human activity, from handicraft to high tech, but is most commonly applied to industrial design, in which raw materials are transformed into finished goods on a large scale. Such finished goods may be sold to other manufacturers for the production of other, more complex products, such as aircraft, household appliances, furniture, sports equipment or automobiles, or sold to wholesalers, who in turn sell them to retailers, who then sell them to end users and consumers.

Exam Probability: **Medium**

37. *Answer choices:*
(see index for correct answer)

- a. personal values
- b. Sarbanes-Oxley act of 2002
- c. corporate values
- d. Manufacturing

Guidance: level 1

:: ::

_________ are electronic transfer of money from one bank account to another, either within a single financial institution or across multiple institutions, via computer-based systems, without the direct intervention of bank staff.

Exam Probability: **High**

38. *Answer choices:*
(see index for correct answer)

- a. Electronic funds transfer
- b. deep-level diversity
- c. levels of analysis
- d. imperative

Guidance: level 1

:: Game theory ::

To _________ is to make a deal between different parties where each party gives up part of their demand. In arguments, _________ is a concept of finding agreement through communication, through a mutual acceptance of terms—often involving variations from an original goal or desires.

Exam Probability: **Medium**

39. *Answer choices:*
(see index for correct answer)

- a. Compromise
- b. Trembling hand perfect equilibrium
- c. Rationalizability
- d. Swap regret

Guidance: level 1

:: Contract law ::

A _________ is a legally-binding agreement which recognises and governs the rights and duties of the parties to the agreement. A _________ is legally enforceable because it meets the requirements and approval of the law. An agreement typically involves the exchange of goods, services, money, or promises of any of those. In the event of breach of _________, the law awards the injured party access to legal remedies such as damages and cancellation.

Exam Probability: **Low**

40. *Answer choices:*

(see index for correct answer)

- a. Samenlevingscontract
- b. Pirate code
- c. Contract
- d. Implied authority

Guidance: level 1

:: ::

Walter Elias Disney was an American entrepreneur, animator, voice actor and film producer. A pioneer of the American animation industry, he introduced several developments in the production of cartoons. As a film producer, Disney holds the record for most Academy Awards earned by an individual, having won 22 Oscars from 59 nominations. He was presented with two Golden Globe Special Achievement Awards and an Emmy Award, among other honors. Several of his films are included in the National Film Registry by the Library of Congress.

Exam Probability: **Low**

41. *Answer choices:*

(see index for correct answer)

- a. open system
- b. Walt Disney
- c. imperative
- d. corporate values

Guidance: level 1

:: E-commerce ::

IBM _________ also known as WCS is a software platform framework for e-commerce, including marketing, sales, customer and order processing functionality in a tailorable, integrated package. It is a single, unified platform which offers the ability to do business directly with consumers , with businesses , indirectly through channel partners , or all of these simultaneously. _________ is a customizable, scalable and high availability solution built on the Java - Java EE platform using open standards, such as XML, and Web services.

Exam Probability: **High**

42. *Answer choices:*

(see index for correct answer)

- a. Online insurance
- b. WebSphere Commerce
- c. Notice and take down
- d. Social shopping

Guidance: level 1

:: ::

Competition arises whenever at least two parties strive for a goal which cannot be shared: where one`s gain is the other`s loss .

Exam Probability: **High**

43. *Answer choices:*

(see index for correct answer)

- a. surface-level diversity
- b. Competitor
- c. Character
- d. functional perspective

Guidance: level 1

:: Information technology management ::

B2B is often contrasted with business-to-consumer . In B2B commerce, it is often the case that the parties to the relationship have comparable negotiating power, and even when they do not, each party typically involves professional staff and legal counsel in the negotiation of terms, whereas B2C is shaped to a far greater degree by economic implications of information asymmetry. However, within a B2B context, large companies may have many commercial, resource and information advantages over smaller businesses. The United Kingdom government, for example, created the post of Small Business Commissioner under the Enterprise Act 2016 to "enable small businesses to resolve disputes" and "consider complaints by small business suppliers about payment issues with larger businesses that they supply."

Exam Probability: **Medium**

44. *Answer choices:*

(see index for correct answer)

- a. Change control
- b. Multichannel Group
- c. Business-to-business
- d. Storage hypervisor

Guidance: level 1

:: E-commerce ::

The phrase _________ was originally coined in 1997 by Kevin Duffey at the launch of the Global _________ Forum, to mean "the delivery of electronic commerce capabilities directly into the consumer's hand, anywhere, via wireless technology." Many choose to think of _________ as meaning "a retail outlet in your customer's pocket."

Exam Probability: **Low**

45. *Answer choices:*

(see index for correct answer)

- a. Mobimoneybox
- b. Playism
- c. Mobile commerce
- d. AdsML

Guidance: level 1

:: ::

_________ refers to a business or organization attempting to acquire goods or services to accomplish its goals. Although there are several organizations that attempt to set standards in the _________ process, processes can vary greatly between organizations. Typically the word " _________ " is not used interchangeably with the word "procurement", since procurement typically includes expediting, supplier quality, and transportation and logistics in addition to _________ .

Exam Probability: **Low**

46. *Answer choices:*

(see index for correct answer)

- a. Purchasing
- b. levels of analysis
- c. Character
- d. personal values

Guidance: level 1

:: ::

A _________ is a structured form of play, usually undertaken for enjoyment and sometimes used as an educational tool. _________ s are distinct from work, which is usually carried out for remuneration, and from art, which is more often an expression of aesthetic or ideological elements. However, the distinction is not clear-cut, and many _________ s are also considered to be work or art .

Exam Probability: **Medium**

47. *Answer choices:*

(see index for correct answer)

- a. surface-level diversity
- b. interpersonal communication
- c. Game
- d. Character

Guidance: level 1

:: Marketing ::

__________ is a concept introduced in a book of the same name in 1999 by marketing expert Seth Godin. __________ is a non-traditional marketing technique that advertises goods and services when advance consent is given.

Exam Probability: **Medium**

48. *Answer choices:*

(see index for correct answer)

- a. Marchitecture
- b. Need
- c. Permission marketing
- d. Boston matrix

Guidance: level 1

:: Industry ::

A __________ is a set of sequential operations established in a factory where materials are put through a refining process to produce an end-product that is suitable for onward consumption; or components are assembled to make a finished article.

Exam Probability: **High**

49. *Answer choices:*

(see index for correct answer)

- a. Production line
- b. Industrialisation
- c. Takt time
- d. Tube and clamp scaffold

Guidance: level 1

:: Banking ::

A _________ is a financial institution that accepts deposits from the public and creates credit. Lending activities can be performed either directly or indirectly through capital markets. Due to their importance in the financial stability of a country, _________ s are highly regulated in most countries. Most nations have institutionalized a system known as fractional reserve _________ ing under which _________ s hold liquid assets equal to only a portion of their current liabilities. In addition to other regulations intended to ensure liquidity, _________ s are generally subject to minimum capital requirements based on an international set of capital standards, known as the Basel Accords.

Exam Probability: **Low**

50. *Answer choices:*

(see index for correct answer)

- a. Sibos
- b. Gold key
- c. Bank
- d. Retail banking

Guidance: level 1

:: ::

Senior management, executive management, upper management, or a _________ is generally a team of individuals at the highest level of management of an organization who have the day-to-day tasks of managing that organization — sometimes a company or a corporation.

Exam Probability: **High**

51. *Answer choices:*

(see index for correct answer)

- a. Management team
- b. Sarbanes-Oxley act of 2002
- c. interpersonal communication
- d. corporate values

Guidance: level 1

:: Business law ::

A _________ is a business entity created by two or more parties, generally characterized by shared ownership, shared returns and risks, and shared governance. Companies typically pursue _________ s for one of four reasons: to access a new market, particularly emerging markets; to gain scale efficiencies by combining assets and operations; to share risk for major investments or projects; or to access skills and capabilities.

Exam Probability: **High**

52. *Answer choices:*

(see index for correct answer)

- a. Joint venture
- b. Novated lease
- c. Negative option billing
- d. Business courts

Guidance: level 1

:: ::

An _________ in international trade is a good or service produced in one country that is bought by someone in another country. The seller of such goods and services is an _________ er; the foreign buyer is an importer.

Exam Probability: **Medium**

53. *Answer choices:*

(see index for correct answer)

- a. empathy
- b. Export
- c. information systems assessment
- d. hierarchical perspective

Guidance: level 1

:: ::

A _________ or _________ s is a type of footwear and not a specific type of shoe. Most _________ s mainly cover the foot and the ankle, while some also cover some part of the lower calf. Some _________ s extend up the leg, sometimes as far as the knee or even the hip. Most _________ s have a heel that is clearly distinguishable from the rest of the sole, even if the two are made of one piece. Traditionally made of leather or rubber, modern _________ s are made from a variety of materials. _________ s are worn both for their functionality protecting the foot and leg from water, extreme cold, mud or hazards or providing additional ankle support for strenuous activities with added traction requirements , or may have hobnails on their undersides to protect against wear and to get better grip; and for reasons of style and fashion.

Exam Probability: **High**

54. *Answer choices:*

(see index for correct answer)

- a. Boot
- b. Sarbanes-Oxley act of 2002
- c. open system
- d. functional perspective

Guidance: level 1

:: Price fixing convictions ::

_________ AG is a German multinational conglomerate company headquartered in Berlin and Munich and the largest industrial manufacturing company in Europe with branch offices abroad.

Exam Probability: **High**

55. *Answer choices:*

(see index for correct answer)

- a. YKK Group
- b. Anheuser-Busch InBev
- c. Siemens
- d. Danish Christmas Tree Growers Association

Guidance: level 1

:: ::

A _________ is a person who trades in commodities produced by other people. Historically, a _________ is anyone who is involved in business or trade. _________ s have operated for as long as industry, commerce, and trade have existed. During the 16th-century, in Europe, two different terms for _________ s emerged: One term, meerseniers, described local traders such as bakers, grocers, etc.; while a new term, koopman (Dutch: koopman, described _________ s who operated on a global stage, importing and exporting goods over vast distances, and offering added-value services such as credit and finance.

Exam Probability: **Medium**

56. *Answer choices:*

(see index for correct answer)

- a. deep-level diversity
- b. information systems assessment
- c. surface-level diversity
- d. Merchant

Guidance: level 1

:: E-commerce ::

_________ is the business-to-business or business-to-consumer or business-to-government purchase and sale of supplies, work, and services through the Internet as well as other information and networking systems, such as electronic data interchange and enterprise resource planning.

Exam Probability: **High**

57. *Answer choices:*

(see index for correct answer)

- a. E-procurement
- b. Customer Access and Retrieval System
- c. Digital currency
- d. MonkeySports

Guidance: level 1

:: ::

_________ refers to the overall process of attracting, shortlisting, selecting and appointing suitable candidates for jobs within an organization. _________ can also refer to processes involved in choosing individuals for unpaid roles. Managers, human resource generalists and _________ specialists may be tasked with carrying out _________ , but in some cases public-sector employment agencies, commercial _________ agencies, or specialist search consultancies are used to undertake parts of the process. Internet-based technologies which support all aspects of _________ have become widespread.

Exam Probability: **Low**

58. *Answer choices:*

(see index for correct answer)

- a. functional perspective
- b. personal values
- c. Recruitment
- d. hierarchical perspective

Guidance: level 1

:: Commodities ::

In economics, a _________ is an economic good or service that has full or substantial fungibility: that is, the market treats instances of the good as equivalent or nearly so with no regard to who produced them. Most commodities are raw materials, basic resources, agricultural, or mining products, such as iron ore, sugar, or grains like rice and wheat. Commodities can also be mass-produced unspecialized products such as chemicals and computer memory.

Exam Probability: **High**

59. *Answer choices:*

(see index for correct answer)

- a. Commoditization
- b. Commodity money
- c. IRely
- d. Sample grade

Guidance: level 1

Business ethics

Business ethics (also known as corporate ethics) is a form of applied ethics or professional ethics, that examines ethical principles and moral or ethical problems that can arise in a business environment. It applies to all aspects of business conduct and is relevant to the conduct of individuals and entire organizations. These ethics originate from individuals, organizational statements or from the legal system. These norms, values, ethical, and unethical practices are what is used to guide business. They help those businesses maintain a better connection with their stakeholders.

:: Management ::

__________ or executive pay is composed of the financial compensation and other non-financial awards received by an executive from their firm for their service to the organization. It is typically a mixture of salary, bonuses, shares of or call options on the company stock, benefits, and perquisites, ideally configured to take into account government regulations, tax law, the desires of the organization and the executive, and rewards for performance.

Exam Probability: **Low**

1. *Answer choices:*

(see index for correct answer)

- a. Planning
- b. Swarm Development Group
- c. PDCA
- d. Executive compensation

Guidance: level 1

:: Socialism ::

_________ is a label used to define the first currents of modern socialist thought as exemplified by the work of Henri de Saint-Simon, Charles Fourier, Étienne Cabet and Robert Owen.

Exam Probability: **Low**

2. *Answer choices:*
(see index for correct answer)

- a. Utopian socialism
- b. Bolivarian Revolution
- c. Class conflict
- d. HaNoar HaOved VeHaLomed

Guidance: level 1

:: Writs ::

In common law, a writ of _________ is a writ whereby a private individual who assists a prosecution can receive all or part of any penalty imposed. Its name is an abbreviation of the Latin phrase _________ pro domino rege quam pro se ipso in hac parte sequitur, meaning "[he] who sues in this matter for the king as well as for himself."

Exam Probability: **Medium**

3. *Answer choices:*
(see index for correct answer)

- a. Writ
- b. Writ of assistance
- c. Writ of execution

Guidance: level 1

:: Price fixing convictions ::

_________ AG is a German multinational conglomerate company headquartered in Berlin and Munich and the largest industrial manufacturing company in Europe with branch offices abroad.

Exam Probability: **Low**

4. *Answer choices:*
(see index for correct answer)

- a. Northwest Airlines
- b. AGC Glass Europe
- c. YKK Group
- d. Siemens

Guidance: level 1

:: Management ::

The term _________ refers to measures designed to increase the degree of autonomy and self-determination in people and in communities in order to enable them to represent their interests in a responsible and self-determined way, acting on their own authority. It is the process of becoming stronger and more confident, especially in controlling one`s life and claiming one`s rights. _________ as action refers both to the process of self- _________ and to professional support of people, which enables them to overcome their sense of powerlessness and lack of influence, and to recognize and use their resources. To do work with power.

Exam Probability: **Medium**

5. *Answer choices:*
(see index for correct answer)

- a. Staff management
- b. Competitive heterogeneity
- c. Empowerment
- d. Project cost management

Guidance: level 1

:: ::

The _________ , the Calvinist work ethic or the Puritan work ethic is a work ethic concept in theology, sociology, economics and history that emphasizes that hard work, discipline and frugality are a result of a person`s subscription to the values espoused by the Protestant faith, particularly Calvinism. The phrase was initially coined in 1904–1905 by Max Weber in his book The Protestant Ethic and the Spirit of Capitalism.

Exam Probability: **Medium**

6. *Answer choices:*

(see index for correct answer)

- a. personal values
- b. Protestant work ethic
- c. corporate values
- d. information systems assessment

Guidance: level 1

:: Progressive Era in the United States ::

The Clayton Antitrust Act of 1914 , was a part of United States antitrust law with the goal of adding further substance to the U.S. antitrust law regime; the _________ sought to prevent anticompetitive practices in their incipiency. That regime started with the Sherman Antitrust Act of 1890, the first Federal law outlawing practices considered harmful to consumers . The _________ specified particular prohibited conduct, the three-level enforcement scheme, the exemptions, and the remedial measures.

Exam Probability: **High**

7. *Answer choices:*

(see index for correct answer)

- a. Mann Act
- b. Clayton Act
- c. Clayton Antitrust Act

Guidance: level 1

:: Pyramid and Ponzi schemes ::

_________ was an Italian swindler and con artist in the U.S. and Canada. His aliases include Charles Ponci, Carlo, and Charles P. Bianchi. Born and raised in Italy, he became known in the early 1920s as a swindler in North America for his money-making scheme. He promised clients a 50% profit within 45 days or 100% profit within 90 days, by buying discounted postal reply coupons in other countries and redeeming them at face value in the United States as a form of arbitrage. In reality, Ponzi was paying earlier investors using the investments of later investors. While this type of fraudulent investment scheme was not originally invented by Ponzi, it became so identified with him that it now is referred to as a "Ponzi scheme". His scheme ran for over a year before it collapsed, costing his "investors" $20 million.

Exam Probability: **Low**

8. *Answer choices:*

(see index for correct answer)

- a. Foundation for New Era Philanthropy
- b. Make Money Fast
- c. Investors Overseas Service
- d. Charles Ponzi

Guidance: level 1

:: ::

Sustainability is the process of people maintaining change in a balanced environment, in which the exploitation of resources, the direction of investments, the orientation of technological development and institutional change are all in harmony and enhance both current and future potential to meet human needs and aspirations. For many in the field, sustainability is defined through the following interconnected domains or pillars: environment, economic and social, which according to Fritjof Capra is based on the principles of Systems Thinking. Sub-domains of _________ development have been considered also: cultural, technological and political. While _________ development may be the organizing principle for sustainability for some, for others, the two terms are paradoxical . _________ development is the development that meets the needs of the present without compromising the ability of future generations to meet their own needs. Brundtland Report for the World Commission on Environment and Development introduced the term of _________ development.

Exam Probability: **High**

9. *Answer choices:*

(see index for correct answer)

- a. Character
- b. surface-level diversity
- c. functional perspective
- d. corporate values

Guidance: level 1

:: Minimum wage ::

The _________ are working people whose incomes fall below a given poverty line due to lack of work hours and/or low wages.Largely because they are earning such low wages, the _________ face numerous obstacles that make it difficult for many of them to find and keep a job, save up money, and maintain a sense of self-worth.

Exam Probability: **Medium**

10. *Answer choices:*

(see index for correct answer)

- a. Minimum wage in Taiwan
- b. Guaranteed minimum income
- c. Working poor
- d. Minimum wage in the United States

Guidance: level 1

:: ::

_________ is a private Dominican liberal arts college in Madison, Wisconsin. The college occupies a 55 acres campus overlooking the shores of Lake Wingra.

Exam Probability: **High**

11. *Answer choices:*

(see index for correct answer)

- a. open system
- b. surface-level diversity
- c. functional perspective

- d. deep-level diversity

Guidance: level 1

:: ::

Bernard Lawrence _________ is an American former market maker, investment advisor, financier, fraudster, and convicted felon, who is currently serving a federal prison sentence for offenses related to a massive Ponzi scheme. He is the former non-executive chairman of the NASDAQ stock market, the confessed operator of the largest Ponzi scheme in world history, and the largest financial fraud in U.S. history. Prosecutors estimated the fraud to be worth $64.8 billion based on the amounts in the accounts of _________ `s 4,800 clients as of November 30, 2008.

Exam Probability: **High**

12. *Answer choices:*

(see index for correct answer)

- a. information systems assessment
- b. Sarbanes-Oxley act of 2002
- c. Madoff
- d. co-culture

Guidance: level 1

:: ::

_________ in the United States is a federal and state program that helps with medical costs for some people with limited income and resources. _________ also offers benefits not normally covered by Medicare, including nursing home care and personal care services. The Health Insurance Association of America describes _________ as "a government insurance program for persons of all ages whose income and resources are insufficient to pay for health care." _________ is the largest source of funding for medical and health-related services for people with low income in the United States, providing free health insurance to 74 million low-income and disabled people as of 2017. It is a means-tested program that is jointly funded by the state and federal governments and managed by the states, with each state currently having broad leeway to determine who is eligible for its implementation of the program. States are not required to participate in the program, although all have since 1982. _________ recipients must be U.S. citizens or qualified non-citizens, and may include low-income adults, their children, and people with certain disabilities. Poverty alone does not necessarily qualify someone for _________ .

Exam Probability: **Low**

13. *Answer choices:*

(see index for correct answer)

- a. surface-level diversity
- b. cultural
- c. hierarchical
- d. open system

Guidance: level 1

:: Industry ::

_________ is the manner in which a given entity has decided to address issues of energy development including energy production, distribution and consumption. The attributes of _________ may include legislation, international treaties, incentives to investment, guidelines for energy conservation, taxation and other public policy techniques. Energy is a core component of modern economies. A functioning economy requires not only labor and capital but also energy, for manufacturing processes, transportation, communication, agriculture, and more.

Exam Probability: **Low**

14. *Answer choices:*

(see index for correct answer)

- a. Energy policy
- b. Sexual division of labour
- c. Production line
- d. Mass production

Guidance: level 1

:: Timber industry ::

The _________ is an international non-profit, multi-stakeholder organization established in 1993 to promote responsible management of the world's forests. The FSC does this by setting standards on forest products, along with certifying and labeling them as eco-friendly.

Exam Probability: **Low**

15. *Answer choices:*

(see index for correct answer)

- a. Lumber hooker
- b. Susquehanna Boom
- c. Timber recycling
- d. National Hardwood Lumber Association

Guidance: level 1

:: Corporate crime ::

_________ LLP, based in Chicago, was an American holding company. Formerly one of the "Big Five" accounting firms , the firm had provided auditing, tax, and consulting services to large corporations. By 2001, it had become one of the world's largest multinational companies.

Exam Probability: **High**

16. *Answer choices:*

(see index for correct answer)

- a. Ovson Egg
- b. Compass Group
- c. Anti-corporate

- d. Arthur Andersen

Guidance: level 1

:: Social responsibility ::

The United Nations Global Compact is a non-binding United Nations pact to encourage businesses worldwide to adopt sustainable and socially responsible policies, and to report on their implementation. The _________ is a principle-based framework for businesses, stating ten principles in the areas of human rights, labor, the environment and anti-corruption. Under the Global Compact, companies are brought together with UN agencies, labor groups and civil society. Cities can join the Global Compact through the Cities Programme.

Exam Probability: **Low**

17. *Answer choices:*

(see index for correct answer)

- a. Enterprise 2020
- b. Footprints network
- c. Socially responsible marketing
- d. UN Global Compact

Guidance: level 1

:: Labour law ::

An _________ is special or specified circumstances that partially or fully exempt a person or organization from performance of a legal obligation so as to avoid an unreasonable or disproportionate burden or obstacle.

Exam Probability: **Medium**

18. *Answer choices:*

(see index for correct answer)

- a. Carl Degenkolb
- b. Undue hardship
- c. Matthew W. Finkin
- d. Negligent retention

Guidance: level 1

:: ::

__________ is the collection of mechanisms, processes and relations by which corporations are controlled and operated. Governance structures and principles identify the distribution of rights and responsibilities among different participants in the corporation and include the rules and procedures for making decisions in corporate affairs. __________ is necessary because of the possibility of conflicts of interests between stakeholders, primarily between shareholders and upper management or among shareholders.

Exam Probability: **Medium**

19. *Answer choices:*

(see index for correct answer)

- a. corporate values
- b. Corporate governance
- c. hierarchical
- d. cultural

Guidance: level 1

:: ::

A __________ is a form of business network, for example, a local organization of businesses whose goal is to further the interests of businesses. Business owners in towns and cities form these local societies to advocate on behalf of the business community. Local businesses are members, and they elect a board of directors or executive council to set policy for the chamber. The board or council then hires a President, CEO or Executive Director, plus staffing appropriate to size, to run the organization.

Exam Probability: **Low**

20. *Answer choices:*

(see index for correct answer)

- a. information systems assessment
- b. deep-level diversity
- c. functional perspective
- d. Chamber of Commerce

Guidance: level 1

:: ::

The __________ is an American stock exchange located at 11 Wall Street, Lower Manhattan, New York City, New York. It is by far the world`s largest stock exchange by market capitalization of its listed companies at US$30.1 trillion as of February 2018. The average daily trading value was approximately US$169 billion in 2013. The NYSE trading floor is located at 11 Wall Street and is composed of 21 rooms used for the facilitation of trading. A fifth trading room, located at 30 Broad Street, was closed in February 2007. The main building and the 11 Wall Street building were designated National Historic Landmarks in 1978.

Exam Probability: **Medium**

21. *Answer choices:*
(see index for correct answer)

- a. New York Stock Exchange
- b. similarity-attraction theory
- c. co-culture
- d. personal values

Guidance: level 1

:: Leadership ::

__________ is a theory of leadership where a leader works with teams to identify needed change, creating a vision to guide the change through inspiration, and executing the change in tandem with committed members of a group; it is an integral part of the Full Range Leadership Model. __________ serves to enhance the motivation, morale, and job performance of followers through a variety of mechanisms; these include connecting the follower`s sense of identity and self to a project and to the collective identity of the organization; being a role model for followers in order to inspire them and to raise their interest in the project; challenging followers to take greater ownership for their work, and understanding the strengths and weaknesses of followers, allowing the leader to align followers with tasks that enhance their performance.

Exam Probability: **High**

22. *Answer choices:*

(see index for correct answer)

- a. Motivational Leadership
- b. Tribal Leadership
- c. Superleadership
- d. Moral example

Guidance: level 1

:: ::

The _________ to Fight AIDS, Tuberculosis and Malaria is an international financing organization that aims to "attract, leverage and invest additional resources to end the epidemics of HIV/AIDS, tuberculosis and malaria to support attainment of the Sustainable Development Goals established by the United Nations." A public-private partnership, the organization maintains its secretariat in Geneva, Switzerland. The organization began operations in January 2002. Microsoft founder Bill Gates was one of the first private foundations among many bilateral donors to provide seed money for the partnership.

Exam Probability: **High**

23. *Answer choices:*

(see index for correct answer)

- a. open system
- b. Global Fund
- c. hierarchical perspective
- d. information systems assessment

Guidance: level 1

:: Fraud ::

In the United States, _________ is the claiming of Medicare health care reimbursement to which the claimant is not entitled. There are many different types of _________ , all of which have the same goal: to collect money from the Medicare program illegitimately.

Exam Probability: **Medium**

24. *Answer choices:*

(see index for correct answer)

- a. Money mule
- b. Clothing scam companies
- c. Medicare fraud
- d. Transcript fraud

Guidance: level 1

:: Monopoly (economics) ::

A _________ is a form of intellectual property that gives its owner the legal right to exclude others from making, using, selling, and importing an invention for a limited period of years, in exchange for publishing an enabling public disclosure of the invention. In most countries _________ rights fall under civil law and the _________ holder needs to sue someone infringing the _________ in order to enforce his or her rights. In some industries _________ s are an essential form of competitive advantage; in others they are irrelevant.

Exam Probability: **High**

25. *Answer choices:*

(see index for correct answer)

- a. Regulatory economics
- b. Monopsony
- c. Electricity liberalization
- d. Patent

Guidance: level 1

:: ::

The Federal National Mortgage Association , commonly known as _________ , is a United States government-sponsored enterprise and, since 1968, a publicly traded company. Founded in 1938 during the Great Depression as part of the New Deal, the corporation`s purpose is to expand the secondary mortgage market by securitizing mortgage loans in the form of mortgage-backed securities , allowing lenders to reinvest their assets into more lending and in effect increasing the number of lenders in the mortgage market by reducing the reliance on locally based savings and loan associations . Its brother organization is the Federal Home Loan Mortgage Corporation , better known as Freddie Mac. As of 2018, _________ is ranked #21 on the Fortune 500 rankings of the largest United States corporations by total revenue.

Exam Probability: **High**

26. *Answer choices:*
(see index for correct answer)

- a. imperative
- b. empathy
- c. deep-level diversity
- d. Fannie Mae

Guidance: level 1

:: Renewable energy ::

_________ is the conversion of energy from sunlight into electricity, either directly using photovoltaics , indirectly using concentrated _________ , or a combination. Concentrated _________ systems use lenses or mirrors and tracking systems to focus a large area of sunlight into a small beam. Photovoltaic cells convert light into an electric current using the photovoltaic effect.

Exam Probability: **High**

27. *Answer choices:*
(see index for correct answer)

- a. Biomass briquettes
- b. Solar power
- c. Algae fuel
- d. Market transformation

Guidance: level 1

:: Mortgage ::

In finance, __________ means making loans to people who may have difficulty maintaining the repayment schedule, sometimes reflecting setbacks, such as unemployment, divorce, medical emergencies, etc. Historically, subprime borrowers were defined as having FICO scores below 600, although "this has varied over time and circumstances."

Exam Probability: **High**

28. *Answer choices:*

(see index for correct answer)

- a. AEPROSER
- b. Strategic default
- c. Subprime lending
- d. Higher lending charge

Guidance: level 1

:: Ethically disputed business practices ::

__________ is the trading of a public company`s stock or other securities by individuals with access to nonpublic information about the company. In various countries, some kinds of trading based on insider information is illegal. This is because it is seen as unfair to other investors who do not have access to the information, as the investor with insider information could potentially make larger profits than a typical investor could make. The rules governing __________ are complex and vary significantly from country to country. The extent of enforcement also varies from one country to another. The definition of insider in one jurisdiction can be broad, and may cover not only insiders themselves but also any persons related to them, such as brokers, associates and even family members. A person who becomes aware of non-public information and trades on that basis may be guilty of a crime.

Exam Probability: **Low**

29. *Answer choices:*

(see index for correct answer)

- a. Repo 105
- b. Insider trading
- c. Designer drug

- d. Spamming

Guidance: level 1

:: Leadership ::

__________ is leadership that is directed by respect for ethical beliefs and values and for the dignity and rights of others. It is thus related to concepts such as trust, honesty, consideration, charisma, and fairness.

Exam Probability: **Low**

30. *Answer choices:*

(see index for correct answer)

- a. Ethical leadership
- b. Jewish leadership
- c. Moral example
- d. Authentic leadership

Guidance: level 1

:: Culture ::

__________ is a society which is characterized by individualism, which is the prioritization or emphasis, of the individual over the entire group. __________ s are oriented around the self, being independent instead of identifying with a group mentality. They see each other as only loosely linked, and value personal goals over group interests. __________ s tend to have a more diverse population and are characterized with emphasis on personal achievements, and a rational assessment of both the beneficial and detrimental aspects of relationships with others. __________ s have such unique aspects of communication as being a low power-distance culture and having a low-context communication style. The United States, Australia, Great Britain, Canada, the Netherlands, and New Zealand have been identified as highly __________ s.

Exam Probability: **Medium**

31. *Answer choices:*

(see index for correct answer)

- a. Intracultural
- b. Individualistic culture
- c. cultural framework

- d. High-context

Guidance: level 1

:: Decentralization ::

__________ or sub __________ mainly refers to the unrestricted growth in many urban areas of housing, commercial development, and roads over large expanses of land, with little concern for urban planning. In addition to describing a particular form of urbanization, the term also relates to the social and environmental consequences associated with this development. In Continental Europe the term "peri-urbanisation" is often used to denote similar dynamics and phenomena, although the term __________ is currently being used by the European Environment Agency. There is widespread disagreement about what constitutes sprawl and how to quantify it. For example, some commentators measure sprawl only with the average number of residential units per acre in a given area. But others associate it with decentralization , discontinuity , segregation of uses, and so forth.

Exam Probability: **High**

32. *Answer choices:*

(see index for correct answer)

- a. Leopold Kohr
- b. Regional state
- c. Politics of Somalia
- d. Urban sprawl

Guidance: level 1

:: Data management ::

__________ is a form of intellectual property that grants the creator of an original creative work an exclusive legal right to determine whether and under what conditions this original work may be copied and used by others, usually for a limited term of years. The exclusive rights are not absolute but limited by limitations and exceptions to __________ law, including fair use. A major limitation on __________ on ideas is that __________ protects only the original expression of ideas, and not the underlying ideas themselves.

Exam Probability: **High**

33. *Answer choices:*
(see index for correct answer)

- a. Chunked transfer encoding
- b. Copyright
- c. Data management
- d. Data stream management system

Guidance: level 1

:: Business ethics ::

The __________ are the names of two corporate codes of conduct, developed by the African-American preacher Rev. Leon Sullivan, promoting corporate social responsibility.

Exam Probability: **High**

34. *Answer choices:*
(see index for correct answer)

- a. Linda Peeno
- b. Journal of Business Ethics Education
- c. Sullivan principles
- d. Repugnant market

Guidance: level 1

:: Public relations terminology ::

__________ , also called "green sheen", is a form of spin in which green PR or green marketing is deceptively used to promote the perception that an organization`s products, aims or policies are environmentally friendly. Evidence that an organization is __________ often comes from pointing out the spending differences: when significantly more money or time has been spent advertising being "green" , than is actually spent on environmentally sound practices. __________ efforts can range from changing the name or label of a product to evoke the natural environment on a product that contains harmful chemicals to multimillion-dollar marketing campaigns portraying highly polluting energy companies as eco-friendly.Publicized accusations of __________ have contributed to the term`s increasing use.

Exam Probability: **Low**

35. *Answer choices:*

(see index for correct answer)

- a. Corporate pathos
- b. No comment
- c. PR Gallery
- d. Crisis communication

Guidance: level 1

:: Toxicology ::

_________ or lead-based paint is paint containing lead. As pigment, lead chromate , Lead oxide, , and lead carbonate are the most common forms. Lead is added to paint to accelerate drying, increase durability, maintain a fresh appearance, and resist moisture that causes corrosion. It is one of the main health and environmental hazards associated with paint. In some countries, lead continues to be added to paint intended for domestic use, whereas countries such as the U.S. and the UK have regulations prohibiting this, although _________ may still be found in older properties painted prior to the introduction of such regulations. Although lead has been banned from household paints in the United States since 1978, paint used in road markings may still contain it. Alternatives such as water-based, lead-free traffic paint are readily available, and many states and federal agencies have changed their purchasing contracts to buy these instead.

Exam Probability: **Low**

36. *Answer choices:*

(see index for correct answer)

- a. Halocin
- b. Dioxin Reassessment Report
- c. Antagonism
- d. Thermostability

Guidance: level 1

:: ::

_________ Corporation was an American energy, commodities, and services company based in Houston, Texas. It was founded in 1985 as a merger between Houston Natural Gas and InterNorth, both relatively small regional companies. Before its bankruptcy on December 3, 2001, _________ employed approximately 29,000 staff and was a major electricity, natural gas, communications and pulp and paper company, with claimed revenues of nearly $101 billion during 2000. Fortune named _________ "America`s Most Innovative Company" for six consecutive years.

Exam Probability: **Medium**

37. *Answer choices:*

(see index for correct answer)

- a. cultural
- b. open system
- c. Enron
- d. similarity-attraction theory

Guidance: level 1

:: Business ::

_________ , or built-in obsolescence, in industrial design and economics is a policy of planning or designing a product with an artificially limited useful life, so that it becomes obsolete after a certain period of time. The rationale behind this strategy is to generate long-term sales volume by reducing the time between repeat purchases .

Exam Probability: **Medium**

38. *Answer choices:*

(see index for correct answer)

- a. Business directory
- b. NEWSCYCLE Solutions
- c. Accounting networks and associations
- d. Business strategy mapping

Guidance: level 1

:: False advertising law ::

The Lanham Act is the primary federal trademark statute of law in the United States. The Act prohibits a number of activities, including trademark infringement, trademark dilution, and false advertising.

Exam Probability: **Low**

39. *Answer choices:*

(see index for correct answer)

- a. Lanham Act
- b. POM Wonderful LLC v. Coca-Cola Co.

Guidance: level 1

:: Competition regulators ::

The _________ is an independent agency of the United States government, established in 1914 by the _________ Act. Its principal mission is the promotion of consumer protection and the elimination and prevention of anticompetitive business practices, such as coercive monopoly. It is headquartered in the _________ Building in Washington, D.C.

Exam Probability: **Medium**

40. *Answer choices:*

(see index for correct answer)

- a. Federal Trade Commission
- b. Australian Competition and Consumer Commission
- c. Competition Bureau
- d. Fair Trade Commission

Guidance: level 1

:: United States law ::

The ABA _________, created by the American Bar Association , are a set of rules that prescribe baseline standards of legal ethics and professional responsibility for lawyers in the United States. They were promulgated by the ABA House of Delegates upon the recommendation of the Kutak Commission in 1983. The rules are merely recommendations, or models, and are not themselves binding. However, having a common set of Model Rules facilitates a common discourse on legal ethics, and simplifies professional responsibility training as well as the day-to-day application of such rules. As of 2015, 49 states and four territories have adopted the rules in whole or in part, of which the most recent to do so was the Commonwealth of the Northern Mariana Islands in March 2015. California is the only state that has not adopted the ABA Model Rules, while Puerto Rico is the only U.S. jurisdiction outside of confederation has not adopted them but instead has its own Código de Ética Profesional.

Exam Probability: **High**

41. *Answer choices:*
(see index for correct answer)

- a. judgment notwithstanding the verdict
- b. Pro se

Guidance: level 1

:: Dutch inventions ::

The Fairtrade certification initiative was created to form a new method for economic trade. This method takes an ethical standpoint, and considers the producers first.

Exam Probability: **Medium**

42. *Answer choices:*
(see index for correct answer)

- a. Fairtrade
- b. Dijkstra's algorithm

Guidance: level 1

:: Industrial ecology ::

_________ is a strategy for reducing the amount of waste created and released into the environment, particularly by industrial facilities, agriculture, or consumers. Many large corporations view P2 as a method of improving the efficiency and profitability of production processes by technology advancements. Legislative bodies have enacted P2 measures, such as the _________ Act of 1990 and the Clean Air Act Amendments of 1990 by the United States Congress.

Exam Probability: **High**

43. *Answer choices:*

(see index for correct answer)

- a. Cleaner production
- b. Best available technology
- c. Pollution Prevention
- d. Industrial metabolism

Guidance: level 1

:: ::

_________ refers to a business initiative to increase the access between a company and their current and potential customers through the use of the Internet. The Internet allows the company to market themselves and attract new customers to their website where they can provide product information and better customer service. Customers can place orders electronically, therefore reducing expensive long distant phone calls and postage costs of placing orders, while saving time on behalf of the customer and company.

Exam Probability: **High**

44. *Answer choices:*

(see index for correct answer)

- a. open system
- b. cultural
- c. levels of analysis
- d. co-culture

Guidance: level 1

:: Commercial crimes ::

_________ is an agreement between participants on the same side in a market to buy or sell a product, service, or commodity only at a fixed price, or maintain the market conditions such that the price is maintained at a given level by controlling supply and demand.

Exam Probability: **High**

45. *Answer choices:*
(see index for correct answer)

- a. Pranknet
- b. Skimming
- c. Price fixing
- d. Cartel

Guidance: level 1

:: Labor rights ::

The _________ is the concept that people have a human _________ , or engage in productive employment, and may not be prevented from doing so. The _________ is enshrined in the Universal Declaration of Human Rights and recognized in international human rights law through its inclusion in the International Covenant on Economic, Social and Cultural Rights, where the _________ emphasizes economic, social and cultural development.

Exam Probability: **High**

46. *Answer choices:*
(see index for correct answer)

- a. Kate Mullany House
- b. The Hyatt 100
- c. China Labour Bulletin
- d. Swift raids

Guidance: level 1

:: Agricultural labor ::

The _________ of America, or more commonly just _________ , is a labor union for farmworkers in the United States. It originated from the merger of two workers` rights organizations, the Agricultural Workers Organizing Committee led by organizer Larry Itliong, and the National Farm Workers Association led by César Chávez and Dolores Huerta. They became allied and transformed from workers` rights organizations into a union as a result of a series of strikes in 1965, when the mostly Filipino farmworkers of the AWOC in Delano, California initiated a grape strike, and the NFWA went on strike in support. As a result of the commonality in goals and methods, the NFWA and the AWOC formed the _________ Organizing Committee on August 22, 1966.This organization was accepted into the AFL-CIO in 1972 and changed its name to the _________ Union.

Exam Probability: **Low**

47. *Answer choices:*

(see index for correct answer)

- a. Kibbutz
- b. United Farm Workers
- c. H-2A Visa
- d. Custom harvesting

Guidance: level 1

:: Corporate governance ::

_________ refers to the practice of members of a corporate board of directors serving on the boards of multiple corporations. A person that sits on multiple boards is known as a multiple director. Two firms have a direct interlock if a director or executive of one firm is also a director of the other, and an indirect interlock if a director of each sits on the board of a third firm. This practice, although widespread and lawful, raises questions about the quality and independence of board decisions.

Exam Probability: **Low**

48. *Answer choices:*

(see index for correct answer)

- a. Integrated reporting
- b. Institute of Directors in New Zealand
- c. Institute of Corporate Directors

- d. Proxy firm

Guidance: level 1

:: Law ::

__________ is a body of law which defines the role, powers, and structure of different entities within a state, namely, the executive, the parliament or legislature, and the judiciary; as well as the basic rights of citizens and, in federal countries such as the United States and Canada, the relationship between the central government and state, provincial, or territorial governments.

Exam Probability: **High**

49. *Answer choices:*
(see index for correct answer)

- a. Comparative law
- b. Constitutional law

Guidance: level 1

:: Water law ::

The __________ is the primary federal law in the United States governing water pollution. Its objective is to restore and maintain the chemical, physical, and biological integrity of the nation`s waters; recognizing the responsibilities of the states in addressing pollution and providing assistance to states to do so, including funding for publicly owned treatment works for the improvement of wastewater treatment; and maintaining the integrity of wetlands. It is one of the United States` first and most influential modern environmental laws. As with many other major U.S. federal environmental statutes, it is administered by the U.S. Environmental Protection Agency , in coordination with state governments. Its implementing regulations are codified at 40 C.F.R. Subchapters D, N, and O .

Exam Probability: **Medium**

50. *Answer choices:*
(see index for correct answer)

- a. The Helsinki Rules on the Uses of the Waters of International Rivers

- b. Clean Water Act
- c. Correlative rights doctrine
- d. Water quality law

Guidance: level 1

:: ::

A _________ is a problem offering two possibilities, neither of which is unambiguously acceptable or preferable. The possibilities are termed the horns of the _________ , a clichéd usage, but distinguishing the _________ from other kinds of predicament as a matter of usage.

Exam Probability: **High**

51. *Answer choices:*

(see index for correct answer)

- a. personal values
- b. open system
- c. Dilemma
- d. surface-level diversity

Guidance: level 1

:: Corporate scandals ::

The _________ was a privately held international group of financial services companies controlled by Allen Stanford, until it was seized by United States authorities in early 2009. Headquartered in the Galleria Tower II in Uptown Houston, Texas, it had 50 offices in several countries, mainly in the Americas, included the Stanford International Bank, and said it managed US$8.5 billion of assets for more than 30,000 clients in 136 countries on six continents. On February 17, 2009, U.S. Federal agents placed the company into receivership due to charges of fraud. Ten days later, the U.S. Securities and Exchange Commission amended its complaint to accuse Stanford of turning the company into a "massive Ponzi scheme".

Exam Probability: **Medium**

52. *Answer choices:*

(see index for correct answer)

- a. Stanford Financial Group

- b. Lynn Brewer
- c. Guinness share-trading fraud
- d. Patent encumbrance of large automotive NiMH batteries

Guidance: level 1

:: Nepotism ::

_________ is the granting of favour to relatives in various fields, including business, politics, entertainment, sports, religion and other activities. The term originated with the assignment of nephews to important positions by Catholic popes and bishops. Trading parliamentary employment for favors is a modern-day example of _________ . Criticism of _________ , however, can be found in ancient Indian texts such as the Kural literature.

Exam Probability: **Low**

53. *Answer choices:*

(see index for correct answer)

- a. Crachach
- b. Nepotism
- c. Cardinal-nephew
- d. Ethnic nepotism

Guidance: level 1

:: Offshoring ::

A _________ is the temporary suspension or permanent termination of employment of an employee or, more commonly, a group of employees for business reasons, such as personnel management or downsizing an organization. Originally, _________ referred exclusively to a temporary interruption in work, or employment but this has evolved to a permanent elimination of a position in both British and US English, requiring the addition of "temporary" to specify the original meaning of the word. A _________ is not to be confused with wrongful termination. Laid off workers or displaced workers are workers who have lost or left their jobs because their employer has closed or moved, there was insufficient work for them to do, or their position or shift was abolished . Downsizing in a company is defined to involve the reduction of employees in a workforce. Downsizing in companies became a popular practice in the 1980s and early 1990s as it was seen as a way to deliver better shareholder value as it helps to reduce the costs of employers . Indeed, recent research on downsizing in the U.S., UK, and Japan suggests that downsizing is being regarded by management as one of the preferred routes to help declining organizations, cutting unnecessary costs, and improve organizational performance. Usually a _________ occurs as a cost cutting measure.

Exam Probability: **Low**

54. *Answer choices:*
(see index for correct answer)

- a. Offshore company
- b. Body shopping
- c. Global labor arbitrage
- d. Layoff

Guidance: level 1

:: United States federal defense and national security legislation ::

The USA _________ is an Act of the U.S. Congress that was signed into law by President George W. Bush on October 26, 2001. The title of the Act is a contrived three letter initialism preceding a seven letter acronym , which in combination stand for Uniting and Strengthening America by Providing Appropriate Tools Required to Intercept and Obstruct Terrorism Act of 2001. The acronym was created by a 23 year old Congressional staffer, Chris Kyle.

Exam Probability: **Medium**

55. *Answer choices:*
(see index for correct answer)

- a. Patriot Act
- b. USA PATRIOT Act

Guidance: level 1

:: ::

In ecology, a _________ is the type of natural environment in which a particular species of organism lives. It is characterized by both physical and biological features. A species` _________ is those places where it can find food, shelter, protection and mates for reproduction.

Exam Probability: **Low**

56. *Answer choices:*
(see index for correct answer)

- a. Habitat
- b. information systems assessment
- c. co-culture
- d. personal values

Guidance: level 1

:: ::

A _________ is an astronomical body orbiting a star or stellar remnant that is massive enough to be rounded by its own gravity, is not massive enough to cause thermonuclear fusion, and has cleared its neighbouring region of _________ esimals.

Exam Probability: **Low**

57. *Answer choices:*
(see index for correct answer)

- a. deep-level diversity
- b. Planet
- c. interpersonal communication
- d. surface-level diversity

Guidance: level 1

:: Professional ethics ::

In the mental health field, a _________ is a situation where multiple roles exist between a therapist, or other mental health practitioner, and a client. _________ s are also referred to as multiple relationships, and these two terms are used interchangeably in the research literature. The American Psychological Association Ethical Principles of Psychologists and Code of Conduct is a resource that outlines ethical standards and principles to which practitioners are expected to adhere. Standard 3.05 of the APA ethics code outlines the definition of multiple relationships. Dual or multiple relationships occur when.

Exam Probability: **Low**

58. *Answer choices:*

(see index for correct answer)

- a. professional conduct
- b. Dual relationship
- c. Continuous professional development

Guidance: level 1

:: Workplace ::

In business management, _________ is a management style whereby a manager closely observes and/or controls the work of his/her subordinates or employees.

Exam Probability: **Low**

59. *Answer choices:*

(see index for correct answer)

- a. Workplace revenge
- b. Workplace incivility
- c. Work etiquette
- d. Micromanagement

Guidance: level 1

Accounting

Accounting or accountancy is the measurement, processing, and communication of financial information about economic entities such as businesses and corporations. The modern field was established by the Italian mathematician Luca Pacioli in 1494. Accounting, which has been called the "language of business", measures the results of an organization's economic activities and conveys this information to a variety of users, including investors, creditors, management, and regulators.

:: Partnerships ::

Articles of partnership is a voluntary contract between/among two or more persons to place their capital, labor, and skills into business, with the understanding that there will be a sharing of the profits and losses between/among partners. Outside of North America, it is normally referred to simply as a _________ .

Exam Probability: **High**

1. *Answer choices:*

(see index for correct answer)

- a. Partnership agreement
- b. Uniform Limited Partnership Act
- c. Revised Uniform Limited Partnership Act
- d. Revised Uniform Partnership Act

Guidance: level 1

:: Financial statements ::

_________ s - are the "Financial statements of a group in which the assets, liabilities, equity, income, expenses and cash flows of the parent company and its subsidiaries are presented as those of a single economic entity", according to International Accounting Standard 27 "Consolidated and separate financial statements", and International Financial Reporting Standard 10 " _________ s".

Exam Probability: **High**

2. *Answer choices:*
(see index for correct answer)

- a. PnL Explained
- b. Government financial statements
- c. Quarterly finance report
- d. Consolidated financial statement

Guidance: level 1

:: Real estate valuation ::

_________ or OMV is the price at which an asset would trade in a competitive auction setting. _________ is often used interchangeably with open _________ , fair value or fair _________ , although these terms have distinct definitions in different standards, and may or may not differ in some circumstances.

Exam Probability: **Medium**

3. *Answer choices:*
(see index for correct answer)

- a. Zillow
- b. Market value
- c. Sales comparison approach
- d. Rate base

Guidance: level 1

:: Loans ::

In corporate finance, a _________ is a medium- to long-term debt instrument used by large companies to borrow money, at a fixed rate of interest. The legal term " _________ " originally referred to a document that either creates a debt or acknowledges it, but in some countries the term is now used interchangeably with bond, loan stock or note. A _________ is thus like a certificate of loan or a loan bond evidencing the fact that the company is liable to pay a specified amount with interest and although the money raised by the _________ s becomes a part of the company`s capital structure, it does not become share capital. Senior _________ s get paid before subordinate _________ s, and there are varying rates of risk and payoff for these categories.

Exam Probability: **High**

4. *Answer choices:*

(see index for correct answer)

- a. Bridge loan
- b. Second lien
- c. Small Business Lending Index
- d. Debenture

Guidance: level 1

:: Debt ::

A _________ is a monetary amount owed to a creditor that is unlikely to be paid and, or which the creditor is not willing to take action to collect for various reasons, often due to the debtor not having the money to pay, for example due to a company going into liquidation or insolvency. There are various technical definitions of what constitutes a _________ , depending on accounting conventions, regulatory treatment and the institution provisioning. In the USA, bank loans with more than ninety days` arrears become "problem loans". Accounting sources advise that the full amount of a _________ be written off to the profit and loss account or a provision for _________ s as soon as it is foreseen.

Exam Probability: **Low**

5. *Answer choices:*

(see index for correct answer)

- a. Bad debt
- b. Debt adjustment

- c. Household debt
- d. Bailout

Guidance: level 1

:: Management accounting ::

__________ accounting is a traditional cost accounting method introduced in the 1920s, as an alternative for the traditional cost accounting method based on historical costs.

Exam Probability: **High**

6. *Answer choices:*

(see index for correct answer)

- a. Standard cost
- b. Accounting management
- c. Direct material total variance
- d. Institute of Management Accountants

Guidance: level 1

:: SEC filings ::

__________ is a prescribed regulation under the US Securities Act of 1933 that lays out reporting requirements for various SEC filings used by public companies. Companies are also often called issuers , filers or registrants .

Exam Probability: **Medium**

7. *Answer choices:*

(see index for correct answer)

- a. Form 10-12B
- b. Regulation S-K
- c. Form 10-K405
- d. Form F-4

Guidance: level 1

:: Payment systems ::

A _________ is a bond of the redeemable transaction type which is worth a certain monetary value and which may be spent only for specific reasons or on specific goods. Examples include housing, travel, and food _________ s. The term _________ is also a synonym for receipt and is often used to refer to receipts used as evidence of, for example, the declaration that a service has been performed or that an expenditure has been made. _________ is a tourist guide for using services with a guarantee of payment by the agency.

Exam Probability: **Low**

8. *Answer choices:*

(see index for correct answer)

- a. Sri Lanka Interbank Payment System
- b. EDesk
- c. Voucher
- d. Demand draft

Guidance: level 1

:: ::

_________ is the collection of mechanisms, processes and relations by which corporations are controlled and operated. Governance structures and principles identify the distribution of rights and responsibilities among different participants in the corporation and include the rules and procedures for making decisions in corporate affairs. _________ is necessary because of the possibility of conflicts of interests between stakeholders, primarily between shareholders and upper management or among shareholders.

Exam Probability: **High**

9. *Answer choices:*

(see index for correct answer)

- a. information systems assessment
- b. hierarchical
- c. Character
- d. Corporate governance

Guidance: level 1

:: Types of business entity ::

A sole _________ , also known as the sole trader, individual entrepreneurship or _________ , is a type of enterprise that is owned and run by one person and in which there is no legal distinction between the owner and the business entity. A sole trader does not necessarily work `alone`—it is possible for the sole trader to employ other people.

Exam Probability: **Low**

10. *Answer choices:*
(see index for correct answer)

- a. S.A.
- b. Limited company
- c. Dual-listed company
- d. Proprietorship

Guidance: level 1

:: E-commerce ::

_________ is an e-commerce payment system used in the Netherlands, based on online banking. Introduced in 2005, this payment method allows customers to buy on the Internet using direct online transfers from their bank account.

Exam Probability: **Low**

11. *Answer choices:*
(see index for correct answer)

- a. Online food ordering
- b. IDEAL
- c. ESewa
- d. Mobify

Guidance: level 1

:: Accounting in the United States ::

The __________ is the internal audit profession`s most widely recognized advocate, educator, and provider of standards, guidance, and certifications. Established in 1941, the IIA today serves more than 200,000 members from more than 170 countries and territories. IIA`s global headquarters are in Lake Mary, Fla., United States.

Exam Probability: **Low**

12. *Answer choices:*

(see index for correct answer)

- a. Federal Accounting Standards Advisory Board
- b. Governmental Accounting Standards Board
- c. Institute of Internal Auditors
- d. Certified Government Financial Manager

Guidance: level 1

:: Taxation ::

__________ is an estimate of the market value of a property, based on what a knowledgeable, willing, and unpressured buyer would probably pay to a knowledgeable, willing, and unpressured seller in the market. An estimate of __________ may be founded either on precedent or extrapolation. __________ differs from the intrinsic value that an individual may place on the same asset based on their own preferences and circumstances.

Exam Probability: **Medium**

13. *Answer choices:*

(see index for correct answer)

- a. Tax Freedom Day
- b. Intra-European Organisation of Tax Administrations
- c. Voluntary taxation
- d. Income tax and gambling losses

Guidance: level 1

:: Competition (economics) ::

In taxation and accounting, _________ refers to the rules and methods for pricing transactions within and between enterprises under common ownership or control. Because of the potential for cross-border controlled transactions to distort taxable income, tax authorities in many countries can adjust intragroup transfer prices that differ from what would have been charged by unrelated enterprises dealing at arm's length . The OECD and World Bank recommend intragroup pricing rules based on the arm's-length principle, and 19 of the 20 members of the G20 have adopted similar measures through bilateral treaties and domestic legislation, regulations, or administrative practice. Countries with _________ legislation generally follow the OECD _________ Guidelines for Multinational Enterprises and Tax Administrations in most respects, although their rules can differ on some important details.

Exam Probability: **Medium**

14. *Answer choices:*

(see index for correct answer)

- a. Economic forces
- b. School choice
- c. Wantrapreneur
- d. Tax competition

Guidance: level 1

:: International accounting organizations ::

The _________ is the global organization for the accountancy profession. Founded in 1977, IFAC has more than 175 members and associates in more than 130 countries and jurisdictions, representing nearly 3 million accountants employed in public practice, industry and commerce, government, and academe. The organization supports the development, adoption and implementation of international standards for accounting education, ethics, and the public sector as well as audit and assurance. It supports four independent standard-setting boards, which establish international standards on ethics, auditing and assurance, accounting education, and public sector accounting. It also issues guidance to encourage high quality performance by professional accountants in business and small and medium accounting practices.

Exam Probability: **Low**

15. *Answer choices:*
(see index for correct answer)

- a. Confederation of Asian and Pacific Accountants
- b. International Federation of Accountants
- c. Asia-Pacific Management Accounting Association
- d. World Congress of Accountants

Guidance: level 1

:: Real estate ::

Amortisation is paying off an amount owed over time by making planned, incremental payments of principal and interest. To amortise a loan means "to kill it off". In accounting, amortisation refers to charging or writing off an intangible asset`s cost as an operational expense over its estimated useful life to reduce a company`s taxable income.

Exam Probability: **Low**

16. *Answer choices:*
(see index for correct answer)

- a. Affordable housing
- b. Chambre de bonne
- c. Contingent interest
- d. Amortization

Guidance: level 1

:: ::

__________ science is the application of science to criminal and civil laws, mainly—on the criminal side—during criminal investigation, as governed by the legal standards of admissible evidence and criminal procedure.

Exam Probability: **Medium**

17. *Answer choices:*
(see index for correct answer)

- a. Sarbanes-Oxley act of 2002
- b. hierarchical perspective
- c. surface-level diversity
- d. Forensic

Guidance: level 1

:: Legal terms ::

_________ is a state of prolonged public dispute or debate, usually concerning a matter of conflicting opinion or point of view. The word was coined from the Latin controversia, as a composite of controversus – "turned in an opposite direction," from contra – "against" – and vertere – to turn, or versus , hence, "to turn against."

Exam Probability: **Low**

18. *Answer choices:*

(see index for correct answer)

- a. Legislative veto
- b. Controversy
- c. Innominate jury
- d. Abstract of judgment

Guidance: level 1

:: ::

_________ is the consumption and saving opportunity gained by an entity within a specified timeframe, which is generally expressed in monetary terms. For households and individuals, " _________ is the sum of all the wages, salaries, profits, interest payments, rents, and other forms of earnings received in a given period of time."

Exam Probability: **High**

19. *Answer choices:*

(see index for correct answer)

- a. hierarchical perspective
- b. personal values
- c. similarity-attraction theory
- d. Income

Guidance: level 1

:: Management accounting ::

_________ is a method of identifying and evaluating activities that a business performs, using activity-based costing to carry out a value chain analysis or a re-engineering initiative to improve strategic and operational decisions in an organization.

Exam Probability: **Medium**

20. *Answer choices:*

(see index for correct answer)

- a. Semi-variable cost
- b. Hedge accounting
- c. Activity-based management
- d. Fixed assets management

Guidance: level 1

:: Corporate crime ::

_________ LLP, based in Chicago, was an American holding company. Formerly one of the "Big Five" accounting firms , the firm had provided auditing, tax, and consulting services to large corporations. By 2001, it had become one of the world`s largest multinational companies.

Exam Probability: **Medium**

21. *Answer choices:*

(see index for correct answer)

- a. Arthur Andersen
- b. Walter Forbes
- c. Holdings of American International Group
- d. John Peter Galanis

Guidance: level 1

:: Management accounting ::

_________ s are costs that change as the quantity of the good or service that a business produces changes. _________ s are the sum of marginal costs over all units produced. They can also be considered normal costs. Fixed costs and _________ s make up the two components of total cost. Direct costs are costs that can easily be associated with a particular cost object. However, not all _________ s are direct costs. For example, variable manufacturing overhead costs are _________ s that are indirect costs, not direct costs. _________ s are sometimes called unit-level costs as they vary with the number of units produced.

Exam Probability: **High**

22. *Answer choices:*
(see index for correct answer)

- a. Institute of Management Accountants
- b. Backflush accounting
- c. Variable cost
- d. Job costing

Guidance: level 1

:: Asset ::

In financial accounting, an _________ is any resource owned by the business. Anything tangible or intangible that can be owned or controlled to produce value and that is held by a company to produce positive economic value is an _________ . Simply stated, _________ s represent value of ownership that can be converted into cash . The balance sheet of a firm records the monetary value of the _________ s owned by that firm. It covers money and other valuables belonging to an individual or to a business.

Exam Probability: **Medium**

23. *Answer choices:*
(see index for correct answer)

- a. Asset
- b. Fixed asset

Guidance: level 1

:: Actuarial science ::

The __________ is the greater benefit of receiving money now rather than an identical sum later. It is founded on time preference.

Exam Probability: **Medium**

24. *Answer choices:*
(see index for correct answer)

- a. Expected shortfall
- b. Time value of money
- c. Actuarial present value
- d. Model risk

Guidance: level 1

:: Business law ::

An __________ is a natural person, business, or corporation that provides goods or services to another entity under terms specified in a contract or within a verbal agreement. Unlike an employee, an __________ does not work regularly for an employer but works as and when required, during which time they may be subject to law of agency. __________ s are usually paid on a freelance basis. Contractors often work through a limited company or franchise, which they themselves own, or may work through an umbrella company.

Exam Probability: **Medium**

25. *Answer choices:*
(see index for correct answer)

- a. OHADA
- b. Personal Property Security Act
- c. Relational contract
- d. Independent contractor

Guidance: level 1

:: Hazard analysis ::

Broadly speaking, a _________ is the combined effort of 1. identifying and analyzing potential events that may negatively impact individuals, assets, and/or the environment ; and 2. making judgments "on the tolerability of the risk on the basis of a risk analysis" while considering influencing factors . Put in simpler terms, a _________ analyzes what can go wrong, how likely it is to happen, what the potential consequences are, and how tolerable the identified risk is. As part of this process, the resulting determination of risk may be expressed in a quantitative or qualitative fashion. The _________ is an inherent part of an overall risk management strategy, which attempts to, after a _________ , "introduce control measures to eliminate or reduce" any potential risk-related consequences.

Exam Probability: **High**

26. *Answer choices:*

(see index for correct answer)

- a. Hazardous Materials Identification System
- b. Risk assessment
- c. Swiss cheese model

Guidance: level 1

:: Asset ::

In accounting, a _________ is any asset which can reasonably be expected to be sold, consumed, or exhausted through the normal operations of a business within the current fiscal year or operating cycle . Typical _________ s include cash, cash equivalents, short-term investments , accounts receivable, stock inventory, supplies, and the portion of prepaid liabilities which will be paid within a year.In simple words, assets which are held for a short period are known as _________ s. Such assets are expected to be realised in cash or consumed during the normal operating cycle of the business.

Exam Probability: **Medium**

27. *Answer choices:*

(see index for correct answer)

- a. Fixed asset
- b. Current asset

Guidance: level 1

:: Generally Accepted Accounting Principles ::

A __________ is a reduction of the recognized value of something. In accounting, this is a recognition of the reduced or zero value of an asset. In income tax statements, this is a reduction of taxable income, as a recognition of certain expenses required to produce the income.

Exam Probability: **High**

28. *Answer choices:*
(see index for correct answer)

- a. Historical cost
- b. Write-off
- c. Standard Business Reporting
- d. Treasury stock

Guidance: level 1

:: Mathematical finance ::

In economics and finance, __________ , also known as present discounted value, is the value of an expected income stream determined as of the date of valuation. The __________ is always less than or equal to the future value because money has interest-earning potential, a characteristic referred to as the time value of money, except during times of negative interest rates, when the __________ will be more than the future value. Time value can be described with the simplified phrase, "A dollar today is worth more than a dollar tomorrow". Here, `worth more` means that its value is greater. A dollar today is worth more than a dollar tomorrow because the dollar can be invested and earn a day`s worth of interest, making the total accumulate to a value more than a dollar by tomorrow. Interest can be compared to rent. Just as rent is paid to a landlord by a tenant without the ownership of the asset being transferred, interest is paid to a lender by a borrower who gains access to the money for a time before paying it back. By letting the borrower have access to the money, the lender has sacrificed the exchange value of this money, and is compensated for it in the form of interest. The initial amount of the borrowed funds is less than the total amount of money paid to the lender.

Exam Probability: **Low**

29. *Answer choices:*
(see index for correct answer)

- a. Present value
- b. Snell envelope
- c. Markov switching multifractal
- d. No-arbitrage bounds

Guidance: level 1

:: Finance ::

__________ , in finance and accounting, means stated value or face value. From this come the expressions at par , over par and under par .

Exam Probability: **Low**

30. *Answer choices:*
(see index for correct answer)

- a. High-net-worth individual
- b. Par value
- c. Pet banks
- d. Wrap account

Guidance: level 1

:: Generally Accepted Accounting Principles ::

In accounting, __________ , gross margin, sales profit, or credit sales is the difference between revenue and the cost of making a product or providing a service, before deducting overheads, payroll, taxation, and interest payments. This is different from operating profit . Gross margin is the term normally used in the U.S., while __________ is the more common usage in the UK and Australia.

Exam Probability: **Low**

31. *Answer choices:*
(see index for correct answer)

- a. Long-term liabilities
- b. Deprival value
- c. Treasury stock
- d. Gross profit

Guidance: level 1

:: ::

_________ is the field of accounting concerned with the summary, analysis and reporting of financial transactions related to a business. This involves the preparation of financial statements available for public use. Stockholders, suppliers, banks, employees, government agencies, business owners, and other stakeholders are examples of people interested in receiving such information for decision making purposes.

Exam Probability: **Medium**

32. *Answer choices:*

(see index for correct answer)

- a. Sarbanes-Oxley act of 2002
- b. Financial accounting
- c. surface-level diversity
- d. process perspective

Guidance: level 1

:: Insolvency ::

_________ is the process in accounting by which a company is brought to an end in the United Kingdom, Republic of Ireland and United States. The assets and property of the company are redistributed. _________ is also sometimes referred to as winding-up or dissolution, although dissolution technically refers to the last stage of _________ . The process of _________ also arises when customs, an authority or agency in a country responsible for collecting and safeguarding customs duties, determines the final computation or ascertainment of the duties or drawback accruing on an entry.

Exam Probability: **Low**

33. *Answer choices:*

(see index for correct answer)

- a. Liquidation
- b. Personal Insolvency Arrangement
- c. Conservatorship
- d. George Samuel Ford

Guidance: level 1

:: Accounting terminology ::

Accounts are typically defined by an identifier and a caption or header and are coded by account type. In computerized accounting systems with computable quantity accounting, the accounts can have a quantity measure definition.

Exam Probability: **Medium**

34. *Answer choices:*

(see index for correct answer)

- a. outstanding balance
- b. Fund accounting
- c. Chart of accounts
- d. Account

Guidance: level 1

:: United States federal income tax ::

Under United States tax law, the _________ is a dollar amount that non-itemizers may subtract from their income before income tax is applied. Taxpayers may choose either itemized deductions or the _________, but usually choose whichever results in the lesser amount of tax payable. The _________ is available to US citizens and aliens who are resident for tax purposes and who are individuals, married persons, and heads of household. The _________ is based on filing status and typically increases each year. It is not available to nonresident aliens residing in the United States . Additional amounts are available for persons who are blind and/or are at least 65 years of age.

Exam Probability: **Medium**

35. *Answer choices:*

(see index for correct answer)

- a. Personal Casualty Gains
- b. Standard deduction
- c. 1256 Contract
- d. Rabbi trust

Guidance: level 1

:: Credit cards ::

The __________ Company, also known as Amex, is an American multinational financial services corporation headquartered in Three World Financial Center in New York City. The company was founded in 1850 and is one of the 30 components of the Dow Jones Industrial Average. The company is best known for its charge card, credit card, and traveler`s cheque businesses.

Exam Probability: **Medium**

36. *Answer choices:*

(see index for correct answer)

- a. Rail travel card
- b. American Express
- c. CardLab
- d. North American Bancard

Guidance: level 1

:: Asset ::

__________ s, also known as tangible assets or property, plant and equipment , is a term used in accounting for assets and property that cannot easily be converted into cash. This can be compared with current assets such as cash or bank accounts, described as liquid assets. In most cases, only tangible assets are referred to as fixed. IAS 16 defines __________ s as assets whose future economic benefit is probable to flow into the entity, whose cost can be measured reliably. __________ s belong to one of 2 types:"Freehold Assets" – assets which are purchased with legal right of ownership and used,and "Leasehold Assets" – assets used by owner without legal right for a particular period of time.

Exam Probability: **Medium**

37. *Answer choices:*

(see index for correct answer)

- a. Fixed asset
- b. Current asset

Guidance: level 1

:: ::

__________ is a means of protection from financial loss. It is a form of risk management, primarily used to hedge against the risk of a contingent or uncertain loss

Exam Probability: **Medium**

38. *Answer choices:*
(see index for correct answer)

- a. personal values
- b. open system
- c. Insurance
- d. interpersonal communication

Guidance: level 1

:: Financial ratios ::

The __________ shows the percentage of how profitable a company`s assets are in generating revenue.

Exam Probability: **Medium**

39. *Answer choices:*
(see index for correct answer)

- a. Capital adequacy ratio
- b. Retention rate
- c. Sales density
- d. Operating margin

Guidance: level 1

:: Business ethics ::

In accounting and in most Schools of economic thought, __________ is a rational and unbiased estimate of the potential market price of a good, service, or asset. It takes into account such objectivity factors as.

Exam Probability: **Low**

40. *Answer choices:*
(see index for correct answer)

- a. Fair value
- b. Walmarting
- c. Eating your own dog food
- d. Sweatshop

Guidance: level 1

:: Free accounting software ::

A __________ is the principal book or computer file for recording and totaling economic transactions measured in terms of a monetary unit of account by account type, with debits and credits in separate columns and a beginning monetary balance and ending monetary balance for each account.

Exam Probability: **Low**

41. *Answer choices:*
(see index for correct answer)

- a. Frontaccounting
- b. Ledger
- c. TurboCASH
- d. HomeBank

Guidance: level 1

:: Organizational behavior ::

__________ is the state or fact of exclusive rights and control over property, which may be an object, land/real estate or intellectual property. __________ involves multiple rights, collectively referred to as title, which may be separated and held by different parties.

Exam Probability: **High**

42. *Answer choices:*
(see index for correct answer)

- a. Micro-initiative
- b. Satisficing
- c. Organizational justice
- d. Ownership

Guidance: level 1

:: Financial accounting ::

A __________ is an ownership interest in a corporation with enough voting stock shares to prevail in any stockholders` motion. A majority of voting shares is always a __________ . When a party holds less than the majority of the voting shares, other present circumstances can be considered to determine whether that party is still considered to hold a controlling ownership interest.

Exam Probability: **Low**

43. *Answer choices:*

(see index for correct answer)

- a. SEC filing
- b. Controlling interest
- c. Advance payment
- d. Intellectual capital

Guidance: level 1

:: Management accounting ::

An __________ allows a company to provide a monetary value for items that make up their inventory. Inventories are usually the largest current asset of a business, and proper measurement of them is necessary to assure accurate financial statements. If inventory is not properly measured, expenses and revenues cannot be properly matched and a company could make poor business decisions.

Exam Probability: **High**

44. *Answer choices:*

(see index for correct answer)

- a. Inventory valuation
- b. Profit center
- c. Management control system
- d. Double counting

Guidance: level 1

:: Manufacturing ::

_________ costs are all manufacturing costs that are related to the cost object but cannot be traced to that cost object in an economically feasible way.

Exam Probability: **Low**

45. *Answer choices:*

(see index for correct answer)

- a. Can seamer
- b. Calender
- c. Manufacturing overhead
- d. Manufacturing engineering

Guidance: level 1

:: Accounting in the United States ::

_________ were documents issued by the Committee on Accounting Procedure between 1938 and 1959 on various accounting problems. They were discontinued with the dissolution of the Committee in 1959 under a recommendation from the Special Committee on Research Program. In all, 17 bulletins were issued; however, the lack of binding authority over AICPA`s membership reduced the influence of, and compliance with the content of the bulletins. The _________ have all been superseded by the Accounting Standards Codification .

Exam Probability: **Low**

46. *Answer choices:*

(see index for correct answer)

- a. American Institute of Certified Public Accountants
- b. Uniform Certified Public Accountant Examination
- c. Institute of Internal Auditors
- d. Other comprehensive basis of accounting

Guidance: level 1

:: Stock market ::

A _________ , securities exchange or bourse, is a facility where stock brokers and traders can buy and sell securities, such as shares of stock and bonds and other financial instruments. _________ s may also provide for facilities the issue and redemption of such securities and instruments and capital events including the payment of income and dividends. Securities traded on a _________ include stock issued by listed companies, unit trusts, derivatives, pooled investment products and bonds. _________ s often function as "continuous auction" markets with buyers and sellers consummating transactions via open outcry at a central location such as the floor of the exchange or by using an electronic trading platform.

Exam Probability: **Medium**

47. *Answer choices:*
(see index for correct answer)

- a. Non-voting stock
- b. Immediate or cancel
- c. Stock Exchange
- d. Mr. Market

Guidance: level 1

:: Television terminology ::

A nonprofit organization , also known as a non-business entity, _________ organization, or nonprofit institution, is dedicated to furthering a particular social cause or advocating for a shared point of view. In economic terms, it is an organization that uses its surplus of the revenues to further achieve its ultimate objective, rather than distributing its income to the organization`s shareholders, leaders, or members. Nonprofits are tax exempt or charitable, meaning they do not pay income tax on the money that they receive for their organization. They can operate in religious, scientific, research, or educational settings.

Exam Probability: **Medium**

48. *Answer choices:*
(see index for correct answer)

- a. Satellite television
- b. Not-for-profit
- c. multiplexing

- d. nonprofit

Guidance: level 1

:: Management accounting ::

_________ is an accountancy practice, the aim of which is to provide an offset to the mark-to-market movement of the derivative in the profit and loss account. There are two types of hedge recognized. For a fair value hedge the offset is achieved either by marking-to-market an asset or a liability which offsets the P&L movement of the derivative. For a cash flow hedge some of the derivative volatility into a separate component of the entity`s equity called the cash flow hedge reserve. Where a hedge relationship is effective , most of the mark-to-market derivative volatility will be offset in the profit and loss account. _________ entails much compliance - involving documenting the hedge relationship and both prospectively and retrospectively proving that the hedge relationship is effective.

Exam Probability: **Low**

49. *Answer choices:*

(see index for correct answer)

- a. Constraints accounting
- b. Hedge accounting
- c. Investment center
- d. Certified Management Accountant

Guidance: level 1

:: Financial ratios ::

The _________ is a financial ratio indicating the relative proportion of shareholders` equity and debt used to finance a company`s assets. Closely related to leveraging, the ratio is also known as risk, gearing or leverage. The two components are often taken from the firm`s balance sheet or statement of financial position , but the ratio may also be calculated using market values for both, if the company`s debt and equity are publicly traded, or using a combination of book value for debt and market value for equity financially.

Exam Probability: **Medium**

50. *Answer choices:*
(see index for correct answer)

- a. Risk-adjusted return on capital
- b. Payout ratio
- c. Debt-to-equity ratio
- d. Days payable outstanding

Guidance: level 1

:: Accounting terminology ::

_________ is money owed by a business to its suppliers shown as a liability on a company`s balance sheet. It is distinct from notes payable liabilities, which are debts created by formal legal instrument documents.

Exam Probability: **Low**

51. *Answer choices:*
(see index for correct answer)

- a. Impairment cost
- b. Internal auditing
- c. Capital appreciation
- d. Accounts payable

Guidance: level 1

:: Financial statements ::

A Statement of changes in equity and similarly the statement of changes in owner`s equity for a sole trader, statement of changes in partners` equity for a partnership, statement of changes in Shareholders` equity for a Company or statement of changes in Taxpayers` equity for Government financial statements is one of the four basic financial statements.

Exam Probability: **High**

52. *Answer choices:*
(see index for correct answer)

- a. Quarterly finance report
- b. Consolidated financial statement
- c. PnL Explained
- d. Statement of retained earnings

Guidance: level 1

:: Accounting ::

_________ are designed to facilitate the process of journalizing and posting transactions. They are used for the most frequent transactions in a business. For example, in merchandising businesses, companies acquire merchandise from vendors, and then in turn sell the merchandise to individuals or other businesses. Sales and purchases are the most common transactions for the merchandising businesses. A business such as a retail store will record the following transactions many times a day for sales on account and cash sales.

Exam Probability: **Low**

53. *Answer choices:*

(see index for correct answer)

- a. Special journals
- b. Merdiban
- c. KashFlow
- d. Accounting records

Guidance: level 1

:: Project management ::

_________ is the widespread practice of collecting information and attempting to spot a pattern. In some fields of study, the term " _________ " has more formally defined meanings.

Exam Probability: **High**

54. *Answer choices:*

(see index for correct answer)

- a. Libyan Project Management Association
- b. Outcomes theory
- c. Karol Adamiecki
- d. Theory X and Theory Y

Guidance: level 1

:: Financial ratios ::

In finance, the _________ , also known as the acid-test ratio is a type of liquidity ratio which measures the ability of a company to use its near cash or quick assets to extinguish or retire its current liabilities immediately. Quick assets include those current assets that presumably can be quickly converted to cash at close to their book values. It is the ratio between quickly available or liquid assets and current liabilities.

Exam Probability: **Medium**

55. *Answer choices:*

(see index for correct answer)

- a. Calmar ratio
- b. Average accounting return
- c. Quick ratio
- d. EV/EBITDA

Guidance: level 1

:: Debt ::

A _________ is a party that has a claim on the services of a second party. It is a person or institution to whom money is owed. The first party, in general, has provided some property or service to the second party under the assumption that the second party will return an equivalent property and service. The second party is frequently called a debtor or borrower. The first party is called the _________ , which is the lender of property, service, or money.

Exam Probability: **Low**

56. *Answer choices:*

(see index for correct answer)

- a. Peak debt
- b. Debt crisis
- c. Consumer debt
- d. Odious debt

Guidance: level 1

:: Stock market ::

_________ is a form of stock which may have any combination of features not possessed by common stock including properties of both an equity and a debt instrument, and is generally considered a hybrid instrument. _________ s are senior to common stock, but subordinate to bonds in terms of claim and may have priority over common stock in the payment of dividends and upon liquidation. Terms of the _________ are described in the issuing company`s articles of association or articles of incorporation.

Exam Probability: **Medium**

57. *Answer choices:*

(see index for correct answer)

- a. Preferred stock
- b. Growth investing
- c. Intermarket analysis
- d. Flash trading

Guidance: level 1

:: Economic globalization ::

_________ is an agreement in which one company hires another company to be responsible for a planned or existing activity that is or could be done internally,and sometimes involves transferring employees and assets from one firm to another.

Exam Probability: **Low**

58. *Answer choices:*

(see index for correct answer)

- a. reshoring
- b. global financial

Guidance: level 1

:: Accounting software ::

_________ is any item or verifiable record that is generally accepted as payment for goods and services and repayment of debts, such as taxes, in a particular country or socio-economic context. The main functions of _________ are distinguished as: a medium of exchange, a unit of account, a store of value and sometimes, a standard of deferred payment. Any item or verifiable record that fulfils these functions can be considered as _________ .

Exam Probability: **Low**

59. *Answer choices:*

(see index for correct answer)

- a. Teaspiller
- b. Invoiceit
- c. Boeing Calc
- d. Chrysler Comprehensive Compensation System

Guidance: level 1

INDEX: Correct Answers

Foundations of Business

1. c: Description

2. d: Commerce

3. : Entrepreneurship

4. a: Return on investment

5. c: Credit

6. b: Restructuring

7. : Empowerment

8. a: Number

9. b: Business plan

10. a: Selling

11. c: Technology

12. b: Trademark

13. b: Import

14. a: Security

15. d: Payment

16. d: Incentive

17. c: Audience

18. a: Accounts receivable

19. : Management

20. a: Manufacturing

21. b: Insurance

22. c: ASEAN

23. : ITeM

24. c: Currency

25. : Investment

26. b: Authority

27. : Revenue

28. : Fraud

29. b: Board of directors

30. c: Bankruptcy

31. c: Creativity

32. b: Expense

33. a: Consumer Protection

34. c: Interest rate

35. b: Limited liability

36. c: Marketing strategy

37. d: Energies

38. d: Privacy

39. d: Working capital

40. c: Solution

41. : Present value

42. a: Human resources

43. : Trade agreement

44. d: Specification

45. a: Threat

46. d: Officer

47. : Integrity

48. b: Project

49. c: Exercise

50. a: Buyer

51. c: Project management

52. d: Stock

53. : Mission statement

54. b: Competitive advantage

55. b: Frequency

56. a: Strategic alliance

57. : Dividend

58. c: Loan

59. : Regulation

Management

1. a: Interaction

2. b: Empowerment

3. d: Trade

4. : Customs

5. b: Subsidiary

6. : Cost

7. b: Size

8. c: Fixed cost

9. d: Intellectual property

10. d: Partnership

11. : Sharing

12. : Mission statement

13. : Project team

14. d: Philosophy

15. c: Protection

16. d: Social capital

17. c: Research and development

18. a: Code

19. d: Political risk

20. d: Contingency theory

21. d: Transactional leadership

22. c: Kaizen

23. : Synergy

24. b: Overtime

25. a: Management system

26. a: Offshoring

27. a: Change management

28. a: Collaboration

29. c: Cash flow

30. c: Justice

31. a: Facilitator

32. b: Firm

33. c: Bargaining

34. : Skill

35. a: Enabling

36. d: Case study

37. : Schedule

38. c: Standardization

39. d: Franchising

40. : Transformational leadership

41. d: Job design

42. c: Patent

43. d: Consultant

44. a: Management

45. : European Union

46. d: Entrepreneur

47. d: Project manager

48. b: Compromise

49. c: Integrity

50. : Office

51. a: American Express

52. : Intranet

53. a: Span of control

54. c: Situational leadership

55. c: Motivation

56. a: Balanced scorecard

57. a: Job description

58. c: Sexual harassment

59. : Supply chain

Business law

1. b: Probate

2. a: Marketing

3. a: Ford

4. c: First Amendment

5. b: Utility

6. c: Complaint

7. : Sole proprietorship

8. a: Void contract

9. : Federal government

10. b: Parol evidence

11. d: Trustee

12. d: Supreme Court

13. b: Appeal

14. d: Estoppel

15. c: Insurable interest

16. a: Accord and satisfaction

17. a: Collective bargaining

18. d: Private law

19. : Real property

20. b: Appellate Court

21. a: Operation of law

22. : Operating agreement

23. b: Lease

24. b: Revocation

25. b: Identity theft

26. c: Product liability

27. a: Dividend

28. c: Categorical imperative

29. : Reasonable person

30. : Economic espionage

31. a: Option contract

32. d: Firm

33. d: Procedural law

34. d: Insider trading

35. a: Prohibition

36. b: Inventory

37. : Foreign Corrupt Practices Act

38. c: Social responsibility

39. d: S corporation

40. c: Statute of limitations

41. d: Authority

42. d: Plaintiff

43. a: Testimony

44. c: Utilitarianism

45. d: Incentive

46. c: Affidavit

47. d: Credit

48. b: Judicial review

49. b: Condition precedent

50. : Specific performance

51. b: Affirmative action

52. b: Advertisement

53. a: Executory contract

54. a: National Labor Relations Board

55. a: Labor relations

56. a: Restraint of trade

57. d: Clayton Act

58. b: Misrepresentation

59. a: Service mark

Finance

1. b: Financial management

2. : Financial crisis

3. d: Exercise

4. : Factory

5. c: Income

6. b: Capital budgeting

7. : Normal balance

8. c: Current asset

9. d: Financial market

10. : Cost of capital

11. d: Risk premium

12. a: Double taxation

13. : Book value

14. a: Income statement

15. c: Going concern

16. b: Historical cost

17. a: Operating expense

18. d: Absorption costing

19. b: Choice

20. b: Investment

21. a: Adjusting entries

22. a: Competition

23. c: Financial instrument

24. a: Budget

25. b: Land

26. c: Utility

27. : Yield curve

28. b: Stock exchange

29. : Maturity date

30. b: Hedge fund

31. d: Rate risk

32. b: Liquidation

33. a: Convertible bond

34. : Total cost

35. a: Corporation

36. d: Indirect costs

37. d: Receipt

38. b: Cost of goods sold

39. : Expected return

40. : Bank of America

41. : Cost allocation

42. a: Income tax

43. : Good

44. c: Board of directors

45. d: Intangible asset

46. : Social security

47. a: Debtor

48. b: Conservatism

49. : Inventory

50. a: Credit

51. b: Call option

52. c: Exchange rate

53. d: Incentive

54. a: Cash equivalent

55. c: Commercial paper

56. c: Deferral

57. d: Present value

58. c: Municipal bond

59. : Future value

Human resource management

1. c: Authoritarianism

2. c: Arbitration

3. b: Open shop

4. : Management

5. b: Organizational culture

6. d: Brainstorming

7. c: Physician

8. c: Mergers and acquisitions

9. a: Collaboration

10. c: McDonnell Douglas Corp. v. Green

11. d: Job enlargement

12. c: Picketing

13. c: Free Trade

14. d: Nearshoring

15. c: Service Employees International Union

16. c: Problem solving

17. : Pattern bargaining

18. : Executive search

19. c: Vesting

20. : Severance package

21. c: Payroll

22. b: Glass ceiling

23. b: Partnership

24. c: Wage

25. a: Interactional justice

26. a: Pay grade

27. a: Hostile work environment

28. b: Golden parachute

29. b: Onboarding

30. : Knowledge management

31. c: Business process outsourcing

32. b: Seniority

33. a: Coaching

34. b: Telecommuting

35. b: Card check

36. : Needs analysis

37. a: Training and development

38. d: National Labor Relations Act

39. d: Supply chain

40. d: Cost

41. c: Layoff

42. : Discipline

43. a: National Association of Colleges and Employers

44. a: Virtual team

45. d: UNITE HERE

46. a: Employee Polygraph Protection Act

47. d: Human resources

48. b: Just cause

49. a: Bargaining unit

50. a: Culture shock

51. a: Whistleblower

52. : Employee handbook

53. : Employee surveys

54. b: Centralization

55. c: Mediation

56. : Licensure

57. : Asbestos

58. a: Undue hardship

59. : Social contract

Information systems

1. : Clickstream

2. d: Threat

3. : Code

4. b: Pop-up ad

5. b: Virtual world

6. d: Structured query language

7. c: Business process management

8. a: Business model

9. d: Enterprise resource planning

10. : Interoperability

11. c: Data link

12. a: Privacy

13. a: Social media

14. c: Statistics

15. : Big data

16. : Accessibility

17. c: Blog

18. a: Monopoly

19. a: World Wide Web

20. d: Knowledge management

21. a: Botnet

22. a: Positioning system

23. : Google

24. a: Groupware

25. : Throughput

26. b: Enterprise systems

27. d: Database management system

28. a: Master data management

29. c: Network management

30. d: Packet switching

31. b: Collision

32. a: Netflix

33. c: Query language

34. c: Unstructured data

35. a: Government-to-business

36. c: Verisign

37. a: Commercial off-the-shelf

38. b: Business process reengineering

39. a: Information ethics

40. c: Utility computing

41. : Data integrity

42. c: Expert system

43. a: American Express

44. d: ITunes

45. c: Data cleansing

46. c: Service-oriented architecture

47. a: Computer-integrated manufacturing

48. a: Domain name

49. a: Innovation

50. a: PeopleSoft

51. b: Peer production

52. a: Asset

53. a: Information management

54. : Documentation

55. a: Diagram

56. b: Authentication protocol

57. b: Content management

58. d: Copyright

59. a: Database

Marketing

1. a: Interview

2. a: Advertising agency

3. a: Data analysis

4. : Services marketing

5. d: Clayton Act

6. b: Wholesale

7. c: Commercialization

8. a: Hearing

9. d: Brand

10. b: Social media

11. c: Marketing management

12. : Copyright

13. b: Forecasting

14. a: Evaluation

15. c: Competition

16. a: Adoption

17. : Database

18. c: Expense

19. d: Supply chain

20. d: Social networking

21. b: Competitive advantage

22. b: E-commerce

23. a: Technology

24. c: Market development

25. a: Committee

26. a: Trademark

27. : Integrated marketing

28. d: Consideration

29. : Image

30. d: Customer

31. d: Sales

32. a: Marketing strategy

33. d: Total cost

34. : Information system

35. : Subsidiary

36. d: Strategic alliance

37. : Return on investment

38. : Advertisement

39. d: Shopping

40. : Early adopter

41. b: Economies of scale

42. a: Marketing mix

43. c: Qualitative research

44. a: Interactive marketing

45. b: Competitor

46. d: Commodity

47. c: Cost-plus pricing

48. a: Intellectual property

49. d: Business marketing

50. b: Organizational structure

51. : Comparative advertising

52. d: Infomercial

53. a: Product placement

54. a: Exchange rate

55. c: Disintermediation

56. : Marketing communications

57. a: Publicity

58. a: Marketing channel

59. c: Distribution channel

Manufacturing

1. d: Third-party logistics

2. b: Paper

3. c: Technical support

4. : Service quality

5. b: Lead

6. b: Forecasting

7. : Total productive maintenance

8. b: Coating

9. a: Information management

10. d: Design of experiments

11. b: Consortium

12. a: Vendor relationship management

13. : Electronic data interchange

14. : Extended enterprise

15. : Kanban

16. : Original equipment manufacturer

17. a: Heat transfer

18. d: Catalyst

19. d: Pattern

20. c: Synergy

21. d: Reverse auction

22. : Blanket

23. : Pareto analysis

24. d: Consensus

25. c: Poka-yoke

26. b: E-procurement

27. a: Supply chain network

28. a: Process control

29. c: Durability

30. a: Process capability

31. b: Change management

32. a: Request for quotation

33. : Thomas Register

34. a: Throughput

35. c: Sales

36. : Purchasing

37. b: Schedule

38. a: Ball

39. : Materials management

40. d: Turbine

41. c: Tool

42. : Sputnik

43. c: Value engineering

44. a: Sensitivity analysis

45. b: Good

46. : Sony

47. : Volume

48. a: Procurement

49. : Time management

50. d: Quality assurance

51. a: Kaizen

52. d: Water

53. a: Mary Kay

54. b: Strategy

55. : Concurrent engineering

56. c: Voice of the customer

57. b: Zero Defects

58. a: Reflux

59. d: Steel

Commerce

1. : Information system

2. a: E-commerce

3. a: Policy

4. : Adoption

5. a: Property

6. d: Revenue

7. d: Entrepreneur

8. a: Insurance

9. : Jurisdiction

10. c: Chief executive officer

11. a: DigiCash

12. : Bill of lading

13. d: Freight forwarder

14. a: Transaction cost

15. b: Wall Street Journal

16. b: Direct marketing

17. c: Asset

18. d: Standing

19. b: Front office

20. a: Market structure

21. d: Monopoly

22. : Logo

23. : Advertising

24. b: Loyalty

25. d: Customer satisfaction

26. a: Yield management

27. a: Semantic

28. d: Project

29. b: Contribution margin

30. b: Wholesale

31. b: Dutch auction

In the social sciences and life sciences, a _________ is a research method involving an up-close, in-depth, and detailed examination of a subject of study , as well as its related contextual conditions.

Exam Probability: **Low**

36. *Answer choices:*

(see index for correct answer)

- a. pilot project
- b. explanatory research
- c. Preference test
- d. Case study

Guidance: level 1

:: Project management ::

Some scenarios associate "this kind of planning" with learning "life skills". _________ s are necessary, or at least useful, in situations where individuals need to know what time they must be at a specific location to receive a specific service, and where people need to accomplish a set of goals within a set time period.

Exam Probability: **Medium**

37. *Answer choices:*

(see index for correct answer)

- a. Project cycle management
- b. Gantt chart
- c. Project network
- d. DICE framework

Guidance: level 1

:: ::

_________ or standardisation is the process of implementing and developing technical standards based on the consensus of different parties that include firms, users, interest groups, standards organizations and governments. _________ can help maximize compatibility, interoperability, safety, repeatability, or quality. It can also facilitate commoditization of formerly custom processes. In social sciences, including economics, the idea of _________ is close to the solution for a coordination problem, a situation in which all parties can realize mutual gains, but only by making mutually consistent decisions. This view includes the case of "spontaneous _________ processes", to produce de facto standards.

Exam Probability: **High**

38. *Answer choices:*
(see index for correct answer)

- a. process perspective
- b. information systems assessment
- c. Standardization
- d. empathy

Guidance: level 1

:: Marketing ::

_________ is based on a marketing concept which can be adopted by an organization as a strategy for business expansion. Where implemented, a franchisor licenses its know-how, procedures, intellectual property, use of its business model, brand, and rights to sell its branded products and services to a franchisee. In return the franchisee pays certain fees and agrees to comply with certain obligations, typically set out in a Franchise Agreement.

Exam Probability: **Low**

39. *Answer choices:*
(see index for correct answer)

- a. Klondike Big Inch Land Promotion
- b. Content Curation Marketing
- c. Emailing
- d. Franchising

Guidance: level 1

:: Leadership ::

__________ is a theory of leadership where a leader works with teams to identify needed change, creating a vision to guide the change through inspiration, and executing the change in tandem with committed members of a group; it is an integral part of the Full Range Leadership Model. __________ serves to enhance the motivation, morale, and job performance of followers through a variety of mechanisms; these include connecting the follower`s sense of identity and self to a project and to the collective identity of the organization; being a role model for followers in order to inspire them and to raise their interest in the project; challenging followers to take greater ownership for their work, and understanding the strengths and weaknesses of followers, allowing the leader to align followers with tasks that enhance their performance.

Exam Probability: **Low**

40. *Answer choices:*

(see index for correct answer)

- a. Ethical leadership
- b. Maintenance actions
- c. Servant leadership
- d. Three levels of leadership model

Guidance: level 1

:: Human resource management ::

__________ is a core function of human resource management and it is related to the specification of contents, methods and relationship of jobs in order to satisfy technological and organizational requirements as well as the social and personal requirements of the job holder or the employee. Its principles are geared towards how the nature of a person`s job affects their attitudes and behavior at work, particularly relating to characteristics such as skill variety and autonomy. The aim of a __________ is to improve job satisfaction, to improve through-put, to improve quality and to reduce employee problems .

Exam Probability: **Medium**

41. *Answer choices:*

rect answer)

- a. Human resource accounting
- b. Illness rate
- c. Adecco Group North America
- d. Job design

Guidance: level 1

:: Monopoly (economics) ::

A _________ is a form of intellectual property that gives its owner the legal right to exclude others from making, using, selling, and importing an invention for a limited period of years, in exchange for publishing an enabling public disclosure of the invention. In most countries _________ rights fall under civil law and the _________ holder needs to sue someone infringing the _________ in order to enforce his or her rights. In some industries _________ s are an essential form of competitive advantage; in others they are irrelevant.

Exam Probability: **Medium**

42. *Answer choices:*
(see index for correct answer)

- a. Tesco Town
- b. Intellectual property
- c. Patent
- d. Herfindahl index

Guidance: level 1

:: ::

A _________ is a professional who provides expert advice in a particular area such as security , management, education, accountancy, law, human resources, marketing , finance, engineering, science or any of many other specialized fields.

Exam Probability: **High**

43. *Answer choices:*
(see index for correct answer)

- a. empathy

32. c: Automation

33. : Economics

34. : Cost structure

35. a: Budget

36. a: Preference

37. d: Manufacturing

38. a: Electronic funds transfer

39. a: Compromise

40. c: Contract

41. b: Walt Disney

42. b: WebSphere Commerce

43. b: Competitor

44. c: Business-to-business

45. c: Mobile commerce

46. a: Purchasing

47. c: Game

48. c: Permission marketing

49. a: Production line

50. c: Bank

51. a: Management team

52. a: Joint venture

53. b: Export

54. a: Boot

55. c: Siemens

56. d: Merchant

57. a: E-procurement

58. c: Recruitment

59. : Commodity

Business ethics

1. d: Executive compensation

2. a: Utopian socialism

3. d: Qui tam

4. d: Siemens

5. c: Empowerment

6. b: Protestant work ethic

7. b: Clayton Act

8. d: Charles Ponzi

9. : Sustainable

10. c: Working poor

11. : Edgewood College

12. c: Madoff

13. : Medicaid

14. a: Energy policy

15. : Forest Stewardship Council

16. d: Arthur Andersen

17. d: UN Global Compact

18. b: Undue hardship

19. b: Corporate governance

20. d: Chamber of Commerce

21. a: New York Stock Exchange

22. : Transformational leadership

23. b: Global Fund

24. c: Medicare fraud

25. d: Patent

26. d: Fannie Mae

27. b: Solar power

28. c: Subprime lending

29. b: Insider trading

30. a: Ethical leadership

31. b: Individualistic culture

32. d: Urban sprawl

33. b: Copyright

34. c: Sullivan principles

35. : Greenwashing

36. : Lead paint

37. c: Enron

38. : Planned obsolescence

39. a: Lanham Act

40. a: Federal Trade Commission

41. c: Model Rules of Professional Conduct

42. c: Fair Trade Certified

43. c: Pollution Prevention

44. : Global reach

45. c: Price fixing

46. : Right to work

47. b: United Farm Workers

48. : Interlocking directorate

49. b: Constitutional law

50. b: Clean Water Act

51. c: Dilemma

52. a: Stanford Financial Group

53. b: Nepotism

54. d: Layoff

55. a: Patriot Act

56. a: Habitat

57. b: Planet

58. b: Dual relationship

59. d: Micromanagement

Accounting

1. a: Partnership agreement

2. d: Consolidated financial statement

3. b: Market value

4. d: Debenture

5. a: Bad debt

6. a: Standard cost

7. b: Regulation S-K

8. c: Voucher

9. d: Corporate governance

10. d: Proprietorship

11. b: IDEAL

12. c: Institute of Internal Auditors

13. : Fair market value

14. : Transfer pricing

15. b: International Federation of Accountants

16. d: Amortization

17. d: Forensic

18. b: Controversy

19. d: Income

20. c: Activity-based management

21. a: Arthur Andersen

22. c: Variable cost

23. a: Asset

24. b: Time value of money

25. d: Independent contractor

26. b: Risk assessment

27. b: Current asset

28. b: Write-off

29. a: Present value

30. b: Par value

31. d: Gross profit

32. b: Financial accounting

33. a: Liquidation

34. c: Chart of accounts

35. b: Standard deduction

36. b: American Express

37. a: Fixed asset

38. c: Insurance

39. : Return on assets

40. a: Fair value

41. b: Ledger

42. d: Ownership

43. b: Controlling interest

44. a: Inventory valuation

45. c: Manufacturing overhead

46. : Accounting Research Bulletins

47. c: Stock Exchange

48. b: Not-for-profit

49. b: Hedge accounting

50. c: Debt-to-equity ratio

51. d: Accounts payable

52. d: Statement of retained earnings

53. a: Special journals

54. : Trend analysis

55. c: Quick ratio

56. : Creditor

57. a: Preferred stock

58. c: Outsourcing

59. : Money

CPSIA information can be obtained
at www.ICGtesting.com
Printed in the USA
LVHW062137311019
635718LV00025B/611/P

9 781538 852453